OLD BILL WILLIAMS, *Mountain Man*

University of Oklahoma Press : *Norman*

OLD
BILL WILLIAMS
MOUNTAIN MAN

BY ALPHEUS H. FAVOUR

With an Introduction by William Brandon

Library of Congress Catalog Card Number: 62-10767

Copyright © 1936 by the University of North Carolina Press. Assigned 1962 to the University of Oklahoma Press. New edition copyright © 1962 by the University of Oklahoma Press, Norman, Publishing Division of the University. Manufactured in the U.S.A. First printing of the new edition, 1962; second printing, 1981; third printing, 1983.

INTRODUCTION

History, as with the old saw about how to write a play, is not written but rewritten. One of the recent revisions in the history of western America has concerned the time of the mountain men, roughly the period from about 1810 to the 1840's. This was previously regarded as a misty, colorful, but rather minor interlude between the headline appearances of Lewis and Clark (pre-1810) and the pioneers in covered wagons (post-1840). But it is now coming to be regarded as a period of considerable importance in the westward story. The mountain men, not at all meaning to lead the course of empire but only hunting beaver, have nevertheless been promoted to major historical stature. They are the new heroes in today's version of that wonderful romance between the young United States and its western star. Their time, in the words of a present-day historian of the fur trade, Dale Morgan, was "a golden age in the history of the West."

This concept was less than current when Alpheus H. Favour's *Old Bill Williams, Mountain Man* was first published, forty-four years ago. Since then, biographies of mountain men have become so stylish that we've been getting them almost by the brigade. Mountain doings of the great fur trade days have been industriously worked and reworked and year by year have lost their blur; the great names among the mountain men have been shined to a magnificent luster. Favour's study of Old Bill Williams has been increasingly enhanced thereby. It is the only full-length account of Old Bill's rip-roaring career, thus providing an essential chapter in the mountain man epic.

William Sherley Williams was born during the American Revolution, a child of the early frontier. In his young manhood he became an itinerant preacher and appointed himself a missionary to the Osages, at the time the mightiest Indian nation of the nearer prairie West. The Osages converted young Preacher Bill rather than the other way around, and from this point on he forsook civilization and made the wilderness his home.

He was a master trapper and so he signed his name, but he never aspired to be a local business leader in the Rocky Mountain fur trade, as did such mountain boys as Jed Smith, Jim Bridger, Tom Fitzpatrick, and Old Henry Fraeb. Sometimes when he fell in with a brigade of trappers he "naturally assumed the leadership," but informally if so; he had no particular fame as a captain of men, as did Jed Smith or Joseph Reddeford Walker. He lived more with Indians, perhaps, than did any other prominent mountain man and had to a surpassing degree a gift for their languages and notions, but no one would have dreamed of Old Bill as a responsible and trusted government Indian agent, as were Tom Fitzpatrick and Kit Carson in their later years. He had more education than was common for the mountains, and wrote a fine flowing hand, but he had "no glory," as the young Easterner Albert Pike wrote of him in 1834, "except in the woods."

He was one of the guides of the Sibley survey of the Santa Fe Trail in 1825, and he was a guide with two different Frémont expeditions some twenty years later, but he also distinguished himself during the Mexican War, so it was said, by pretending to be an Indian war party and throwing a scare into the green troops of the Army of the West, just for an innocent frolic, Old Bill being a fun-loving lad of nearly sixty at the time. His sense of endeavor was intensely personal, cached deep beneath the crust of many years and many adventures. He never achieved acclaim as an official guide to equal or even approach the renown of such influential openers of the West as Kit Carson or Tom Fitzpatrick. Although he spent a continuous forty years roaming strange countries from the Mississippi to the Pacific, the last twenty-four or so centering in the region of the Colorado Rockies, he left no record of exploration to equal or even approach that of Jed Smith, the greatest explorer among the mountain men, whose career in the West totaled eight years.

Old Bill's travels were his own affair. Unlike Indians and the other mountain men, he liked to go alone—so much so that one of his many sobriquets was Old Solitaire. He was proud of his feats of valor, endurance, and skill, and he felt no need of companions for protection. This desire for solitude may have stemmed in part from his secretiveness about his beaver hunting, at which by common consent and his own admission he was the champion of the mountains. Part of it may have stemmed from his tendency toward mysticism, which appeared to grow with the years.

He was a controversial figure in his own time and has remained so ever since. According to some of the tales he was vicious and treacherous, but according to others he was kind and trustworthy. Above all he epitomized the wildness of the mountain men; among all that tattered, tough, and untrammeled company, he was the most tattered, the toughest, and notoriously the least trammeled. His drunken sprees were magnificent; his escapades were legendary. No one has presented him as a candidate for the greatest of the mountain men; he was only the most interesting.

His life came to a close with a dramatic thunderclap of a climax that might have been composed by Schiller. He swindled his friends, the Tabeguache Utes, out of their spring catch of furs to go on a mighty Taos drunk, capped the betrayal by leading soldiers against a band of Indians that included some of these same Tabeguache people, was badly wounded in the ensuing battle, and while recovering from his wound took on the hopeless task of trying to lead the fourth Frémont expedition across the Rockies in midwinter. All his ability could not accomplish this, as he told Frémont before the attempt was begun. But he made the try. The Fourth Expedition ended in tragedy and disaster, enshrining Old

Bill in another controversy that has persisted to the present day. He disappeared while returning to the mountains in an effort to bring out some of the expedition's baggage. The place, time, and manner of his death are left to guesswork. As befits a folk hero, he simply vanished in the mountain mists.

Old Bill's biographer, Alpheus Hoyt Favour, was born in 1880, of Puritan stock, in Natick, Massachusetts. Following an impeccable education in law and settlement work in New York with the reformer Charles Parkhurst, he moved to Prescott, Arizona, in 1917. There he founded a successful law firm, served as a member of the Arizona State Senate and that body's leading legal authority, became a collector of books and guns, and became interested in the life and times of Old Bill Williams. To the north, near Williams, Arizona, is Bill Williams Mountain, and not far northwest of Prescott are found the headwaters of Bill Williams Fork of the Colorado; Old Bill's stamp was left over a sizable hunk of the Southwest as well as the southern Rockies. But the fascination of the eminent, utterly respectable lawyer, of Puritanical background and cultured upbringing, with the life of leathery, lousy, godless Old Bill is by no means the least interesting aspect of this book.

Favour brought to the work the considerable gifts of a dedicated amateur, in the best sense of the word. Except for a monograph on Arizona state laws he had written nothing else, but Old Bill emerges clothed with color and authority. The findings of more recent scholarship dispute some details, such as the account of Old Bill's death which Favour is inclined to credit, but the genuine enthusiasm of the narrative, the attention given to the historical context of persons and events, and the devotion to seeking what may be found of truth and reality more than offset occasional lapses. Favour died in 1939, three years after the first publication of *Old Bill Williams*. In the years since, the book has touched a book's best destiny, that of exerting a special and lasting influence.

One further point about Old Bill's legend remains to be mentioned. During his own time, nearly everyone in the mountains who could write recorded some mention of him. The English travel writer of the Far West in the 1840's, George Frederick Augustus Ruxton, wrote of Old Bill so vividly that he created a type, a recognizable character that has lived ever since in western fiction and western movies—the past master plainsman, the eccentric old-timer, the weathered rock of experience scarred by Taos lightning and ancient demigodly deeds, the old scout who is seldom sober and never wrong. We have seen him in films times without number. Here he is in the original, as he really was.

William Brandon

MONTEREY, CALIFORNIA

ACKNOWLEDGMENT

THE GATHERING of the material for this book has been a congenial task. It has afforded an opportunity to meet and know many interesting people and to make new friends. Everywhere I have met with uniform courtesy and a spirit of sympathetic co-operation. To all who have helped I take this opportunity of expressing my thanks. I am especially under obligation to William Bork, my efficient scout and investigator; to Senator Carl Hayden for his help in my search of government records in Washington; to my friend William P. Stuart, the editor of the Prescott *Evening Courier*, for his advice; to my fellow townswoman, Miss Sharlot M. Hall, for her counsel and constant admonition that nothing ever written has been lost; and to the Huntington Library of San Marino, California, and to Mrs. Charles G. McGehee of Bowling Green Plantation, Woodville, Mississippi, for the use of manuscripts and the assistance given me in my research work. My main prop and co-worker has been my good wife, Eva, who encouraged me to depart, at least temporarily, from my chosen profession, the law.

Alpheus H. Favour

PRESCOTT, ARIZONA

CONTENTS

ILLUSTRATIONS

OLD BILL WILLIAMS, *Mountain Man*

CHAPTER ONE

Mountain Men

THE CLOSE of the Revolutionary War did not bring peace to the country west of the Allegheny Mountains. The control of New Orleans by the Spaniards, the uncertainty of the land policy, coupled with the Indian problem, for many years kept this section in a turmoil. The westerners developed a hostile attitude towards the newly formed federal government which did not subside until Louisiana was purchased from France at the beginning of the new century.

By that treaty of cession the inhabitants of the Mississippi Valley acquired an outlet to the sea; most of our people believed at the time that we were also getting a definite territory west of the river, but in reality we were acquiring only a claim to an unbounded area. Nevertheless this new territory beyond the Mississippi, with its prairies, mountains, and rivers, peopled by many Indian tribes, from the start drew people westward. As the years went by, the number moving into the new area steadily increased. They came from every walk of life seeking adventure and fortune from hunting, trapping, and trading. As time passed there developed from these adventurers a distinct type known as mountain men. These mountain men were the natural product of their environment. In turn, it was this class of men who, without purpose on their part, helped the United States to change its claims to the

3

territorial limits of Louisiana into actual possession, with international recognition.

We of today are accustomed to surround the soldiers of the Revolution and the frontiersmen with a halo of glory, heaping praises upon their behavior and deeds, but in their own time, viewed from the standpoint of their contemporaries, all this idealization was lacking; and had we lived in those days, we should have heard doubt, reproach, and even charges of treason against some we now count among our national heroes. How many would suppose that during the period between 1787 and 1794, after this country had gained its independence, some of the very men who had fought to gain this independence, felt that the government they had created had so failed that they were willing to give up their citizenship and seek freedom under the flag of the Spanish king? This is exactly what happened, however, in the case of Joseph Williams, the father of the famous mountain man, as well as in the case of Daniel Boone, Moses Austin, the father of Stephen F. Austin of Texas, and many others prominent in the frontier life of that day.

At the close of the Revolution, Spain held the west bank of the Mississippi and with the Floridas on the east controlled the outlet to the sea. In 1762, France ceded the Colony or Province of Louisiana to Spain. The following year, as the result of the Seven Years' War in Europe and the French and Indian War in America, France ceded Canada to England. The peace of November 30, 1782, between the United States and England, recognized our independence and established the boundaries of our territory, which were the Mississippi on the west and Florida on the south.

During this period the United States was faced with two very difficult western problems; first, the creation of a system of control of the public domain, which was ceded by most of the original thirteen colonies to the central government; and second, the welfare of those who were then in that country, particularly in regard to protection from the Indians and to the use of the Mississippi as a waterway for their trade. A solution of the first problem was reached, but the latter became more troublesome as the years went by and was solved only by the purchase of Louisiana in 1803.

Much discussion took place in the Continental Congress under the Articles of Confederation, in respect to these public lands. Many acts were proposed, but the results were visible only in the Land Ordinance of 1785. Before the Northwest Ordinance of 1787, providing for the form of government for the territory, was adopted, the army had twice been instructed to drive out those who were occupying these public lands. True, it was generally conceded that there would be a flow of settlers to the West, but until the older communities and their finances were better regulated, it was not thought well to drain these sections of their population, since it was better to build up the economic prosperity of the merchants and manufacturers in the settled communities before starting new settlements in the West. This feeling was especially pronounced in New England, where it was even held that men who might move over the mountains should be treated as members of a family who had run away from home, and should be left to shift for themselves.

Thomas Scott, a congressman from western Pennsylvania, was one of the leaders in the movement to outline a land policy on broad principles. He made it clear in his speeches that in his opinion the people were going to enter into the public domain whether Congress provided legal means or not, and that for the sake of law and order, as well as for the revenue to be derived from the sale of land, a land policy should be definitely determined.[1]

George Washington was of the same opinion. He felt that if Congress did not take action at once, the people would turn elsewhere for protection. On October 10, 1784, he wrote to Governor Harrison of Virginia, from personal observation, "The western states stand as it were, upon a pivot. A touch of a feather would turn them either way."[2]

[1] 1 Cong., 1 sess., *Annals of Congress*, 427–30.
[2] Benjamin Horace Hibbard, *History of the Public Land Policies*, 34.

Congressman Scott also pointed out the "superior encourage-ment held out to the people settling on the other side of the river Mississippi [in Spanish territory], where the soil is fertile, and the climate equally agreeable." He also read a "kind of proclama-tion issued by the governor of the Spanish posts at the Illinois," which contained "an invitation to all persons inclined to settle in the Western country, offering as inducements, lands without charge, exemptions from taxes, protection in civil and religious liberties, besides provision and implements of husbandry."[3]

The Spaniards were keenly alive to the situation. Baron de Carondelet, governor of Louisiana from 1791 to 1797,[4] had circu-lars printed in the English language and distributed throughout the western country, in which he offered farming implements and land as inducement to settle in the province. This he did with his eyes wide open to the dangers to the government from these settlers, for "no man of his time had a keener appreciation than Carondelet of the menace to the Spanish Empire in the westward thrust of American frontiersmen." He said of them, "A carbine and a little cornmeal in a sack is sufficient for an American to range the forests alone for a month."[5]

As the result of the Spaniards' invitation to come in and settle west of the Mississippi, Colonel George Morgan, a native of New Jersey, long interested in western lands, made an arrangement with the Spaniard Gardoqui for a tract of land for a colony in what is now a part of southern Missouri, at New Madrid. Coloni-zation across the river centered in New Madrid, Ste Geneviève, and St. Louis.

The Spaniards played fast and loose in the game. General Ber-nado de Gálvez, governor of the Indies and conqueror of the British posts of Pensacola and Mobile during the period of the Revolution, directed the governor of Louisiana, under date of

[3] 1 Cong., 1 sess., *Annals of Congress*, 646–49.
[4] Francisco Luis Hector de Carondelet was born of a distinguished Burgundian family. His mother had an Irish father and a Spanish mother. Carondelet married a Spanish noblewoman and through the influence of her family received his appointment to the governorship of Louisiana.
[5] Eugene C. Barker, *Life of Stephen F. Austin*, 7.

June 27, 1784, to notify "all inhabitants of the district that the English and the United States of America do not have the right that they claim to the free navigation of the Mississippi, for the treaty of the 30th of November, 1782, on which they base it, cannot fix the limits of that which England did not possess, the two banks of said river being already at that time occupied by our arms."[6] The governor was cautioned to see to it that it was made clear to all who violated the order that their goods would be confiscated and legal action taken.

In the meantime the western lands were being filled with settlers and this section was growing in population. These people found that the transportation of their farm products, their furs, and other articles of trade across the mountains to the Atlantic was too costly. There was only one profitable outlet, and that was to the sea by way of the river.

The attitude of the Atlantic states almost brought the matter to open warfare. North Carolina passed a law ceding the area beyond the mountains to the federal government, leaving the inhabitants with no means to raise money for defense against the Indians, and making no provision for future economic development. This great area practically set adrift, shortly attempted the organization of the Independent State of Franklin. This state lasted only a short time, but its brief existence shows the spirit of the men of that territory during those years. They were headed then, as in former times, by such leaders as Colonel John Sevier, known among his followers as "Nolichucky Jack," under whom many of them and their families had fought during the Revolution. It was the same Colonel Sevier who had received the commendation of the North Carolina Assembly for his "voluntary, distinguished, and eminent services" at King's Mountain, in 1790. North Carolina attempted to pacify the malcontents. The cession act was repealed and the western territory reannexed, but not before some blood had been shed, nor before Governor Sevier, the head of the new state, had written to Don Diego de Gardoqui,

[6] Gálvez to Gov. *ad int.* of Louisiana, June 27, 1784–Houch Papers Spanish MSS "A," 1784–1805. Wisconsin Historical Library.

the Spanish ambassador, proposing an independent state under Spanish protection.

General James Wilkinson, a native of Maryland and a veteran of the Revolution, had moved to Kentucky in 1784. Wilkinson was badly in need of money, and he undertook a trading venture to New Orleans in 1787. Being very skillful in his negotiations and manipulations, he was not long in procuring from the Spanish governor, Miró, an agreement which almost amounted to a trade monopoly. In addition to his trade arrangement, he received substantial sums of money and was commissioned to undertake the separation of the West from the United States.[7] Unquestionably, Wilkinson sensed the temper of the people of his section and believed he could depend upon them to support his efforts to that end.

Besides Sevier's plans and Wilkinson's schemes, James Robertson, of Watauga, wrote a letter to the Creek Indian, McGillivray, suggesting that such a separation of the West from the seacoast states would eventually take place, for they would manage in some way to enter into a satisfactory arrangement with the powers that controlled the Mississippi. He stated that this must come about because the interests of the eastern and western countries were so diverse.

An effort was made by the United States to adjust matters with Spain. In 1781 Congress authorized John Jay to negotiate a trade treaty with Spain, waiving free navigation of the Mississippi; Spain had not yet acted upon Jay's proposals when the ending of the American Revolution caused him to withdraw them.

George Rogers Clark, the man who had conquered the Ohio country for the United States during the Revolution by capturing Kaskaskia from the French and Vincennes from the British, proposed to lead troops down the Mississippi, against the Spaniards, if they persisted in their attitude.

A gentleman in Ohio wrote a letter to a friend in Boston which, although extreme, showed the general sentiment of the people.

[7] *American State Papers, Miscellaneous,* I, 936–39, II, 80–95.

He said, "to sell us, and make us vassals to the merciless Spaniards, is a grievance not to be borne. The parliamentary acts which occasioned our revolt from Great Britain were not so barefaced and intolerable." He further stated they could raise twenty thousand troops and could probably increase this number from the annual immigration of from two to four thousand. He referred to George Rogers Clark's having taken Vincennes, and said they were determined that the Spaniards should not trade up the river. He also stated that preparations were being made whereby the Spaniards would be driven from the mouth of the Mississippi, and if the United States would not come in and help the settlers beyond the mountains, they would certainly get help from some other source, and he suggested that Great Britain stood ready to assist them. He ended his letter with the direct challenge, "You are as ignorant of this country as Great Britain was of America. These hints, if rightly improved, may be of some service; if not, blame yourselves for the neglect."[8]

We can conclude that Spanish duplicity and failure of the settlers to agree among themselves were the chief reasons matters did not take a more serious turn during these troublesome years.

The doubt and misunderstanding in the Mississippi Valley were quieted in 1803. The United States purchased the Louisiana Territory from France after it had been secretly ceded to that nation by Spain. The acquisition of Louisiana assured the domination of the United States in North America, afforded a field for expansion, provided opportunity for colonization, satisfied the land desire of the nation, and, with the exception of the Revolutionary War, was the most important event in our history. The story of that period from the signing of the treaty with France in 1803, down to the completion of the Gadsden Purchase in 1853, with the intervening settlements of boundary questions in the acquisition of Texas, the treaty with England agreeing on the boundary as the forty-ninth parallel, the acquisition of territory in the war with Mexico, and the relinquishment of all claims to the territory

[8] *Secret Journals of Congress,* IV, 320–23.

by Spain, England, and Russia, indeed seemed like the working out of the "Manifest Destiny" of the country as claimed by Senator Thomas H. Benton, who coined the expression.

In a general way, Louisiana was a name for the country lying west of the Mississippi River. This territory had been discovered by the French, and whatever settlements had been made and whatever commerce in the fur trade had been carried on within its boundaries, had been the work of the French. The principal settlement down the river was the shipping port of New Orleans, and up the river was the small trading community of St. Louis, with a population of about a thousand inhabitants, mostly of French extraction. In her purchase, the United States had acquired all that France possessed or could claim.

England, by her treaty with France, had previously acquired all of the Canadian holdings formerly held and claimed by France, particularly that portion lying north of the Mississippi River and west to and including the Oregon country, and also claimed a considerable part of the territory acquired through the Louisiana Purchase by the United States. Notwithstanding the several treaties which Spain had made, this latter country still claimed all of the country lying east of New Mexico, nearly to the Mississippi River and as far north as the Missouri River, her claims being based on conquest, discovery, and settlement in the Río Grande Valley. Russia also had a vague undetermined claim to a large part of the North American continent which lay adjacent to her holdings along the Bering Strait and down into the Oregon country.

Louisiana was a great, unexplored territory, inhabited by Indians, the names of many of the tribes being unknown to the countries claiming the land occupied by these tribes. At many points, the United States, Spain, England, and Russia each claimed the same territory; yet not one of these nations in any sense occupied the country claimed. At the time of the Purchase, New Mexico had been a settled community for nearly two hundred years. Up and down the Río Grande were built many pueblos or communities. From the time of the Coronado Expedition, down through the years, the Spaniards and Mexicans from the Río

Grande Valley had gone into the mountains and plains of that country lying to the east and north of the Sangre de Cristo Mountains, almost as far as the Missouri River, on trading and trapping excursions with the Indians. Like the other nationalities, they made no settlements; neither did they remain long to trade and trap.

All through the country lying north of the Missouri River and in the Northwest, the Hudson's Bay Company[9] and other English companies were active. They pursued much the same methods as the French had used so successfully before them in their dealings with the Indians, establishing posts and conducting extensive business in the fur trade.

In the Northwest the Russians had carried on some trade with the Indians, but had never penetrated to any extent inland, nor had they founded any settlements. One Russian, Baranov, had established himself as almost a monarch, but it takes more than one man to hold an empire.

Therefore, at the time the Louisiana Purchase was made, there was an open race among four nations, each with claims which could be ripened into rights if properly developed and exercised. England, Spain, and Russia failed because they did not or could not produce a type of man like the free trapper and the mountain man.

When the cession was assured, James Madison instructed Mr. Livingston to look up the records of the Treaty of San Ildefonso and the Treaty of Utrecht to find out just what they showed in reference to the boundaries of the acquired territory. It was generally claimed by this country, aside from the New Orleans end of the territory, where the Sabine River marked the boundary with Texas, that the Rocky Mountains bounded it on the west, and that the territory included all of the waters of the Arkansas, Missouri, and Mississippi rivers. However, since nobody knew the location of the headwaters of the Arkansas and their relation

[9] The Company was chartered May 2, 1670, under the name of "The Governor and Company of adventurers of England trading into Hudson Bay," or it was commonly known as the Hudson's Bay Company.—H. M. Chittenden, *History of the American Fur Trade of the Far West*, I, 87.

to the upper Río Grande, the extent of the Rockies, or the location of the headwaters of the Missouri and the Mississippi, these terms did not mean very much at that time except, as Jefferson said of the purchase, it "has more than doubled the area of the United States, and the new parts are not inferior to the old in soil, climate, production and important communications."

Mr. Livingston inquired of the minister of foreign affairs, Mr. Talleyrand, what were the boundaries and what France had intended to take from Spain when she acquired Louisiana. Mr. Talleyrand in answer replied, "I can give you no direction; you have made a noble bargain for yourself and I suppose you will make the most of it." How well this country made the most of the bargain is demonstrated by positive proof when we reflect that there were added to our states from this territory, Louisiana, Missouri, Arkansas, Iowa, Minnesota, North and South Dakota, Nebraska, Kansas, Wyoming, Montana, and indirectly all of the other states lying west of the Mississippi.

President Jefferson saw perhaps as clearly as anyone the possibilities of the great territory if prompt action were taken to establish a legal right to all of the country which might be claimed in the area we had purchased. Immediately on the transfer to the United States, he sent out the previously planned Lewis and Clark expedition from St. Louis. It started the same year the Upper Province was transferred to the Americans. At the head of this exploring party was Meriwether Lewis, captain in the United States Army, former private secretary to President Jefferson, and a relative of the Williams family. Second in command was Lieutenant William Clark, a brother of George Rogers Clark. The expedition set out in the spring of 1804 from St. Louis, with forty-two men, traveled across the unknown territory to the Columbia River, came in sight of the Pacific, and was back in St. Louis in the fall of 1806, thus forging the first official tie which was to bind this great expanse of the continent to the United States.

The expedition of Lewis and Clark across an untraveled land, meeting and mastering new conditions, successfully treating with heretofore strange Indian tribes, and overcoming the problems of food and the forces of nature, stands out as a great epic in American exploration. Although Lewis was at the head, his magnanimity and generosity in sharing the honor of the expedition with his lieutenant, William Clark, so that it has come to be known as the Lewis and Clark Expedition, have reflected even more honor on him by the sharing, than had he assumed the credit alone.

Not waiting for the return of the Lewis and Clark expedition, President Jefferson had Lieutenant Zebulon M. Pike sent out on an exploring expedition to the headwaters of the Mississippi. The young officer left in August of 1805 and returned in April of the next year, having successfully traversed that part of the country where the Mississippi heads and which formed the northerly boundary of the Purchase. Upon Pike's return to St. Louis he was immediately dispatched on a second expedition. At the head of twenty soldiers, he left St. Louis to accompany a band of Osages to western Missouri; and after this was accomplished, he proceeded to the headwaters of the Red River. Pike traveled up the Arkansas and over the mountains, invading Spanish territory.

The Spaniards, hearing of the Pike expedition, sent Lieutenant Don Facundo Malgares with a party of soldiers to head off the American; the Spanish force left Santa Fe and proceeded generally in a northeasterly direction as far as the country of the Pawnees. They failed to find the Pike party and returned to Santa Fe, later arresting him when he entered Spanish territory, and taking him to Chihuahua. He was returned to the United States across Texas. Thus it seems that Spain was claiming, on that date, the territory as far as the Missouri River and was willing to resort to force to maintain this claim.

Following the Lewis and Clark and the Pike explorations, other government-sponsored parties were sent out over the years following, until by the year 1820, Washington had fairly accurate knowledge of the territory west of the Mississippi which this nation claimed. It should be noted, however, that up to the end of the second decade, we had only hunters and trappers in the country west of the Mississippi, and no mountain men in the sense the term later came to be used. The early expeditions were successful in accumulating information about the physical character of the territory, the fauna and flora, and the several tribes of Indians. All this was used later to advantage in the negotiations with the other countries, when boundaries were discussed. It was after 1820, however, when the real test of sovereignty came, namely, that of possession with power to hold. During this period the mountain men had come upon the stage.

Usually "history has concerned itself greatly with the forms of government and the records of politicians and parties."[10] This is hardly the case in tracing the history of the Louisiana Purchase during the first half of the nineteenth century. Then history was influenced by the adventures, deeds, and records of individuals. Among these the hunters, free trappers, fur traders, and mountain men were the chief actors. A few of them have left diaries, journals, and letters, but these are fragmentary and meager, and the records of their accomplishments, for the most part, have been lost. They had few friends or means through which to proclaim their accomplishments. Then, too, many persons in positions of importance were willing to assume and did take credit which rightfully should have gone to others.

It was a period and a region in which home and family played little or no part. It was a struggle of the individual against nature, and the men of that area failed or succeeded through their own efforts. The fur trapper relied on his ability to cope with the natives, the French *voyageurs*, and the English company traders. The "I" played the great part, with politics and government far in the background; and this period marked the high point in the dependence on self which has never been surpassed in the history of the pioneers of the world's frontiers. In driving back the Indians and overcoming the wilderness of the Ohio Valley, Kentucky, and Tennessee, there had been developed a certain type of pioneer—the hunter and Indian fighter. The westward flow of migration over the Appalachians had filled up the places where these trappers and hunters had roamed and hunted. The home seekers with their families crowded in and took up land.

10 J. T. Adams, *Epic of America*, 47.

The wilderness west of the Mississippi offered an asylum and a continuance of the old life, and many took advantage of it. Here was a great domain, a land as rich as or richer than the land they had left, with even better hunting grounds and more fur-bearing animals and only the Indians to contend with. In the early years the hunters and trappers who pushed ever westward were older men. They were migrating for the reason they could not adapt themselves to the new order back home. This type constituted the bulk of the immigration into the new territory until after the War of 1812.

After the settlement of the war with England in 1814, we find a larger number of immigrants, adventurers, and traders, with a sprinkling of families seeking new homes and going into the land covered by the Louisiana Purchase. This movement was induced somewhat by the fact that panic conditions in the East had reduced many to destitution and the West afforded new opportunity. Consequently there drifted across the river, principally into St. Louis, discharged soldiers, bankrupts, adventurers, criminals, merchants, preachers, farmers, lawyers, young men and old, from every state in the Union and every walk of life, each seeking fortune or adventure. From these were recruited the trappers, hunters, and traders. By 1820 it was estimated there were one thousand trappers and hunters in the Missouri River country.[11] Out of them were developed the finished product—the mountain men.

The accounts we have of the trappers during the first twenty years of the century are marked with hardship and disaster, caused in large part by the fact that the trappers were not accustomed to the life or were not experienced to meet situations as they arose. During this period it seems as if luck played the largest hand in the game. True, unless a man had physical strength, could endure thirst, scanty rations, and fatigue, and had determination, courage, and fortitude, he could not hope to get on. Many fell victims to the Indians; some died from hunger, some from exposure, and others from disease. One is impressed, in reading the early history,

11 *Missouri Intelligencer* (September 7, 1822).

by the tremendous mortality among these men. As time passed, life became easier for these hunters and trappers, as they began to learn what to avoid and what to prepare for.

There never was a truer application of the evolutionary theory of "survival of the fittest" than there was among the men of the plains and mountains of that day. They learned to overcome thirst by knowing where the water holes were to be found, to conquer hunger by not running out of provisions, to escape destruction from hostile Indians by anticipating and outwitting their enemies. They could live on the country, were cunning, daring, courageous, and at times half-savage. Nature became an open book to them. They understood the Indian better than he did himself. These men so trained in the life, were known to the Indians as "bad medicine," and to the Mexicans, Californians, and English as a force to reckon with at all times.

At the end of the first two decades of a century of possession of the Louisiana Purchase, we find men of this type in Santa Fe, under a foreign government, more or less holding the local authorities in contempt and adapting themselves to the ways of the Mexicans. They intermarried with the natives and the Indians, but instead of being absorbed into these foreign peoples, they retained much of their own native culture and exerted influence over those among whom they lived.

The government in New Mexico which followed the Spanish overthrow in 1821 was not opposed to the Americans coming with goods to trade, and thus the door was opened for the Americans; once in, they could not be excluded. These traders supplied the needs of the people, and whatever the government desired with respect to foreigners, trade, of necessity, had to go on.

The early Spanish custom of issuing *guías* (licenses) to anyone who undertook any civil activity was still in force. If one were to hold a fandango, he had to get a *guía;* the same applied to trading, to conducting a store, or even to making a trip.[12] When the

12 A *guía* was a written license issued by the Mexican government for any trading, trapping, or venture of any kind; it was also a customs clearance or letter of safe conduct. It was executed in quadruplicate, one copy given to the

invading host of Americans could not get licenses, they found some way to carry on just the same.

Things began to move in the Southwest in the early twenties. Ewing Young and William Wolfskill, with a party of American trappers, went out from Taos and trapped the San Juan and other tributaries of the Colorado.[13] Sylvester Pattie and his son, James O. Pattie, crossed as traders to Santa Fe in 1824; and in 1825, with a *guía* from the government, they were the first white men to trap the Gila River. James Conklin came in 1825 and settled at Taos. The year before, Willaim Huddart, with a few companions, went out to Taos on a trapping expedition as far north as the Green River. Kit Carson came to Santa Fe in 1826, and then went to Taos to live. Skillful as a mountain man, nevertheless he was always kind, diplomatic, honest, and generous. The Mexicans themselves came to look to him for leadership. He typified the finest type of American of his class. All peoples with whom he associated honored and respected him, and the influence of such a man as Carson can hardly be correctly estimated. As an unofficial representative of this country during these early years, he very considerably raised the prestige of his countrymen among the Indians and the foreigners.

Antoine Roubidoux[14] began trading in New Mexico in 1822, and Charles Beaubien settled there in 1827. Jedediah Smith, never without his Bible and his rifle, made his first trip into California from the mountains in 1826, blazing the trail which many followed later. Richard Campbell in 1827 went out with a party from Santa Fe, making the trip across to San Diego by way of Zuñi, opening new country. In 1828, a brother of Captain William Sublette successfully resisted the seizure of his furs, gathered in the Mexico territory. Between 1829 and 1832, David Jackson and

licensee, one copy kept at the place of issue, one copy sent to the department, and one copy sent to Mexico City. See also Josiah Gregg, *Commerce of the Prairies*, 254.

[13] J. J. Hill, "Ewing Young in the Fur Trade of the Far Southwest," *Oregon Historical Quarterly*, Vol. XXIV (March, 1923), 7.

[14] His name is spelled in many different ways. The spelling here is the same as in the license issued to him in 1823.

Ewing Young went across Arizona into California. Pauline Weaver was trapping in central Arizona by 1830, and from that time on had great influence over the Indians of that section.[15] In 1830, the Spanish Trail from Santa Fe to California was finally opened up, and when William Wolfskill and a party went north through Gunnison country, this trail passed southern Utah and the desert into southern California. Such excursions by American frontiersmen took them into a country which was claimed and held by a foreign nation.

In the central West and Northwest the contest was among the English, Russian, and American interests for control of the country. This struggle had been going on since the days of Lewis and Clark. In 1818, no decision having been reached, the United States and British governments stepped in and laid down new rules for the contenders. The United States and England agreed that for a period of ten years the citizens of each nation should have equal rights in the fur trade and hunting, and at the end of that period an agreement would be reached regarding boundaries. The English felt secure in their ultimate acquisition of that country, with the help of the powerful and well-organized Hudson's Bay Company and the Northwest Fur Company.

By the end of 1828, the same forces were still contending. The Northwest Fur Company had been taken over by the Hudson's Bay Company in 1821, and the American Fur Company had extended its influence until it was the one powerful American interest in the fur trade; yet no marked predominance of influence could be noticed by either of the forces, and the agreement made ten years before was continued indefinitely. The fur companies had not gained much in power, but a noticeable change had taken place in the importance of the free trapper, who had theretofore

[15] Pauline Weaver was born in White County, Tennessee, in 1800. He came west in 1820 and from 1830 spent his time between Arizona and California. He guided the Mormon Battalion from the headwaters of the Gila into California in 1846–47. Weaver worked for Hudson's Bay Company for a time. He became a free trapper, rendered valuable service to the early whites in Arizona and California, in keeping the Indians friendly, and served as a scout to the military in Arizona, in 1865. He died in 1867.—See Sharlot M. Hall, *Pauline Weaver, Trapper and Mountain Man*, Prescott Arizona Courier Print, 1929.

been overlooked or not considered by the contending powers. Many employees of the fur companies had given up employment with them and had become independent trappers. To be a free trapper gave a man engaged in that calling a standing which an employee of a company did not have. Moreover, the trappers and the mountain men had increased in numbers during the period and they now were in every nook and cranny of the Rocky Mountains, alternately living among the Indians, fighting the Indians, and trading with the Indians.

Any fair student of the history of this period and territory must acknowledge that these mountain men performed a service to their country which was very considerable, a service which in the rapid march of events has been almost forgotten. It is true that they were not there to see that no other nation got a foothold. Patriotism and love of their native land were not the reasons why these adventurers were following this life. The average mountain man resented every effort of the government to exercise any control over his actions. These men, in some instances, had come from parents who were opposed to the established order, or in a number of cases were in the mountains to avoid the consequences of law violations back in their home communities. This class of men as a rule gave little emphasis to government, and none at all to law. They wanted to be left alone, and so long as the constituted authorities did not interfere with their life as mountain men, they were satisfied.

Yet, in results obtained we must say the mountain men played an important part in enabling the government to make the most of the Purchase. It seemed a simple matter for leaders like Colonel Frémont to cross the plains and mountains and be in California when the critical moment arrived; it should be noted, however, that he was guided by mountain men over trails discovered by their comrades. General Kearny went direct to Santa Fe in 1846, over a trail well blazed; every foot of the country he passed through had been traveled by mountain men. The Mormon Battalion in the historic march from Fort Independence to Santa Fe followed old trails, and the mountain men guided them from

Santa Fe to California. One might go on indefinitely multiplying cases. Besides the knowledge of the country, the game, feed, and water, a full understanding of the various tribes of Indians was of next importance. In Indian contacts these men were at their best. The mountain men and the Indians were for the most part on friendly terms, or, if not at peace, then they understood how to take care of themselves by a technique peculiar to themselves.

The English lost control of the country occupied by the Hudson's Bay Company largely by reason of these men. Had there been no mountain men the English influence would have lasted on the West and Northwest, so much so that the present boundary of this country would have been a line farther south. The Indians would have remained a barrier much longer than they did if we had had no men trained in the life of the plains and mountains. In westward travel the immigrants had the services of the eyes and the skill of the mountain men as guides and scouts in their settlement of Oregon, California, and the mountain regions. These men kept the Mexicans busy at home. If they had not, the Mexican authorities might well have crowded north and east of the Sangre de Cristo Mountains. A delay or hesitation by our armies in California or in the Southwest at the time of the Mexican War would have given England a chance to act, and she was ready at the time. The mountain men saved that situation. They played their part and did it well but they have as a class received scant recognition. One of the most noteworthy of them was Old Bill Williams.

CHAPTER TWO

A North Carolina Family

FICTION AND FACT have been so mixed in the fragmentary account we have of the life of Bill Williams on the plains and in the western mountains that, although he stands out in most of them as a prominent mountain man and master trapper, in many ways he has come to be regarded as a legendary character. Certain of his characteristics are always emphasized in the records of his doings: his early calling as an itinerant preacher in Missouri; his efforts as a missionary among the Osages; his eccentric habits; his drinking of quantities of strong liquor; his ability to speak many different Indian tongues; and, finally, his capability as a hunter and his peculiar method of Indian fighting. Search the records as you may, Old Bill Williams never seems to have had any youth, for he is usually referred to as a trapper who had been many years in the West. A number of different versions of his death have been given, ranging from a ceremonial execution as a medicine man of the Utes in the Southwest to a violent death at the hands of the Blackfeet in the Northwest. The stories told of Williams are more varied than those of any other man of his time, and leave the casual reader in uncertainty as to the real man, or in doubt, indeed, if there ever did exist such a character outside of fiction.

The real truth is that William Sherley Williams, afterward known as Bill Williams, or Old Bill, was born on January 3, 1787, on Horse Creek, a branch of the Pacolet, under Skyuka Mountain, in Rutherford County, North Carolina,[1] and he was killed by the Utes on the upper Río Grande in southern Colorado on March 14, 1849. His life coincides with and touches upon many phases of our national growth from the time of the Revolutionary War to the end of the westward expansion. His parents lived in a part of the country where doubt and misunderstanding of the leaders of our country had become the common attitude of the people toward the government. His kinsfolk were among the Regulators of North Carolina, and his father, although a Revolutionary soldier with years of service, emigrated into what was then a foreign land.

William Sherley Williams, born in the early days of the American Republic, lived under Spanish authority as a boy, and started his own career at the time Jefferson, Livingston, and Monroe effected the Louisiana Purchase. In manhood he became a part of the life of the plains and mountains. He saw the Indians pushed back, the New Mexicans dispossessed, and California taken—all in one lifetime.

Lives are usually influenced by the conditions surrounding them; in turn, events are controlled by the people. This was never better illustrated than in the career of Bill Williams. As we follow him through life, we find him a member of an average early American family, then a trapper and hunter, finally emerging into one of the most noted of the mountain men. Likewise we can follow in his career the changes and developments of the West from a wilderness of the Louisiana Purchase of 1803 into a compact section of our country at the time of his death.

Tracing the history of the ancestors of William Sherley Williams, we find running through the lines a restless, wandering, independent spirit. The Musicks and Lewises came to Virginia from Wales, stayed for a time, and then, feeling that perhaps the family fortunes would prosper more in South Carolina, moved to that state. There things did not work out in just the way they

[1] From family Bible, in possession of C. E. Vaughan of Owensville, Missouri; Mr. Vaughan is the grandson of a sister of William S. Williams.

had planned and they again moved, this time to the mountainous district of the western part of North Carolina.[2]

[2] William Terrell Lewis, *Genealogy of the Lewis Family in America from the Middle of the Seventeenth Century down to the Present Time*, 56, 57–61, 187, 188–97; and also the family Bible in possession of C. E. Vaughan, a great grandson of Joseph Williams and Sarah Williams, shows the family history as follows:

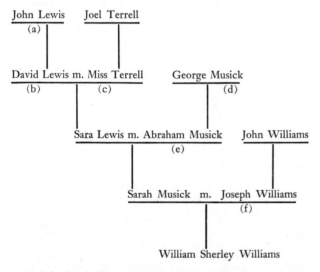

(a) John Lewis, Sr., was born in Wales, England, resided for a time in Denbighshire, England, before coming to America. He accompanied the Mostyn Family to Hanover County, Virginia, in 1675.

(b) David Lewis was the son of John Lewis, born about 1685 in Hanover County, Virginia. He was married three times, had two sets of children, and was preparing to enter into a fourth marriage, when he died in 1779, in his ninety-fourth year, from drinking excessively of cold water after chopping down a tree. He first married Miss Terrell about 1717 and there were born eight children: William, b. 1718; Susannah, b. 1720; Hannah, b. 1722; Sarah, b. 1724, Hanover County, Virginia; David Jr., b. 1726; John, b. 1728; Joel, b. 1730; Anna, b. 1733; his wife died in 1734. He married a second time; had no children. Later he moved, in 1750, to Albemarle County, Virginia, and married Mary McGrath Hart, the widow of Dr. Hart of Philadelphia, and there were three children born: Elizabeth, b. 1754; Col. James, b. 1756; and Miriam, b. 1759.

(c) Miss Terrell, wife of David Lewis, was a staunch Cavalier supporter, the daughter of a Joel Terrell.

(d) George Musick's origin was in Wales, Great Britain. At an early age he was picked up as a foundling; he knew nothing of his family, only that his name was George. "He proved to be a very smart boy and extremely fond of music, so they called him 'George Musick' or Music." He was a loyal supporter of the

On his father's side, his ancestors had given up their home in Wales and had come to the new country. They, too, had located in western North Carolina. Considering the temper of the settlers in this region, it was not strange that Joseph Williams should join the Revolutionists and fight for those things that the colonies had declared against in their Declaration of Independence. The recollection of the family is that he served a number of years in the

---

cause of Charles I, and when Cromwell came into power he left the country and migrated to Virginia.

(e) Abraham Musick, son of George Musick was probably born in Virginia about 1717; he married Sarah Lewis, the fifth child of the first marriage of David Lewis. To this union were born eleven children, the first nine being born in Virginia and the other two in South Carolina. Terrell, b. 1748, who married her cousin Abraham Musick; Lewis, b. 1750, a Revolutionary soldier who fought as one possessed, said to have killed sixty of the enemy. After the War he engaged in several Indian campaigns. While fighting the Cherokees in Rutherford County, North Carolina, he was killed accidentally by one of his own men, although there was some doubt if the killing was not premeditated; John, b. 1752, dying in early life; Joel, b. 1754, drowned in South Carolina; Sarah, b. April 28, 1756, in Hanover County, Virginia, became the mother of William S. Williams and early a member of the Baptist Church. William, b. 1758, also a Revolutionary soldier, was brave even to being reckless. He was an unusually handsome man and one of wonderful physique, "very tall and athletic, fair skin and blue eyes." Residing in Rutherford County, North Carolina, after the War, he fell in love with Miss Winifred Hannon, niece of Col. John Earle of that county, a prominent soldier of the Revolution. Her family objected to his attentions, making every effort to break off the attachment, but were unsuccessful, for the young couple eloped, going to Spanish Louisiana. It was after his uncle William that the son of his sister Sarah was named; Susannah, b. 1760; David, b. 1763, Albemarle County, Virginia, and known as Col. David, was two years of age when the family moved from Virginia to South Carolina in 1765. In 1773 his father moved into Rutherford County, North Carolina. In 1777 during the Revolution, the Cherokees became active and the family moved into a fort until 1779. Enlisted at 16 and served through Revolutionary War. Most of time spent in fighting Indians on the frontier. Fought at Guilford Court House, North Carolina, under General Greene. Moved to Illinois in 1794 and married Prudence Whiteside, the daughter of Dr. James Whiteside formerly of Rutherford County, North Carolina, for whom the Whiteside Station was named. Moved to St. Louis in 1795, settled at Florissant. Soldier in War of 1812; raised a company of horsemen and served on the frontier where he got his title; member of Missouri State Legislature and presidential elector; Jehoiada, b. 1765; Ephraim, b. 1767, who married his cousin, Terrell Musick; and James, b. 1769.

(f) Joseph Williams was born in North Carolina, the son of John Williams, who was born in Wales, England, migrating to America. Joseph Williams was a soldier in the Revolutionary War, serving through the entire seven years in the Virginia, North Carolina, and South Carolina campaigns, and was wounded. He was married about 1777 in Rutherford County, North Carolina.

Continental Line in the various campaigns during the Revolution in that section of the country.[3] Coming from Rutherford County and west of King's Mountain, there is little doubt but that he took part in that celebrated battle on the mountain top, in which Major Ferguson was killed, 250 of the enemy soldiers killed or wounded, and over 600 taken prisoners, with 1,500 stands of arms. This was one of the most important battles of the Revolution, for it encouraged and established the faith of the cause in the minds of many of the Americans. In this battle there were twenty-two cousins of the Musick and Lewis families engaged on the American side.[4]

We know that the Musicks were educated, as education went in that day, were proud of their refusal to follow the Cromwell regime, gloried in the fact that they were Cavaliers, and knew the Washington family, Sarah Musick being personally known to George Washington. Even in after years, under strange frontier conditions, she named a daughter Mary, after Mary Stuart, Queen of Scots, and another daughter Arabella, after Arabella Stuart, "Queen of England for a day."[5]

While the war was still going on, Joseph Williams and Sarah Musick were married, about 1777, joining together two of almost pure Welsh blood, and during the next ten years there were four sons born: the oldest child, James, on March 27, 1778; the second son, Micajah, on February 16, 1783; the third, Lewis, afterwards a prominent divine in Missouri, on May 16, 1784; and William Sherley on January 3, 1787.[6] Mrs. Williams' parents and brothers were near neighbors, each with substantial families, her father having a family of nine, with six slaves.[7]

In the meantime, much had been happening west of the Appalachians, and the Williams and Musick families began to feel the

[3] *History of Cole, Moniteau, (etc.) Counties, Missouri*, Goodspeed Publishing Co., 1128.
[4] Lewis, *op cit.*, 196.
[5] Family Bible in possession of C. E. Vaughan.
[6] Family Bible in possession of C. E. Vaughan; also Lewis, *op. cit.*, 191.
[7] *Heads of Families, First Census of the United States, 1790, North Carolina*, 116, 119.

westward urge so common in that day. Just why Joseph Williams left his home in North Carolina we do not know. After the Revolution he had sold the government land grant of 274 acres[8] received in payment for his thirty-six months as a private in the Continental Line, and had purchased a farm in southwestern North Carolina; he had also acquired more land in the neighborhood.[9] Apparently he was settled with his family. It may be that the stories of land over the mountains urged them. It may be that the North Carolina farm did not turn out as he expected. Perhaps, too, soldiering had made him restless or the spirit of the time urged the move. It has been said that Joseph Williams was an itinerant preacher in Kentucky.[10] He might have preached on the way, for many talked on religion whenever the occasion arose. It is doubtful that he was regularly engaged in preaching, for farming was his calling before he left North Carolina and after he came into the region of the Louisiana Purchase.

In any event, the Williams family gave up their North Carolina home and moved across the Blue Ridge into the area of doubt and misunderstanding. This time they passed through Tennessee, Kentucky, and southern Illinois, and finally, in the year 1794, made their way into the Spanish country lying to the west of the Mississippi River.

[8] *Roster of Soldiers from North Carolina in American Revolution* (published by Daughters of the American Revolution of North Carolina, 1932), 266.

[9] Records of Register of Deeds, Rutherford County, North Carolina.

[10] St. Louis *Globe-Democrat* (Dec. 24, 1911).—In the Sunday magazine of this issue is an article describing an interview with an aged man of Mexican origin, then 102 years of age, Jesús Rupert Valdez Archeleuta, who claimed to have known Williams and to have made trips with the mountain man, over a period of twenty-eight years.

CHAPTER THREE

Early Life in Missouri

THE NORTH CAROLINIAN and his wife, Sarah, sold their Horse Creek farm in the mountains of North Carolina in July, 1794,[1] said good-bye to their friends and relatives, and with their four small boys joined the westward march. In the fall of that year, or the early spring of the next, they had made their way to White-side Station, the town on the east side of the Mississippi River, opposite St. Louis.[2] The former Revolutionary soldier went across the river and made arrangements for the entry of his family into Spanish territory. In taking that step, he was expatriating himself from the county for which he had only recently fought. It took a stout heart to forsake the land of his birth and go to one where a different language was spoken, but courage was common to all pioneers of that day.

St. Louis was then a village of less than one thousand people, mostly of French extraction, and their language, customs, and life were quite different from anything that Joseph Williams had experienced up to that time. Most of the activities in the Upper Louisiana district centered in St. Louis. The Spanish authorities

[1] Deed from Joseph Williams and wife to Isaac Cloud (July 23, 1794), conveying their farm of one hundred fifty acres.—Book M-Q, 237, Register of Deeds, Rutherford County, North Carolina.

[2] *History of Cole, Moniteau (etc.) Counties, Missouri*, 1128; also Lewis, *op. cit.*, 191.

were welcoming people like the Williams family, giving each family a lot within the village of St. Louis, where a home could be built, and the use of a larger tract outside for farming and livestock.

Into this simple, easygoing tolerant, fun-loving French community, these strangers came, their youngest boy, William, being then some seven or eight years of age. They were made to feel at home, and, after all, they were not so far away from their home folks. They had relatives across the river at Whiteside, and Mrs. Williams' father and mother and other members of the family came then or shortly after. In many ways it was a relief to them to be in a peaceful country where politics were unimportant. Then, too, the country suited them and they settled down.

The Spanish government, recognizing the desire of these immigrants to own land, set up laws by which their land hunger could be satisfied. The policy was to grant two hundred arpens to each settler or head of the family, fifty arpens for each child, and twenty for each slave, with a limit of eight hundred arpens to one applicant.[3] An arpen was a measure of land containing 0.8512 of an English acre. The number of arpens which the government would grant to a settler depended on the ability of the homesteader to cultivate and improve the land.[4]

The prospective landowner picked out the tract he wanted and settled on it, and after four years of living on the land, he was qualified to petition the government for a grant of the title, not unlike our own homestead requirements of a later date. If the preliminaries were complied with, the claimant could then petition the *Señor Teniente General* or "Lord High Commissioner" for a survey and at the same time take his oath of allegiance to the Spanish king. A check was made by the officials, and if everything was in order, the survey was made and the settler put in legal possession of the tract surveyed. That constituted his title.

On August 26, 1796, Joseph Williams made application for the survey of a tract of eight hundred arpens northwest of St. Louis.[5]

---

[3] *American State Papers, Public Lands*, VIII, 803.
[4] *Ibid.*, 795.
[5] *Ibid.*, 853.

The authorities waived the requirements as to residence on the Williams application—not an unusual thing for them to do. Indeed, in many instances it was not demanded that the requirements be carried out to the letter, especially if a settler gave promise of becoming an addition to the community. If a settler had a wife and family, in addition to other qualifications, his application was sure to receive favorable attention. Even after Joseph Williams selected the land for his farm, the family continued to make their home in St. Louis, for on September 23, 1795, another son, John W., was born there, claimed by the family to be the first American white child born in St. Louis.[6]

Since the Roman Catholic religion was the only faith recognized by the government, and its observance was a part of the oath of allegiance to the king, it was required that one should become a *bon Catholique* before he could become a citizen. We do not know how this Protestant North Carolinian squared his conscience in this particular; it may be he took the oath with mental reservations as others had done. At any rate, on April 10, 1800, the survey having been made and all formalities having been complied with, Zenon Trudeau, the lieutenant governor of Upper Louisiana, granted to Joseph Williams 800 arpens, or some 680 acres of land, on the south bank of the Missouri, designated Survey No. 282.[7] Williams did not get anything of great value, for land was then selling for a few cents an arpen, the total value being less than one hundred dollars. The tract selected by Joseph Williams was situated at the point of a sweep of the river, on the west side of the old Boone Trace, the main highway from St. Louis up the Missouri River, and was some twelve miles distant from St. Louis, about opposite the town of St. Charles.[8]

[6] Joseph Williams paid taxes in St. Louis as late as 1811.—John T. Scharf, *History of St. Louis City & County*, 192.

[7] *American State Papers, Public Lands*, VIII, 852. See also Records of the Land Department of Secretary of State, Jefferson City Missouri, Volume B of Private Claims, 175. The final survey was made in 1818, and the grant was located in what is now Township 45 North, Range 5 East, of the 5th Principal Meridian, St. Louis County.

[8] See E. Dupre, *Atlas of the City and County of St. Louis by Congressional Townships* (1838).

At a later period, at one of the high waters of the Missouri River, the channel was cut across the narrow part of the bend about a mile north of the Williams farm, leaving an island between their home and the river; and that which was the old bed of the river now is called Crève-Coeur Creek. This Spanish grant to Joseph Williams was confirmed to him after the American occupation.[9]

Some time between 1796 and 1798, the family moved from St. Louis to the farm, or plantation, as Joseph Williams called the place. He built a log house, cleared some ground, and settled down. Other children came along, and here the boy William grew up in a family of nine children.[10]

Both Joseph Williams and his wife could read and write and had a fair background in the fundamentals and in history, all of which gave them a standing in a community where few had any education whatsoever. Following the practice of the period, the parents passed on to their children such knowledge as they had in reading, writing, and arithmetic. Besides the help of their parents, these Williams children at various periods had the advantage of a limited school training, in which they received instruction from hired teachers.

The earliest schools in this pioneer community were held in the settlers' cabins, often with parents and children studying the alphabet together. If the teacher received anything more than his keep, it was so much per head. Often the traveling pedagogue supplemented his teaching with doing odd chores or regular work about the farm or plantation. Not all who claimed ability were educated, even in the common learning of the day. It is related that one of these prospective teachers met with a few of the men of a community near St. Louis and was being examined in regard to his qualifications. He was asked if the earth was round or flat. The candidate answered "he was not quite sure, but was prepared to teach it either way." That reply rather stumped the examining committee; they suspended the questioning, drew apart, and con-

[9] *American State Papers, Public Lands*, II, 699.
[10] Benjamin Franklin was born January 19, 1798; Mary, also called Polly, September 15, 1800; Olivia, January 1, 1803; and Arabella on December 4, 1806.

sulted together. The committee then returned and announced to the candidate they had come to the conclusion that perhaps it would be just as well not to introduce any new methods and he could teach the flat theory, if engaged.[11]

The Williams children had the advantage of a regular school, at least during one year. It was opened at Owen Station, close by their farm. Here the children of the neighborhood, of all ages, along with some children of Indians, received instruction in fundamentals. Bill Williams in his later life indicated he had received more education than the average boy of that period. He could read, keep accounts, had an excellent general knowledge, and wrote a good hand.

During the period of Williams' boyhood, St. Louis was the center of the fur trade and the distributing point for such trading and trapping as went on west of the Mississippi. Important in the fur trade were the French *voyageurs*,[12] with their keelboats and barges going up and down the river, within sight of the Williams home. The *coureurs de bois*[13] traveled over the old Trace, past the Williams cabin, going into trapping country and returning to St. Louis laden with their packs of furs. All this became part of young Bill Williams' life. He grew up, from his first remembrance, in the atmosphere of that trade and early began to realize its importance. His father, however, never seemed to have identified himself with the trade, but occupied himself with farming, stock raising, trading, sugar making in season, and buying and selling real estate when the opportunity arose.[14]

Life in the Joseph Williams household was indeed simple; to get sufficient to eat was the main thing. Whatever business was

[11] John R. Musick, *Stories of Missouri*, 73, 74, 76.

[12] Those who worked on the early water transportation and became adept in handling of canoes and boats on the lakes and rivers. They were for the most part the French and Creoles, this class constituting the large majority of those employed in the fur trade. Later the term was improperly applied to the French trappers or any Frenchmen engaged in various branches of the trade.

[13] Meaning travelers of the woods, a term applied to the French fur trader operating independently, a sort of pack peddler going from tribe to tribe.

[14] There are records in the City Hall of Records, St. Louis, Missouri, Archives, French and Spanish IV, (No. 1) 73, 76, of these contracts made by Joseph Williams from 1800 to 1803, involving sugar making and land interests.

done was carried on by barter. It was a time when there was little or no formality in such dealings, and even in real estate transactions when the trade was settled, we find the contracting parties shaking hands and considering the bargain complete without any written document.

Some years later, Judge Henry Baldwin of the Supreme Court of the United States, in deciding a land title in this district, stated that few of that time could read or write. Judge Baldwin said many of the inhabitants "were in the trade with Orleans, Mackinaw, and the Indian tribes, who attended little to village concerns, and still less to village property, when, on a public sale, its price was eight cents an arpen . . . and was therefore passed from hand to hand by parol, with less formality than the sale of a beaver skin, which a bunch of wampum would buy. . . . Still less did such a race of men, as the boatmen and hunters of the west, who by mutual agreement gave one thing, and took another, whether land or peltry, on a fair exchange by the shake of the hand, ever imagine that a common field lot would ever be worth, when lying waste, a pack of furs, or that no evidence of its sale would be admissible, on a question of whose it was, unless by deed."[15]

It remained a distinctive characteristic of the business of that day that a man's word was as good as a written contract. This continued to be the rule on the plains and in the Rocky Mountains during the period when the boundaries of the Louisiana Purchase were taking form. If a man said he would do anything, nothing further was needed; that constituted his bond, and men were more jealous of their good name in carrying out their contracts than of any other human attainment.

Even more simple than the business method was the home life under which Bill Williams grew up. A one- or two-room log house, with either a dirt floor or rough boards, constituted the living quarters. The cooking was done at the fireplace or over a fire built outside the cabin. The furniture of the house was of the very crudest sort—all made from such lumber as could be cut on the premises with a whipsaw. As a rule there were few cook-

---

[15] *U. S. Supreme Court Reports*, 12 Peters 447-48.

ing utensils—an iron kettle, a skillet, and a few dishes. All of the utensils of the housewife in many families could be packed on horseback with no inconvenience.[16]

The family retired after supper, as soon as darkness came, and were up before sunrise. With little or no money, and with imported cloth goods selling at prohibitive prices, it was but a natural consequence that homespun cloth should be used. Each family kept a few sheep, from which a supply of wool was obtained, and a little cotton was raised. Each family carded its own wool, spun the thread, and made homespun cloth on the rude looms. Many followed the practice set by the Indians in the use of dressed skins for making their moccasins and clothing.

If surplus produce were raised, it could not be sold, since there were no markets, or any people with the means to buy. Consequently each family supplied its own needs, and if there was an excess, it was given to friends or neighbors.

Nature had endowed this section with a lavish hand. There was no need to provide feed for the stock during the winter months, since the native grasses furnished plenty of forage the year round. The country was teeming with game, and such time as men could get off from the work about the plantation was spent in the woods and on the river.

In these early frontier surroundings, under which young Williams grew up, religion played an important part in the life of the community. The law required that all must be Catholic. The padres were the guides, teachers, and counselors of the people. These gay, happy, easygoing French people combined with their religious duties on Sunday, their celebrations, dances, games, and parties. When the religious services were over, the remainder of the day was given to enjoyment. Strange as it may seem, there were both religious tolerance and a total lack of bigotry on the part of the inhabitants, notwithstanding the laws pertaining to religion. Bill Williams' mother had been a member of the Bap-

[16] A good idea of the household possessions of the Williams family can be gained from the papers in the Estate of Joseph Williams, upon which the above and succeeding narrative is to a great extent based.—City Civil Court, St. Louis, Missouri, Probate Division, Case No. 350. See also Scharf, *op. cit.*, 1870.

tist faith in North Carolina. His father, while not so devout, was nevertheless what would be called a professing Christian.[17]

Notwithstanding the acceptance of the Catholic religion by the family at the time they became citizens of the territory, they apparently continued to hold the same faith as before, without interference from the government officials or their neighbors. Sarah Williams was a recognized authority on the Bible, so much so that whenever questions would arise among her friends and neighbors regarding the history, characters, or references in the Bible, she was usually appealed to and her decision was accepted as final.[18] From his earliest youth, Bill Williams grew up in a home where religion was always evident. True, until after the Louisiana Purchase, there were no regular meetings or churches; yet even before that time, in many ways, in the Williams home the importance of religion was emphasized.

The first itinerant preacher who visited the Williams home, was the Reverend John Clark. Born in Scotland, he had been, in turn, sailor, privateer, pirate, an impressed seaman in the English Navy, deserter, school teacher, and finally minister on the frontier. Preaching by Protestants being prohibited by law west of the river, Clark was accustomed to slip clandestinely across from his home in Illinois, visit and minister to the scattered settlers, and then return to his own side of the river. These visits of his were, however, known to the big-hearted lieutenant governor of Upper Louisiana, Zenon Trudeau. His Excellency could see no great harm in what Clark was doing, especially since most of those whom he visited were friends and acquaintances of the Governor. Trudeau found a solution for the situation, without allowing the law of the land to be violated, his record as governor to be attacked, or his friends to be annoyed; he would send word to Father Clark that preaching by non-Catholics was not allowed, and if Clark were found in the country after three days, he would be put in the jail. This message, however, was not sent to the

[17] J. C. Maples and R. P. Rider, *Missouri Baptist Biography*, II, 284.
[18] *History of Cole, Moniteau, (etc.) Counties, Missouri*, 1128.

itinerant preacher until the Governor was sure he had had opportunity to make his rounds of the scattered settlers.

Once the neighbors got up a petition to the Governor asking for permission to hold services in their homes, at which the Reverend Mr. Clark would preach. They sent Abraham Musick, Jr., a cousin of Mrs. Williams, to present it personally to Governor Trudeau. His Excellency publicly and officially rejected the petition, then invited the petitioner to his home, gave him a dinner, at the same time solemnly warning his guest against putting a steeple on his house, ringing any bells, or allowing his children to be baptized by anyone but the parish priest. Then, with a twinkle in his eye, he poured out a glass of good wine, handed it to his friend, saying, "Mark you, if your friend John Clark comes to see you, your neighbor calls, you talk, you pray, you read the Bible, you sing, that's all right; you are all good Catholics."[19]

When Joseph Williams selected his farm in 1796, there was still open land nearer St. Louis, but the river had attracted him. The Osages, Delawares, Shawnees, and other Indians were still numerous in that section where he had selected his home, and continued so until about 1810. Bill's youngest sister, Arabella, recalls that when a small child playing with a little Indian girl, whose mother was employed by Joseph Williams to make maple sugar, she had a scare from a couple of strange Indians. There had been rumors of hostile Indians being in the neighborhood and the Indian woman kept a sharp lookout while attending to her task of keeping the kettles boiling. She heard a noise of someone traveling. The woman hid the white child and the Indian girl each under a large sugar bucket, and cautioned them not to make a sound. Presently two strange Indians came by, looked about, tried to talk to the woman, and went on. It was natural that the Williams boys should become familiar from their earliest childhood with Indian ways.

From the time Bill Williams was nine years of age until he left home, he was thrown constantly in contact with Indian life. Belle

[19] Rev. J. M. Peck, *Father Clark, or The Pioneer Preacher*, 232.

Fontaine trading post[20] lay to the northeast of their home, and many of the Indians going and coming from that post passed by the Williams home. Bill grew up with Indians, learned to speak their language, came to know their ways, thoughts, and habits, could shoot a bow and arrow as well as the Indian boys, and at an early age became an adept in the use of the flintlock gun. The Osages being then in that section of the country, it was with that tribe that he became especially familiar.

The recollections of the Williams family are that Bill Williams had many of the characteristics of his mother; he always had tremendous confidence in his own ability and believed he could do things better than anyone else. Perhaps this is a reflex of the fact that his father and mother always took so much pride in their family connections. He grew up a large, rawboned youth, with red hair and many freckles. He was a ready talker, witty, and quick at repartee. When the Louisiana Purchase was turned over to the United States, the future mountain man was seventeen years of age; he was man grown and, according to the customs of that day, had arrived at man's estate. It may have been the excitement among the people occasioned by the Purchase and the changed conditions brought about by new government, or it may have been a natural desire for adventure that prompted him; in any event he left home that year and started on his career.

[20] Fort Belle Fontaine was the first military post in the Louisiana Purchase, founded in 1805 by order of General James Wilkinson. It was located fourteen miles above St. Louis on the west bank of the Mississippi River, just south of the present bridge crossing the river. It was the site of an old Spanish post. In 1825 it was abandoned.

CHAPTER FOUR

Preacher and Missionary

ON MARCH 9, 1804, the country in and about St. Louis, known as the Upper Province of Louisiana, officially passed from France to the United States. The French had never taken possession of the country, after the cession of 1800, and in order to permit the old French inhabitants to have one more look at their beloved flag, as well as to make the transfer legal, Captain Amos Stoddard, the American commissioner, permitted their flag to replace the Spanish flag, and to remain floating for a day. It was then taken down and the Stars and Stripes displayed, a gracious act, fully appreciated by the older inhabitants. Considering the interest taken in this ceremony, there is little doubt that Bill Williams was there and took part in the celebration.

Outside of the centers of commerce, the change of governments meant very little to the ordinary settler west of the Mississippi, for life went on much the same way after the change as it had before, except that an impetus was given to trade and exploration. People now began to come across the river in greater numbers, and the westward push began in real earnest.

When the United States began to exercise authority, all restrictions on the holding of religious services were removed. Anyone could hold any kind of religious service without fear or hindrance. Spiritual and religious affairs seemed more prominent than ever before. It may be that this was helped along by the religious revival then spreading across the country and being felt by those living west of the Alleghenies.

It was not unusual that young Bill Williams, with religious parents and a religious training, should become converted in this spiritual reawakening. It was a natural step for him to begin to preach; first telling of his own experiences and then, gaining confidence, becoming a regular preacher of the Gospel. One of his marked characteristics in life was always to do well whatever he undertook, and this was true of his initial undertaking. He became an itinerant Baptist parson, following in the faith of his father and mother. The field of his activities was the scattered farms and settlers of Missouri, which at that time extended over an area less than sixty miles from the Mississippi.

These years, in which Bill Williams carried on as an itinerant preacher were always remembered by him, and usually in a boastful way. Uncle Dick Wootton, a mountain man who trapped with Williams in later years, knew nothing of his early life, except that "he was a circuit preacher in the early life in Missouri."[1] William Craig, who helped him steal horses, knew that at one time he "was a minister of the Gospel previous to his becoming a trapper."[2] Albert Pike, who hunted with Williams in the Texas Panhandle, said he "was once a preacher, and afterwards an interpreter in the Osage nation."[3] Williams said of himself that he was so well known on his circuit that even the chickens at the farms he visited knew him, and would exclaim, "Here comes Parson Williams! One of us must be ready for dinner."[4]

There were no churches or organizations among the Protestants during the period Williams was calling the sinners of his circuit to repentance. It was not at all necessary in those days for a person either to be learned or to be asked by any group to preach or to be licensed to serve as a minister of the Gospel. The only

[1] H. L. Conard, *Uncle Dick Wootton*, 201.
[2] Thomas J. Beall, "Recollections of Wm. Craig," *Lewiston* (Idaho) *Tribune* (March 3, 1919).
[3] Albert Pike, *Prose Sketches and Poems*, 37.
[4] Henry Inman, *Old Santa Fe Trail*, 356.

essential was that the individual should feel called to preach and could get persons to listen to his message. The most successful preachers of that day were a combination of exhorter and frontiersman. Whatever the itinerant received as pay for his services was by donation of food, shelter, and clothing from those visited. When these necessities failed to be supplied by his friends, the parson must of necessity fall back on the country for his support. The little money the people had to spend was used to supply their physical needs rather than their spiritual wants.

Bill Williams was not the only member of the family who turned to the ministry. His next older brother, Lewis, as skilled as Bill in the use of the bow and arrow and gun, followed hunting, trapping, and preaching all his life. At least two uncles on his mother's side and several nephews were also Baptist ministers.[5]

Williams' preaching was by exhortation, appealing to the emotions and threatening hell-fire and brimstone to the unrepentant. Those who attended his services often responded in unusual ways to the appeal made. At one of those early Baptist meetings in Missouri, after a stirring appeal to repent and accept the Holy Ghost, one man continued to stand by himself after the crowd had thinned. He repeated over and over again: "Slick as a peeled onion, slick as a peeled onion," each time snapping his fingers. Asked what he meant, he said he had just received the Holy Ghost and it was like a peeled onion to him.[6] From the tales Williams related of his power as a preacher, this incident might well have happened at one of his meetings.

The first services held in the sparsely settled country in which Williams labored were in the settlers' cabins, with only the preacher and the family present. If the visiting parson could command the interest of the settler, he would become a regular visitor, and

[5] Lewis Williams married Nancy Jump in 1805, and there were nine children born to this union. In early life he lived near his father's home north of St. Louis, later moving to Franklin County. He served in the army in the Indian campaign during the War of 1812. He died November 16, 1838.—R. S. Duncan, *History of the Baptists in Missouri*, 79–84.

[6] Wm. S. Bryan and Robert Rose, *A History of the Pioneer Families of Missouri*, 85.

neighbors and friends might be present. As his calls continued, it often happened that the log cabin was not large enough to accommodate all who came, and then, if the weather permitted, the service was held in the open. In this manner, the camp meeting was developed, from the traveling preacher visiting from cabin to cabin. At these early meetings people of all faiths and beliefs attended. The church organization as we know it today from the records of the several churches, did not come into Missouri until after Williams had ceased to ride his circuit.

Some have complained that the religion of these early preachers and their services were prompted by emotions other than religious. They point to the frenzy of these camp meetings, which became nothing less than religious orgies; nevertheless by such means religion was carried on in the new country, outside of the cities and towns. These very agencies laid the foundation for the church organizations we have today, and that strange character, Bill Williams, contributed his part in his own peculiar way in building one of these great faiths.

The Catholic religion was little affected by the change of government; it was firmly established in the towns, with its churches and padres, who occasionally traveled through the country visiting the members of their faith.

The years young Williams was preaching were lean times, from the standpoint of the money he received. It took determination to carry on in such a calling under the conditions that existed. After some five years of preaching he finally gave up his circuit riding. Williams never gave any reason and there is nothing very reliable which sheds light on his decision to leave off preaching. We have several stories of why he quit. One account has it that while preaching to a gathering he noticed a very attractive young lady sitting well toward the front. As the young preacher continued with the service, he glanced now and then in her direction. The young lady seemed considerably pleased at something and smiled broadly back at Williams. Was the smile for him or at him? The thread of his discourse was broken and he began to ramble. Then gripping himself, with his eyes directed over his audience and almost gritting his teeth, he began to draw down fire and brimstone on all, especially on himself. Then a strange thing happened. He did not intend to look at her again, yet some power over which he had no control turned his eyes toward her, although he had told himself he would not look her way. His mind was not on heavenly matters and he became confused and stammering. Could there be any clearer proof to anyone that the Almighty never intended him for one of His servants? Closing up his Bible, he dismissed his audience, and taking up his rifle entered on a new life.[7]

Another account has it that there came into the new land a family from the Far East. In this family was a very beautiful daughter with considerable cultural background. The young minister paid her attention and even asked for her hand in marriage. This she not only refused, but made it plain there was no use in his hoping for any change in her mind at a future moment. The discouraged and disheartened young minister attempted to drown his disappointment in drink. He forthwith got drunk, and, the story runs, that ended his career as a minister.[8] It would hardly seem likely that getting drunk would have disturbed him to that extent, for at the time there was little opposition to the use of liquor even among many of the clergy.

It rather seems likely that young Williams did not give up preaching all at once, that it was a gradual change, as he devoted less time to the calling and more to other lines. His family's recollections are that he trapped and hunted one or two winters and tried teaching, but with indifferent success. Then he moved over and settled among his early boyhood friends, the Osage Indians. This move was prompted by a desire on his part to carry on missionary work among these people. Since some fifteen years of his life after he left the ministry were spent with or near this tribe, we can understand better these years with them if we know something of the background of this tribe.

[7] As told by Judge J. J. Hawkins, formerly of the U. S. Territorial Court of Arizona.
[8] *St. Louis Globe-Democrat* (December 24, 1911).

The Osage Indians, long prior to the Louisiana Purchase, had been one of the powerful nations west of the river. The name itself was a French derivative from *Wazhazhe*, the Indians' own name for the nation.[9] The first mention of this nation was in 1673, when it was said to be located on the Osage River; so for a century and a quarter they had held their own against the pressure from the east and the warlike tribes on the north, west, and south. This nation claimed, and was powerful enough to control, the plains as its hunting grounds, extending west even to the Rocky Mountains. They controlled a scope of country well timbered, plentifully watered, and abounding in game and fur-bearing animals, with the great plains to roam over during the summer season.

The members of this tribe were large, well-proportioned people, many of the men being over six feet in height, with broad visages and broad shoulders which gave the impression of their being even larger than they were. They pierced their ears and used rings and wampum for adornment. One was impressed with the peculiar elevated appearance of the portion of their heads above the ears, which was caused by the binding of the heads of babies to carrying-boards, a custom which was quite commonly practiced by this nation since it was thought it gave the men a bold and manly appearance. The tribe divided about the beginning of the eighteenth century into the Great and Little Osages, yet always maintained friendly relations.

The Osage nations had early carried on trade with the trappers. A number of these adventurers had intermarried with the Osage women and taken up permanent residence among them. One of the early traders among these Indians, prior to the Purchase, was Pierre Chouteau,[10] whose influence, covering a forty-

[9] *Handbook of the American Indians*, Bureau or American Ethnology, Bulletin No. 30, Part 2, 156.—Pronounced Was-sash-eh, according to *American Missionary Register* (February, 1824), Vol. V, 39; or Wah-Sha-She, according to *The Osage Nation and History of Its People* (pamphlet).

[10] (Jean) Pierre Chouteau was born in New Orleans, October 10, 1758. In 1763 he and his brother, Auguste, were in the party which went with La Clede to Ste. Geneviève. Auguste, but thirteen years old, was left in charge of the party by La Clede and journeyed up the river to choose a site for a new fur-trading post. This place was approved by La Clede and named St. Louis. Pierre grew up

year period, practically controlled the destiny of the nation, in
trade, policy, and dealings with the government.

When the young missionary arrived among these Indians, he
knew they worshiped the sun because it gave light, warmth, and
fertility; the moon because it ruled the propagation of the Indians
and animals; the earth because it nourished and supported them;
thunder because it was the source of rain; and also a number of
lesser deities. The medicine man had the supreme word in sickness and in foretelling the outcome of proposed actions. Dreams
were a harbinger of good or evil if properly interpreted.[11] It was
a trying task to substitute for that which they could see a belief
which must be taken on faith. Aside from religion, they were
friendly to Williams, many being acquaintances from boyhood.
It is said that Williams, having renewed his old associations and not
making much headway in proselyting the Osages, offered to trade
with them; that if they would accept the Christian religion, he
would become an Osage, and to this their chiefs and head men
agreed. The bargain did not work out in just the way it was intended, for while it was true that Williams entered wholeheart-
edly into their life, and trapped, hunted, lived, and associated in
every way as an Indian among fellow Indians, the Osages still
revered the sun, moon, earth, and thunder as the all-powerful
spirits. Williams' mother, hearing about this, observed that her
son had got the worst of the bargain, because while Williams had
become two-thirds Osage, the Osages had become only a small
fractional part Christian.[12] His missionary venture was a failure.
He gave up his efforts to convert them and settled among them. In
a short time he was to all intents and purposes a member of that
nation and was recognized as such by their head men and warriors.
Following the usual custom among Indians of naming persons
on account of peculiarity or incident, the Osages named Williams
Pah-hah-soo-gee-ah, by reason of his red hair and his ability to

in the fur trade among the Osages and was engaged in it most of his life. He died
October 10, 1849 at St. Louis.—*Dictionary of American Biography*, IV, 93.

[11] Union Mission Journal (MS, Oklahoma Historical Society, Oklahoma
City), 102.

[12] Recollections of family of Mr. C. E. Vaughan of Owensville, Missouri.

shoot.[13] It is said the Indians even had songs about Williams, which they sang in his honor.

This young man of twenty-six years of age could not well go on single amid such surroundings. He was not insensible to the charms of many of the handsome daughters of nature, and the inevitable took place. Williams was attracted by a maiden of the Grosse Côte, or Big Hill Band, part of the Great Osages. The courtship was conducted in usual Indian fashion, the parents consenting to Williams' suit and accepting the horses and presents offered. The young woman reciprocated his advances, and they were married according to the custom of the tribe, about the year 1813. Perhaps it would be nearer the truth to say he had married his wife and acquired her relatives. The couple set up a lodge and started life. This marriage was not a temporary union but continued until the death of the Indian woman. As was not unusual in such cases, there existed real affection between the white man and the Indian woman. All of this was well known to Williams' father and mother.[14] From the time of his marriage until he left the Great Osages in 1825, his lot was cast with those Indians and he was brought into tribal relations with their great chief, White Hair.

Lack of success had discouraged him in his efforts to convert these Indians to Christianity; living among them had raised doubts in his mind if he really wanted them changed, and when he married into the tribe he was of a mind that his efforts were misdirected. Why bother with the life hereafter? The present was of more concern to him then. One comrade aptly put it, when he said, "Bill laid aside his Christianity and took up his rifle."[15] From that point on, his activities were in paths quite removed from the vocation of an itinerant Baptist preacher, working among Missouri settlers, or a Christian missionary trying to persuade the red men to forsake the religions of their forebears.

[13] Family history, as related by Mr. C. E. Vaughan of Owensville, Missouri, told by Sarah Williams to his grandmother.

[14] Recollections of Mr. C. E. Vaughan.

[15] Micajah McGehee, "Rough Times in Rough Places," from the Narrative of Micajah McGehee, *Century Magazine* (March, 1891), Vol. XLI, 771.

If a traveler in the years following Williams' joining White Hair's tribe had gone some five or six miles up the Marais des Cygnes River[16] from the point where it emptied into the Osage River, in central western Missouri, he would have come on a settlement of queerly shaped Indian huts. They were square or rectangular in shape with steep sloping roofs, the ridgepole being some twenty feet high and the eaves some four or five feet above the ground. The framework was built of logs and saplings and was covered with brush, bark, and mud. The river on which this village stood was known as the Fen or Swamp of the Swans and hence the name, given it by the early French traders. This collection of huts was known as Big Osage Town, being one of the main villages of these Indians; it was ideally located, for it was in the heart of a fine, fertile country, rich in game and well watered. Leading north from this place was a trail which could be easily followed to Fort Osage on the Missouri, seventy-six miles distant; to the south ran another trail, passing to the country inhabited by the Little Osages and the Arkansas Osages and on to Fort Smith in the Arkansas territory, some 150 miles away.

It was in this village Williams lived with his Indian wife, at least during the winter season, for in summer the Great Osages usually scattered far and wide in their rovings. In September, 1814, a daughter was born to him. The baby had red hair like her father, and he named her Mary, after his oldest sister.[17] Not long after the birth of this baby, he had a second child born, another girl, whom he named after his mother, Sarah Williams.

One would have found it difficult to see much difference between this white man and his wife's relatives and friends. He hunted and trapped with them, following their methods in curing the peltries; he joined in their singing, with natural ability and love of music; he danced the ceremonials with full as much enjoyment and feeling as the native sons; if marauding or fighting

[16] Also spelled Marie de Cine, M. De Cigne, Marias de Cygne, Maries des Cygnes, Marias de Seine, Marie de Cein. Pronounced mah-ray d'zine.
[17] The Baptismal Records of St. Francis Church, St. Paul, Kansas. This checks with the Records of Harmony Mission.—See Z. Lewis in the *American Missionary Register*, VI, 273.

45

were planned, he was the first to join. With a multitude of different experiences, his philosophy of life and ideas had undergone a metamorphosis; he was no longer the parson; rather he was on his way to becoming a mountain man. With a perfect speaking knowledge of the language, probably he began to think and dream in the Osage tongue, for he had come to regard dreams in the same manner as his Osage brethren. It was not surprising that the government agents soon saw Williams' value to them as an interpreter and as a medium through whom they could advance the best interests of the trading system then in force among the Indians.

CHAPTER FIVE

With the Osage Indians

WHEN BILL WILLIAMS came to the Osages, the United States government had a definite Indian policy. This policy was the factor and agency system of trade and control. The French and the English had been successful in their handling of the Indian trade through their chartered companies. The first company so formed was the Hudson's Bay Company, owned in part by the British government and in part by private interests. This semi-governmental character of the company gave the English traders tremendous advantage over any competitor in their dealing with the natives. But after the cession of Canada to Great Britain in 1763, independent rivals of the Hudson's Bay Company combined to form the Northwest Fur Company, which carried on a bitter rivalry with the Hudson's Bay Company until the two were amalgamated in 1821.

The first plan adopted by the United States for the handling of the Indians was a modification of the English policy, and was sometimes referred to as the "factor" or "factory" system.[1] The Americans did not go as far as the English went in their policy, for after providing for the handling of all trade through a branch of the War Department, making it a government function, the personnel of the American system was entrusted to government

[1] Chittenden, *op. cit.*, 1, 12–15, and other sources.

employees, entirely eliminating the individual incentive, which the English companies found the primary reason for their success. The factory system, as adopted by the United States, was intended to, and did, control the Indian trade in certain quarters, kept the government informed of the Indian activities, and eliminated much interference with the wards of the government where the system existed.

By the time Bill Williams arrived among the Osages, the system was well established. All Indian affairs were then handled by the War Department. Scattered about on the frontier from the Great Lakes to the Arkansas River, among the Indians, were numerous trading posts designated factories, each in charge of an employee of the War Department, called a factor. Through merchandising outposts, the furs of the Indians were exchanged for such supplies as the red men required, or perhaps more properly speaking, such supplies as the government officials thought they needed.

With the taking over of the Purchase, the very first activity of the government agents, aside from the army occupation, had been to arrange for the setting up of factors' trading posts. The head of the factory system was a superintendent of Indian trade, with headquarters at Georgetown, in what is now the District of Columbia. Under the superintendent were factors, in charge of the trading posts situated among the several tribes of Indians, taking their orders from and making their reports to the superintendent periodically. Each factor had an assistant, or clerk, and an interpreter to carry on the business entrusted to the post. In the principal cities the government also had branch agencies acting as clearinghouses. Some efforts were made to hold the sales of furs in Georgetown, with but indifferent success. These sales in the East were therefore abandoned and the fur trade allowed to resume its normal course at St. Louis.

The first trading post west of the Mississippi was established at Belle Fontaine, with Rodolphe Tillier as factor, Major George C. Sibley as his assistant, and Pierre Loré as the interpreter. The post was described as the "U. S. Factory House, Belle Fontaine, near St. Louis on Upper Louisiana." From the boyhood home of Bill Williams, it was about the same distance as St. Louis, and Williams as a youth was entirely familiar with the trading at that place. The inventory of this factory as of July 1, 1806, shows that it had goods and equipment to a value of $35,712.99½.[2]

The trading post at Belle Fontaine continued to carry on as a government agency until about 1808, when, the trade having moved up the Missouri River to Arrow Rock, in Indian country, the Belle Fontaine factory was discontinued. The new factory at Arrow Rock took its name from a large rock that juts out on the south side of the river, and was situated about twenty miles above the present town of Booneville. Changes took place in those days with considerable rapidity. No sooner was Belle Fontaine discontinued than the Arrow Rock trading post was in full swing. In 1808, Fort Osage was established and remained the chief trading post for the Osage Nation until the system was broken up in 1822. This factory was situated on the south side of the Missouri River, about twelve miles east from the present town of Independence, Missouri. Sibley, Missouri, is now on the site of old Fort Osage. In the early part of 1821 a factory was founded among the Osages at Marais des Cygnes, in the heart of the Osage Nation, about where the present town of Papinsville, Missouri, is situated; Paul Ballio was in charge and Williams was interpreter. Factories were also established at Fort Edward, Fort Smith, Green Bay, and other places convenient for Indian trade and communication with the United States representative in St. Louis.

Not all trade with the Indians was carried on through the factory posts. The governors of the territories had authority to issue licenses to private parties, if satisfied the applicants were men of character and were reliable. At times traders conducted their activities near the Indian country, and often this resulted in the

[2] Report of Rodelphe Tillier, agent July 1, 1806, MS in Retired Files of the Fur Trade, formerly under the War Department in the Department of Interior, Washington, D. C. The use of the half-cent was not that the cent was divided in value; rather, it came from the use of the "bit," today preserved in the common terms in the south and western parts of our country: "two-bits," "four-bits," etc.

developing of settlements. Such was the case of Côte-sans-Dessein, some two miles down stream from the juncture of the Missouri with the Osage, on the south bend. Here a number of French traders had settled and carried on considerable business with the Osage Indians.[3] The volume of exchange which these independents carried on with the Indians did not compete seriously with the factors' trading posts.

The first record we have of Williams' work with the government agency is that of his being a messenger, a fact indicating his familiarity with the country between Arrow Rock and St. Louis. On November 30, 1813, he left Arrow Rock with dispatches from Major George C. Sibley to General William Clark of St. Louis, delivered his dispatch, and left St. Louis on December 15, returning to the trading post.[4] The route traveled took him down the river past his old home. James Bridger[5] began his mountain life among the same surroundings as Bill Williams. They both lived among the Osages and knew each other, being about the same age. On August 6, 1812, Bridger received eleven dollars from George C. Sibley at Fort Osage, for carrying dispatches between "the settlement of the Saline on the Missouri to Fort Osage and back again to the Saline, six days' journey," and again on March 24, 1814, he was paid a like sum at Arrow Rock for eleven

3 Côte-sans-Dessein was founded in 1808. The Indians from the north attacked the place in 1812, and Baptiste Louis Roi, with the assistance of two men and two women, succeeded in repelling the attack. Between 1819 and 1822, Lazarist Father De la Croix made several trips to this place and baptized a number on each occasion.—Reuben Gold Thwaites (ed.), *Early Western Travels 1748–1846*, V, 48 n.; Alfred de Riemaecker, *Joseph et Charles De la Croix*, 71–75.

4 Letter from Wm. Clark to G. C. Sibley dated December 15, 1813, MS in George C. Sibley Papers, Vol. III.

5 James Bridger was apprenticed to learn the blacksmith trade to Phil Creamer of St. Louis. In 1822 he entered the service of Andrew Henry, was with the party in 1823 when the Arickarees attacked General Ashley; was one of the first to discover the South Pass and Great Salt Lake. He was early in the fur trade and remained a central figure for many years; one of the organizers of the Rocky Mountain Fur Company; member of several partnerships; employed by the American Fur Company, associated with Luis Vasquez; in 1843 founded Fort Bridger; served various parties as guide and in government service. Late in life he retired to a farm near west part of Missouri and died there July 17, 1881. He was one of the greatest mountain men.—Chittenden, *op. cit.*, 257–59.

days' "services as an express going to St. Louis and returning to this place with public dispatches."[6]

Jim Bridger must have been born considerably earlier than March 17, 1804, the date given as his natal day by Mr. Chittenden, in his *American Fur Trade*.[7] The fact that Bridger signed his name to the receipts in both instances cited above would also indicate that the usual statement that he was illiterate is not altogether accurate. Possibly this idea came from his signing his name with a cross to the dissolution of the partnership with Sublette, Fitzpatrick, Fraeb, and Gervais and to the organization of a new one with Sublette and Fitzpatrick on June 30, 1834. It was not uncommon in those days for a person to sign his name to one document and make his mark on another. Bill Williams' own mother signed papers both ways.[8]

By 1817, Williams was definitely employed as an interpreter by Major Sibley at the Fort Osage trading post during the spring of 1817, at a salary of $40.00 a month. He was also employed at the post the same spring, in "packing and pressing 78 packs peltry at 33½¢ a pack," and was also paid for "one day's work as a laborer." For the former he received $26.00 and for the latter, $7.75.[9] Besides the receipts he gave for the money received on that day from Major Sibley, Williams signed as a witness on the voucher of Joseph Lajemonierre, when the latter was paid for his work as a laborer.[10] The chirography has one marked characteristic of the man—assurance and confidence in himself. This never grew less as the years went by. (See specimens of Bill Williams' signature.)

Williams made a trip now and then to St. Louis to transact

[6] Receipts by James Bridger to G. C. Sibley, United Sstates Factor at Fort Osage, August 6, 1812, and at Arrow Rock, March 24, 1814, MSS in Retired Files of Indian Fur Trade, Department of the Interior, Washington, D. C.

[7] Chittenden, *op. cit.*, 257. A more recent and excellent work on the life of Bridger seems to carry forward the same date.—J. Cecil Alter, *James Bridger*, 2.

[8] Papers in Estate of Joseph Williams, office of the Clerk of Civil Courts of City of St. Louis, Missouri, Probate Division, case No. 350.

[9] Receipts of Wm. S. Williams to G. C. Sibley, United States Factor, June 30, 1817, MSS in Retired Files of Indian Fur Trade, Department of Interior, Washington, D. C.

[10] Receipt of Joseph Lajemonierre, June 30, 1817, to G. C. Sibley, MS in Retired Files of Indian Fur Trade, Department of the Interior, Washington, D. C.

business, and he also received some mail there.[11] This gave him an opportunity to keep in touch with his family and the outside world. Early in 1821 he was appointed official interpreter at the new factory at Marais des Cygnes. The job was not merely translating from one language to the other; the man must know values and understand the working of the Indian mind. It was the interpreter who either made or broke a trading post.

On January 9, 1820, Bill Williams' father died, having predicted the exact day on which his death would take place. Although his son Bill had not merited his approbation, he gave him an equal share with the other children, his portion being an interest in real estate.[12]

Shortly after his father's death, Edi Musick, a relative, went over to the Osage country, found Bill Williams living at Big Osage Town, and, for $280, bought out his interest in the land he had inherited from his father. This deed is the only record that has come to light of Bill Williams' ever having owned any real estate, and he did not own this for long.[13]

From the records of the Catholic and Protestant missionaries we begin to note the change which was taking place in Bill Williams' outlook on life. The Catholic church had had missionaries among the Osages when they lived farther east, near Kaskaskia, but their efforts had not been made continuously, and not all in the early part of the century.[14] In April, 1822, a Lazarist father, Charles de la Croix, was sent to the Great Osage Nation, after their chieftains had gone to St. Louis to ask *Grand Père des Robes-Noires* (Grandfather of the "Black Robes," as the Indians called these priests) to send them teachers.[15] Fr. de la Croix visited, taught,

[11] Letter advertised for Will S. Williams in *Missouri Gazette* (St. Louis, October 4, 1817).

[12] See Administration Book, 136, 137, office of the Clerk of the Civil Courts of city of St. Louis, Missouri Probate Division.

[13] Deed William S. Williams to James Walton, dated April 28, 1820, recorded June 20, 1820, Book 1, of Deeds, 283. City Hall of Records, St. Louis, Missouri.

[14] Riemaecker, *op. cit.*, 64, 96.

[15] Monseigneur Louis-Guillaume du Bourg, Bishop of New Orleans born on the French island of Martinique, was consecrated Bishop of Louisiana at Rome, 1815. Riemaecker, *op. cit.*, 50.

and baptized them on two trips made during that year. His health was undermined by fever, forcing him to suspend his efforts; then the Jesuits took over the mission he had founded at Florissant, and in 1823 he returned to his home in Belgium.[16]

In 1820 the War Department gave permission to the United Foreign Missionary Society of New York to do missionary work among the Osages. That society established a mission school, called Union, on the Verdigris some 125 miles north of Fort Smith, and another, known as Harmony, on the banks of the Marais des Cygnes not far from Big Osage village in western Missouri.[17] From the records of these two mission schools we have many references to Williams.

The future mountain man at the time was working at the Marais des Cygnes factory with Paul Ballio, and was considered the most skillful interpreter of the Osage and English languages. Williams at first rendered every assistance to the missionaries. He helped them get together a "dictionary of about two thousand words," to translate parts of the Bible and hymns, and to gather material useful in conducting services.[18] This was printed in a book by the Society.[19]

From the records of these missionaries we learn that they were considerably disturbed when they found the Indians "eating the entrails of animals" they had killed, that in matters of religion the Indians had "no correct idea of the one superior God" and were a "people given to idolatry," and that their manners were rude and their habits of living far from clean.[20]

When Father de la Croix visited the Osages in 1822, he seems to have been more favorably impressed. His description of the visit leads us to believe the Padre could enjoy himself almost anywhere. On his first visit a great feast was held, and he describes

[16] *Ibid.*, Chapters XII to XVI.
[17] Article entitled "Civilization of the Indians." *Missouri Intelligencer* (March 27, 1824).
[18] *American Missionary Register*, II, 407; IV, 373. Union Mission Journal (MS), 50.
[19] *The Osage First Book, Washashe Wageressa Pahygreh Tse 1834*, Crocker & Brewster (Copy in Boston Athenaeum).
[20] Union Mission Journal (MS), 102-103.

the "after dinner speeches" of the braves: "After each course of eating the missionary would be condemned to hear the recitation of the prowess of his host; the names of the enemies killed by his hand, and of those whose scalps adorned his buckler."[21] It was among these surroundings that Williams had definitely cast his lot.

On a number of occasions Williams acted as interpreter for the missionaries in the religious services intended for the benefit of the Indians. Once he was asked and consented to translate a sermon to the red men. When the Indians had assembled, Williams asked the minister what text he had selected from which to preach. The minister told him it was to be from the Book of Jonah. Drawing from his years experience with the Indians, Williams advised the good man against telling these Indians the story of Jonah and the whale, for they would never believe the fish story. The man insisted on the talk as he had planned. Williams consented, but with misgiving. The story was told and translated; then an old chief arose and with solemn declaration said, "We have heard several of the white people talk and lie; we know they will lie, but that is the biggest lie we ever heard." Then wrapping his blanket about him, he stalked toward his tipi. The rest of the Indians forthwith arose and without further word, followed the chief, leaving the preacher and Williams alone.[22]

This incident illustrates a prominent Indian characteristic. He would not believe anything which he must take on faith. The Indian must see and himself experience, before he is willing to accept anything as a fact. Williams knew the Indian mind. This trait is perhaps better illustrated in an incident which happened some years later, when Captain Randolph B. Marcy was describing the accomplishments of the white race to a Comanche brave, through a Delaware interpreter. The steam engine was described and the Delaware did fairly well in translating because he himself had seen an engine at one time. The Comanche could not believe him, and the Delaware interpreted his observation of the tale to Captain Marcy as meaning, "Hush, you fool!" Marcy then tried

21 Riemaecker, *op. cit.,* 94.
22 Beall, *op. cit.*

54

to explain the magnetic telegraph and how a message could be sent a thousand miles and an answer returned in ten minutes. The Delaware listened courteously but made no comment, nor did he interpret the substance to the Comanche. Marcy then said, "Explain that to the Comanche"; whereupon the Delaware replied, "I don't think I tell him that, Captain; for the truth is, I don't believe it myself."[23]

Williams' small daughter, Mary, for a time attended the mission school at Harmony. The Indian children in rather limited number did attend the early mission schools, but they never became popular with the Osages; there was decided opposition from the start to their children's going to the schools.

The missionaries were ready to save a soul in any quarter. They became so encouraged by the help Bill Williams gave them in the first days that they prayed "he might be renewed by the Spirit of Grace."[24] It was a hopeless task. Bill Williams was becoming a mountain man, and once headed in that direction, such a man rarely turned back. It may be that the reception of the story of Jonah and the whale by the Indians showed the futility of the missionaries' efforts, or his associations with the missionaries may have hurt his standing with the Indians. He began to show a decided unwillingness to be identified with their work. To them he developed a "selfish and perverse disposition," until finally, when asked by the Reverend Mr. Pixley to "interpret a discourse," he put off answering him for a day, and then definitely refused.[25]

In 1821 war broke out between the Osages and the Cherokees. The fighting was carried on by the Osages principally with bows and arrows, as they were not very well equipped with guns. They had a few "muskets and shotguns," but on a whole made little use of the rifle.[26] The government sent General Henry Atkinson, General E. P. Gaines, and Major William Bradford, from Council Bluffs, to see what could be done about bringing an end to the

[23] Randolph B. Marcy, *Exploration of the Red River of Louisiana*, 33 Cong. 1 sess., *House Exec. Doc.*, 100.
[24] *American Missionary Register*, III, 212.
[25] *Ibid.*, V, 273, 274.
[26] *St. Louis Inquirer* (February 24, 1821).

hostilities. Bill Williams was employed by the officers to go along as interpreter.[27] Leaving the Marais des Cygnes Factory, the party went south to Fort Smith, where they met Colonel Matthew Arbuckle in command of the troops and were assisted by James Miller, the territorial governor. The chiefs and head men of both nations were assembled, and a big talk was held. The meeting was a success, peace was arranged, and a treaty signed,[28] Williams assisting in reconciling the differences between the contending nations.

[27] Union Mission Journal (MS), 137.

[28] Treaty dated Fort Smith, August 7, 1822, between the Cherokee Nation and the Big and Little Osage Nations. Records of the Indian office, Department of the Interior, Washington, D. C.

CHAPTER SIX

Changes in the Indian Trade

SEVERAL CHANGES AND EVENTS took place between 1822 and 1825 which influenced the course of Williams' life. The government discontinued the system of trading through factors. The independent trader came into his own. The Santa Fe trade began in real earnest. Williams' wife died. The Osage Indians were moved out of western Missouri. Major Sibley surveyed a government road to the Spanish settlements.

By the year 1820 the trading policy of the government was being kicked around by everyone. The independent traders as a rule opposed this method of doing business, as it limited their initiative and restricted their operations. The American Fur Company under the leadership of John Jacob Astor was conducting an effective lobby in Washington, to turn the Indian trade over to private interests. The opponents of the system had persuasive arguments. The government was steadily losing money and the system did not seem to be accomplishing the purposes for which it had been adopted. Many in Congress wanted to restrict the liquor trade and were willing to trade off the factors, if that could be accomplished.

The deciding influence was the far western trade up the Missouri River and with Santa Fe. Even when the government posts were in full operation, not all trade had been conducted with the

Indians through these agencies. The American Fur Company had posts on the Missouri, which were supplied out of St. Louis; the Missouri Fur Company carried on some operations along the Missouri; and on the Pacific Coast the Pacific Fur Company was doing much trading.

As early as 1810, attempts had been made to trade with the Santa Fe settlements. In some instances the goods had been seized, the traders had been accused of being spies, and a few merchants had even been thrown into the *calabozos* and kept there for years. Nothing daunted, merchants with stocks of goods left each year for the Southwest. Among these traders we find in 1812, Messrs. Robert McKnight, James Beard; in 1815, Samuel Chambers, Augustus P. Chouteau, and Julius McMunn; and in 1819, David Meriwether, the latter returning some years later as the governor of that territory under the American rule. Colonel Hugh Glenn in 1821 went through to Santa Fe with a caravan and made money. In the same year Captain William Becknell, called the "father of the Santa Fe trade," went out with a party to Santa Fe, meeting with a measure of success. Colonel Braxton Cooper and his son had outfitted a trading party for the Spanish settlements in 1823, going through without mishap from the Indians or the New Mexicans.[1]

All who had gone out to the Spanish settlements brought back glowing tales of the demand for all kinds of merchandise and the prices which could be obtained, and in some instances they had tangible results to show for their efforts.

Congress could not withstand the pressure and on May 6, 1822, abandoned the factory system.[2] A new policy took the place of the old. The new order called for a superintendent of Indian affairs, with headquarters in St. Louis. From him the individuals and the companies could procure licenses to trade among the Indian tribes upon proving responsibility and giving bond. Periodical settlements were to be made between the Indians and the traders; this for the protection of both. In the event any dispute

[1] Gregg, *op. cit.*
[2] *United States Statutes at Large*, III, 682.

arose between the traders and the Indians, the burden of proving the justness of a claim rested upon the shoulders of the trader. This was good in theory but a meaningless provision in actual practice. The new law also prohibited the introduction into Indian territory or sale of intoxicating liquors to the Indians, but this provision was never enforced, to the discredit of the government and with disastrous results to the natives.

The new trade policy probably affected the Indians with whom Bill Williams was living more than any other nation in the West. In 1808 the government had agreed with the Osages to establish and permanently continue at Fort Osage, "at all seasons of the year, a well assorted store of goods for the purpose of bartering with them on moderate terms for their peltries and furs." The government could hardly go on supplying goods through its post after it gave up trading. Richard Graham, the Indian agent, in 1822 made a new treaty, at the Marais des Cygnes, with the Great and Little Osages. He turned over to the Indians merchandise to a value of $2,329.40, and the Indians in turn released the government from its obligation to maintain trading posts.[3] Thus, after having been accustomed for twenty-five years to trade with government agents, the Osages were now turned over to the tender care of the independent trader.

Generally speaking, the new system stimulated western trade. The *Missouri Intelligencer* stated that in less than five months after "the abolition of the United States factories," and after the new law went into effect, "a great activity was prevailing in the operation of the trade; those formerly engaged in it have increased their capital and extended their enterprises; firms have engaged and others are preparing to do so."[4]

General William H. Ashley organized the Rocky Mountain Fur Company in 1822 at St. Louis. In the spring of the next year he went up the Missouri with a strong party and a large stock of goods intended for the Indian trade. In this party were enlisted

[3] *Treaties between the United States of America and the Several Indian Tribes from 1778 to 1837;* treaty dated August 31, 1822, 302, *et seq.*
[4] Issue of September 17, 1822.

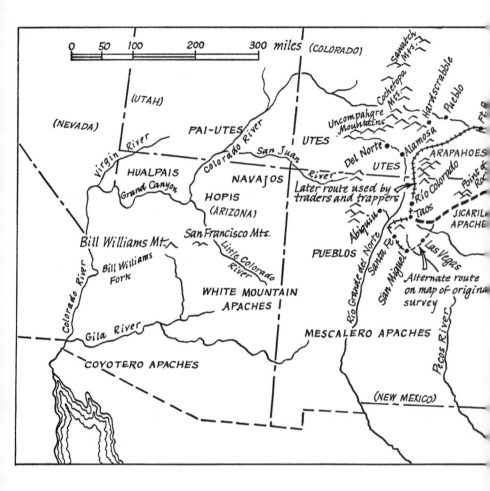

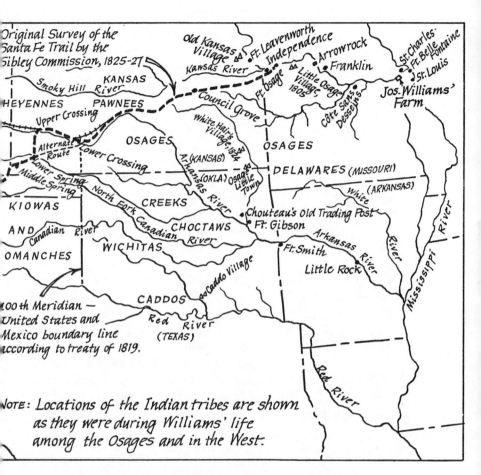

Map illustrating events in the life of Old Bill Williams.

the leading trappers, hunters, and mountain men of the day. The Santa Fe traders took goods of a value of $15,000 by pack animals through to Santa Fe in 1822. Two years later, wagons had been introduced in the trade, and that year goods worth $35,000 went to the Southwest.

One of the earliest to engage in the Santa Fe trade after the new law became operative was Antoine Roubidoux. The first trip he made was typical of many others. On December 29, 1823, he procured authority from General William Clark, superintendent of Indian affairs at St. Louis,[5] to "pass through the Indian country to Council Bluffs,"[6] which at that time was the name of a section of the country where Fort Atkinson was located, some twenty-five miles up the Missouri from the present city of Omaha. Roubidoux, with seventeen men including Charles Beaubien,[7] took his stock of goods by barge up the Missouri to the Fort. At this place he procured another passport from Colònel Henry Leavenworth, the commanding officer in charge of the army post, to "pass through the Indian country lying between this place and the boundary line between the Territory of the United States and New Mexico, in the direction of Santa Fe."[8] Roubidoux was successful in this venture, going through to Santa Fe and returning by the same route. He left Fort Atkinson in September of 1824, and was back at the same place in August of the next year.[9]

Even before the trading posts of the government were abol-

[5] License issued by Wm. Clark, dated December 29, 1823. MS in Huntington Library, San Marino, California. The name is also spelled Antoine Robidoux or Roubideaux.

[6] Council Bluffs was on the west side of the river; it was first called Camp Missouri and was so named by Lewis and Clark; then Fort Atkinson, and later Fort Calhoun.—Chittenden, *op. cit.*, III, 949, 951.

[7] Charles Beaubien was of a fine Canadian family; lived in Santa Fe was part owner of the famous Beaubien and Miranda grant of 1,700,000 acres in New Mexico, the largest single owned tract in the history of the country, which later came into the ownership of Lucien Maxwell, a son-in-law; was appointed one of three circuit judges of New Mexico by General Stephen W. Kearny in 1846; died in 1864.

[8] Permit signed by Colonel Henry Leavenworth. MS in Huntington Library, San Marino, California.

[9] Edgar B. Wesley, "The Diary of James Kennerly," *Missouri Historical Society, Collections*, VI, (No. 1), 50, 75, 78.

ished, Bill Williams had begun to spend less time about the posts and more in trapping and trading on his own account. The work of interpreting did not require all his time, particularly during the trapping seasons, for many of the Indians were away and little was going on at those times to require his services. He was free to go as he pleased and look after his own affairs for the most of the time. His fur catch for the fall of 1821 was considerable. In December of that year the United States factor at "Marias de Cigne," Paul Ballio, paid him by draft the sum of $691.32½. The draft was drawn on "Thomas L. McKenney, Esq. Superintendent of Indian Trade, George Town, Columbia,"[10] through which agency all substantial amounts owing by the factors were paid. In the spring of 1822, Paul Ballio, the factor, reported in his account as having paid to Williams the further sum of $307.57½ by draft;[11] so that Williams during the period of less than a year, carried on a trade to a value of over one thousand dollars, which, taking the circumstances into consideration, indicated much activity on his part, aside from merely living with the Indians.

Paul Ballio and Bill Williams both had married Osage wives. They had been acquainted for years and had been associated in business in the government factory. The Marais des Cygnes factory was closed with the others, and Ballio and Williams were forced to turn to some other activity. They had talked over the situation and were of the opinion there was a good opportunity for them to conduct an independent trading post with their friends, the Osages. It was a very logical decision for them to make. Probably they welcomed a chance to begin trading on their own account. The Indians had been moving west and south, and Ballio and Williams decided to open up farther south. Accordingly, in 1823 they moved some fifty miles southwesterly from the Marais des Cygnes factory and opened a trading post on the

---

[10] Draft of Paul Ballio, United States Factor, December 31, 1821. MS in Retired Files of the Fur Trade, Indian Office, Department of the Interior, Washington, D. C.

[11] Copy of Journal of Paul Ballio, January 1, 1823 (name sometimes spelled Balio). Retired Files of Indian Fur Trade, Department of the Interior, Washington, D. C.

Neosho. These men found it quite different to be in business for themselves, if results meant anything. They were not successful, the chief reason being that they had too liberal a credit policy. Doing business with relatives and friends, the firm of Ballio and Williams both jointly and severally found it impossible to say no. They closed the post and dissolved the partnership. It was not a total loss, for they still had claims against the Osages for the equivalent they had invested. Two years later they got back a small fraction of their money when the Osages sold their holdings to the government, but most was lost.

Williams' next venture showed that he had profited by the experience gained at the Neosho post. He decided he would continue with the Indian trade, but this time he would trade where he had no friends or relatives. He selected the Kickapoos, who lived to the east of the Osages. On May 30, 1824, Richard Graham, the Indian agent, issued a license to him to trade among the Kickapoos at the fork of the Grand River.[12] The Indian trader also included the right to traffic with his home folk, the Osages. We have record of one trade made, a northwest fusil, which was a musket, and it sold for $14.50.[13] The license issued by the Indian agent, was good for one year and called for a bond of five hundred dollars, and the trader, Williams, represented that he had a capital of two thousand dollars. Either Williams had saved something from the Neosho failure, or he still had credit with which to get goods.

This was the last trading he did in Missouri, and no other license was issued to him. That year, 1824, he performed a signal service to the government in connection with the Mad Buffalo incident and at the same time served well his adopted tribesmen.

All the years Williams had lived among the Osage Indians, continuous warfare had been carried on by them with the Pawnees. It

[12] *Report of the Secretary of War Conveying a List of Licenses to Trade with the Indians . . . Quarter Ending September 30, 1826.* 19 Cong., 2 sess., *House Exec. Doc. 86.*

[13] Accounts of Indian Agents, 1822–25, 106. Abstract of Articles Purchased on Account of Presents to Indians in the Quarter from March 1 to June 1, 1824. MS, Kansas Historical Society.

From old unclassified files on the Fur Trade,
Indian Bureau, Department of the Interior, Washington, D. C.

"Besides the receipts he gave for the money received on that day from Major Sibley, Williams signed as a witness on the voucher of Joseph Lajemonierre, when the latter was paid for his work as a laborer. The chirography has one marked characteristic of the man—assurance and confidence in himself. This never grew less as the years went by."

Alfred Jacob Miller, "Mountain Man Preparing Supper,"
from the Porter Collection

"He could progress faster, be less liable to attack, and could secure more peltries in a short time when he had only Bill Williams to look out for. Some called him 'Old Solitaire.'"

was the fixed policy of the Osages to encourage this hostility. They reasoned that with war parties going out, their young men would learn to be brave and would be taught how to fight; moreover, through such war parties they could keep themselves supplied with horses. It was a common practice, amounting practically to a religious custom, to avenge the death of a relative or friend by the killing of an enemy. This is well illustrated by an incident in the life of Tally, one of their great chiefs. Returning to his home from a successful raid on the Pawnees, he found his daughter dying from natural causes. Taking her in his arms after she had passed away, he said, "Now I must go once more to avenge the death of my child."[14] His mourning would continue, he would refrain from shaving or painting his head, and he could not be happy again, or enjoy the blessings of living, until he had avenged her death by killing an enemy. That belief was fundamental and deeply rooted in the minds of the Osages.

In the fall of 1823, a strong war party of some eighty braves, under the leadership of Mad Buffalo,[15] Little Eagle, and other chiefs, conducted a raiding expedition against their old enemies, the Pawnees. At the same time a party of hunters under Major Curtis Welborn was encamped on the Blue River, a branch of the Red River. There existed not the slightest ill feeling or enmity between the Osage raiders and these hunters. Mad Buffalo, in his expedition against the Pawnees, had met with reverses and several braves were killed in the fighting which had taken place, and their deaths must be avenged. The law of the Osages controlled their course. Coming across Major Welborn and his comrades, the Osage braves, under the direction of the chiefs, attacked them on November 17, 1823, killing the Major three white men named Sloan, Lester, and Deterline, and a Negro named Ben, taking thirty horses, and plundering the camp.[16] From the point of view

14 *American Missionary Register*, V, 363.
15 Known also as Cha-to-Kah-Pa-Pe-Sha, or *Shitoka*. He was also one of the chiefs signing the Treaty of Peace between the Cherokees and the Osages, made August 7, 1822.
16 *American Missionary Register*, V, 138–39. *Arkansas Gazette* (October 26, 1824).

of Mad Buffalo he was doing no wrong, but rather was balancing his losses at the hands of the Pawnees.

When the facts of this massacre became known, Colonel Arbuckle, then in charge of the soldiers of that district, demanded of the Osages that they deliver to him the guilty ones, and that they be made to answer for their crime. After six months of negotiations between Arbuckle and the chief men of the tribe, a grand council was arranged, to be held at Cantonment Gibson on the Grand River in Arkansas. Four thousand Indians, including Claremore,[17] Tally, representatives of White Hair's village, and all the chiefs, as well as Mad Buffalo, Little Eagle, and the others involved in the killing, gathered at the Falls of the Verdigris, four miles distant, on June 7, 1824. The next day they came into the cantonment. The question to be decided was whether or not the chiefs should give themselves up and answer for a deed which was, according to their notion, proper and regular. Colonel Arbuckle was the representative of the government. The interpreters were Bill Williams and François Mogré.[18] The government's influence over these Indians was about to be put to the acid test— to get them to consent peaceably to surrender those responsible for the murders. On Bill Williams and his associates there rested tremendous responsibility; the success or failure of the government's efforts depended upon the forcefulness with which these men conveyed Colonel Arbuckle's views to the nation assembled. Because of Arbuckle's handling of the council, and the sound common sense of their great chiefs, the outcome was peaceful. The Colonel, through Williams, explained the laws of the Great White Father, the meaning of a trial, and each step to be taken to arrive at the truth. Each chief in turn arose and expressed himself, and this in turn was translated to the Major. The termination of the council was dramatic. Mad Buffalo arose; "American Chief," he began. "It was by accident that those white people were killed. But at your word, I will go to answer for this offense." Little Eagle

---

[17] The name is spelled Clairmont on the Treaty of 1825; also Clarmore on the treaty between the Osages and Cherokees of 1822.

[18] *American Missionary Register*, V, 303.

then spoke: "Chief, I have never wished to kill white men. No, when they have come to my town, I have, with pleasure, fed them. But since you wish me to go and answer for this affair, I will go." In turn, Little Bear, Little Rattlesnake, and Caddo Killer, all members of the party with Mad Buffalo, arose, assumed the full responsibility for the action of their warriors, and offered to answer to the charge.[19] The Indians parted with their families and friends and were taken into custody. The Colonel promised the prisoners that their friends and families might visit them at their pleasure. Bill Williams and A. P. Chouteau, with members of the tribe, did visit the Indians and assisted in preparing their defense. On October 18, of that year, Mad Buffalo was tried before Judge Andrew Scott, of the Superior Court of Arkansas, at Little Rock, on the charge of murder, and was convicted. The next day the other four chiefs were tried together and Little Eagle was convicted on the same charge, the remaining three being acquitted.[20] Mad Buffalo and Little Eagle were sentenced at the same term by Judge Benjamin Johnson to be hanged.[21]

The trial and result created much interest in the army, among the whites and the Osages. Alexander McNair, the Osage agent, with others, interceded in their behalf with President Monroe,[22] but no action was taken until President John Quincy Adams assumed office, when he issued a full pardon to both Indians on March 21, 1825.[23]

The Osage Nation still stood in the path of the settlers. Already demands had been made of the government that these Indians be moved and their holdings thrown open to settlement. Occasional traders and trappers were passing through. Williams met and talked with them, and he got the news from back home, having kept in touch with affairs through his family and his trips to St.

[19] *Ibid.*, 301–304.

[20] *Arkansas Gazette* (October 19, 1824, and October 26, 1824).

[21] *Hempstead's Court Reports of Arkansas Cases*, 27.

[22] Letter from A. McNair to President Monroe, dated January 30, 1825. MS in Misc. Letter Files for January, February, March, 1825, Office of Secretary of State, Washington, D. C.

[23] Pardons, No. 208, IV, 123. MSS in Office of Chief Clerk of Office of Secretary of State, Washington, D. C.

Louis. In 1822 a legislative committee, consisting of Colonels Boone and Logan, accompanied by one of Williams' brothers, visited the Osage country. They were seeking a site for a capital for the state of Missouri. Williams could see that the days were numbered before the settlers' invasion would become a reality.

CHAPTER SEVEN

The First Santa Fe Survey

GENERAL WILLIAM CLARK traded the Osages out of their holdings on June 2, 1825. A new treaty was entered into by the Great and Little Osages on that date, which ended Bill Williams' connection with those nations. In this treaty provision was made to liquidate the money due him from his trading ventures and to satisfy the claims of his two daughters. For a mere pittance in money, annuities, and goods, the Osage Indians relinquished to the United States their claim to one of the richest tracts ever held by any Indian nation. They gave up practically all of their lands "within the State of Missouri and Territory of Arkansas"[1] with certain reservations.

The treaty was negotiated at St. Louis, and from some of the provisions contained in this document, it would appear that Williams was there in person looking after his own interests and those of his children. He had money due him and he also had two small motherless daughters to think about, his wife having died before 1825.[2] In the treaty these girls each received 640 acres of land "located on the north side of the Marais des Cygnes, at the Double Creek, above Harmony."[3] Williams was not the only white man

[1] *American State Papers, Indian Affairs,* II, 328, *et. seq.;* also *United States Statutes at Large,* VII, 240.
[2] Recollections of family of Mr. C. E. Vaughan.
[3] *American State Papers, Indian Affairs,* II, 588.

among the Osages who had children by an Osage woman, for his children were only two of forty-one children and grandchildren of white fathers and Osage women. The treaty recited that the tribes were "indebted to August P. Chouteau, Paul Ballio and William S. Williams to a large amount, for credits given to them, which they are unable to pay," and asked to have this debt discharged, which was done, Chouteau received $1,000, Ballio $250, and Williams $250, "towards the liquidation of their respective debts due from the said tribes, or nations."[4] The debt referred to grew out of the Neosho post which he and Ballio conducted for a time.

There is not any doubt but that Williams and the others thought each of the allottees would receive the section of land designated by the treaty. Could it be said in any clearer language? No patent, however, was ever granted to any of them. The War Department ruled on September 3, 1838, in reply to a request for a patent by one of the allottees, that the provisions of the treaty of 1825 did not entitle them to a patent of the land, but only the use of the land during their respective lives.[5] This was not accepted by the persons interested, and the question remained unsettled until the treaty of September 29, 1865, wherein the allottees gave up all claims to the land and went over into Indian Territory.

It might well be that at the time of the treaty Williams was asking himself what should be his future. What should he do? Would it be best to settle down with his girls on a tract of land or move on with the Indians, or go to the mountains? The question was settled by Major Sibley's offering him a job as interpreter and guide for a party starting to the Spanish settlements.

It came about in this way. Travel to Santa Fe was not yet reduced to any single route. The traders were still experimenting with the best way to go. Some went from Fort Smith up the Canadian River, and there had to contend with the Osage, Kansas, Pawnee, and Comanche tribes of Indians. Others used the route from Fort Osage to the bend of the Arkansas, encountering these

4 *Ibid.*, 589.
5 Records of the Department of the Interior, XIII, 13.

same tribes. The French trader, with his *voyageurs*, stuck to the Missouri River as far as possible, going up usually to Council Bluffs and then striking across the plains, following generally along the Platte River. On this route the traders had to treat with, and pass through the Pawnees, the Cheyennes, and the Arapahoes. It made little difference which route the Santa Fe traders chose in crossing the United States territory, for when they reached the Mexican dominion they had the Utes, Comanches, and the Apaches to guard against. It was at best a hazardous business. It was apparent that if the army were to protect the trader, the route would have to be defined.

At the suggestion of Governor Alexander McNair, President Monroe urged Congress to lay out a route for the trade between the Missouri and Santa Fe.[6] Senator Benton succeeded in getting Congress to pass an act on March 3, 1825, providing for three commissioners to "mark out a road from the western frontier of the state of Missouri, to the boundary line of the United States, in the direction of Santa Fe of New Mexico." The law directed the marking out of the road and appropriated ten thousand dollars to do the work, and a further sum of twenty thousand dollars to "defray the expenses of treating with the Indians." It was especially provided that nothing should be done towards marking the road until the consent of the Indian tribes, through whose territory the road passed, had been first procured.[7] This was before it was known that General Clark would be able to trade the Osages out of their land, through which the road would run, or the appropriation might never have been made. The President appointed George C. Sibley, Benjamin H. Reeves, and Pierre Menard as commissioners. Menard was prevented from serving on account of sickness, and Thomas Mather took his place.[8]

[6] Message of President Monroe to Congress (May 24, 1824), "In Relation to the Intercourse and Trade now Carried on between the United States and the Mexican Provinces." 18 Cong., 1 sess., *House Exec. Doc. 155, 5.*

[7] *United States Statutes at Large*, IV, 100–101, Statute II, Approved March 3, 1825.

[8] Reeves was from Howard County, Missouri, and resigned as Lieutenant Governor to act as Commissioner. Major Sibley's home was in St. Charles, Mis-

The commissioners selected Mr. Archibald Gamble as secretary and Joseph C. Brown as surveyor, and left St. Louis on July 4, proceeding to Arrow Rock. At that place they rendezvoused and prepared for the expedition. They hired thirty men as guides, chain carriers, wagon masters, and the various other offices incident to such an undertaking.[9]

Sibley, of course, knew the one thing he must do would be to satisfy the Indians through whose territory he was to pass, and who could do that better than Bill Williams? He could talk their language like a native, had married into the tribe, had lived and hunted with them, and had acted as intermediary at a number of important councils with the whites. He also knew that Williams was acquainted with the country lying to the west of the Osages, indeed perhaps as far as Santa Fe, and surely as far as the Arkansas River, for during the years he had lived with the Osages, Williams' trapping and trading excursions had taken him onto the plains in that direction, as the Osages claimed the country clear to the Rocky Mountains for their hunting ground. Major Sibley hired him as interpreter, and he seems to have acted also as guide.[10]

Williams joined the party on August 1 and then went on ahead to arrange for a "Big Talk" with the Osages. Among the men employed by the commissioners was Joseph Reddeford Walker, better known in after years as Captain Joe Walker.[11] This was not

---

souri. He was well known in the Indian trade. Pierre Menard was from Illinois, as was his successor, Thomas Mather.—*Journal of American History*, Vol. III, No. 3 (1909), 468.

[9] *Missouri Intelligencer* (July 9, 1825).

[10] Fort Sutter Papers, Vol. XXXI, No. 126. Huntington Library, San Marino, California.

[11] Joseph Reddeford Walker was born October 13, 1798, in Knoxville, Tennessee. He came to Missouri in 1818, serving for a time as sheriff; went to Taos with Colonel Braxton Cooper, 1821–22; was with the Sibley expedition in 1825, going to Taos, New Mexico; was with Bonneville from 1832, and in California from 1833 to 1834; went from Santa Fe to Los Angeles in 1841; in 1845 piloted the Chiles party from Missouri to California with a sawmill to erect at Sacramento, but on account of Indian troubles was obliged to burn it, together with their wagons; served this same year under Colonel Frémont on his third expedition; led the Walker party to Yavapai County, Arizona, in 1855; and died at Ignacio Valley, California, on October 27, 1876.—W. F. Wagner, *Narrative of Zenas Leonard*, 146, 163.

Walker's first trip away from the frontier, as four years before, with a party of trappers, he had joined Colonel Stephen Cooper and had gone through to Taos with him. That trip was well remembered on account of their great suffering for water while on the way. After joining the Sibley party, Walker spent the remainder of his life on the plains and in the mountains and left his mark in more than half a dozen states. This trip brought together two congenial souls in Bill Williams and Joe Walker. They renewed their acquaintance some eight years later on their horse-stealing expedition into California; and some twenty years later Williams turned aside on his way to Santa Fe to join up with Colonel Frémont on his third expedition and went with him from the headwaters of the Arkansas to the Great Salt Lake country, and for a time they were again members of the same expedition.

The Sibley party proceeded from Fort Osage on one of the then known routes to Santa Fe, which is practically the Santa Fe Trail, as it became known in later years. Josiah Gregg, in his *Commerce of the Prairies*, states that this survey was of "little service to travellers"; yet, if one traces the route he followed in 1831 with the Sibley survey, it is found he went over almost the same road with the exception that their roads separated when Gregg turned off to Santa Fe at the Canadian River, passing through San Miguel. The survey began two miles south of Fort Osage and followed the road to Independence, which was the last white settlement the party encountered before arriving at San Fernando de Taos, commonly called Taos, in the Republic of Mexico.

Williams had no difficulty in arranging for a meeting of the chiefs and head men of the Osages with the commissioners. The meeting was held at "Council Grove, on the river Nee-o-sho, 142 miles a little south of west from Fort Osage."[12] The place derives its name from this council with the Osage Indians. Williams showed his understanding of the people he was dealing with.

[12] The place is about five miles south of McPherson, on the Neosho River, southeastern Kansas, and is now marked by a monument.—*Kansas State Historical Collections*, XVI, 752.

Word of the meeting was sent to the chiefs and warriors. Nothing was hurried. Presents of merchandise were distributed where they would do the most good. By this token the Indians understood they were dealing with a person who would be liberal with them. When the tribe had gathered at the appointed place, a feast was held and more presents were distributed. Then a council was held, in which Williams explained what Major Sibley wanted and each chief gave his views. There was not any difficulty in arranging matters. By an additional sum of five hundred dollars' worth of merchandise, a treaty was drawn up and signed, giving the commissioners the rights they sought.

The Indians agreed to allow them to "survey and mark out a road in such manner as they" might "think proper, through any of the territory owned or claimed by the Great and Little Osage nations." They allowed the free passage of the citizens of the United States and of Mexico over this road, and also extended to them such assistance as they were able to give. The road was defined in a rather unusual manner as the right of passage through their country and extended to a reasonable distance on either side so that travelers thereon might at any time leave the marked route for the purpose of finding sustenance and proper camping places. The last must have been Williams' idea of a road, for it would indicate more the idea of hunting parties crossing the territory than caravans of trade.

The treaty was drawn up and signed on August 10, 1825, by the three commissioners, sixteen chiefs and warriors of the Great and Little Osage tribes, witnessed by the secretary, the surveyor, "W. S. Williams, interpreter," and fifteen of Sibley's men, including "J. R. Walker." The object in getting so many to sign was to give the ceremony all the formality possible, so that the Indians would be the more impressed.[13] Then the Osages were given another feast, the pipe was lighted and passed around, and the council broke up.

[13] Treaty Between the Commissioners and the Great and Little Osages (August 10, 1825), *Indian Affairs, Laws and Treaties*, II, 246. Treaty ratified by Congress (May 3, 1826).—*United States Statutes at Large*, VII, 268.

The white man known to the Indians as the Red-headed Shooter had gone a long way from the time he first came among them, fifteen years before. Then he was just a young paleface, without standing; now he could sit in their council with their chief men and great warriors. Of late years this had happened often; indeed, on many occasions he had with authority spoken for the Great White Father, the President of the United States. His attention to the detail of the ceremonial pipe at the council fire, his command of the Osage language, in all respects were perfect. When he arose in the council and spoke, all listened. It could well be said that Bill Williams in that day was something more than a hunter and trapper. Now he was leaving his friends, indeed his own people in a certain sense. Did he or they realize it was the last council they were to hold together? It would not have made any difference; almost anything in the life of that day was just a happening and was made the most of by Indians and whites.

The Osage treaty out of the way, Williams proceeded on ahead to visit with the Kansas Indians and prepare them for a meeting with the commissioners. He left word to camp at Sora Kansas Creek, now known as Dry Turkey Creek, about sixty-five miles from the Council Grove camp. When the commissioners arrived, the Indians and Williams were waiting for them. Williams again conducted the affair, acting as intermediary and interpreter. His earlier life among the Indians had brought him into contact with this tribe, and he knew them and could talk their dialect. Using much the same approach with these Indians as he had with the Osages, varying it in detail to conform to some special customs of the Kansas Indians, he got them into a proper frame of mind by presents. Then a council was held and the business of the officials carefully stated to the Indians. The business was carried through without any difficulties, and merchandise of about the same amount was distributed as had been given the Osages. A treaty, identical in terms to that made by the Osages, was made. It was signed and witnessed, on August 16, 1825, by the commissioners, the chiefs and head men of the Kansas tribe, and others of the party. Then another feast was held, the pipe smoked, and the council broke up. Both Bill Williams' and Joseph R. Walker's names appear on the treaty as witnesses.[14]

The Osage and Kansas tribes were the only Indians Major Sibley had to treat with, and these being satisfied the party proceeded on to the boundary between the United States and Mexico. In the meantime negotiations had been carried on to work out an arrangement whereby the road might be marked from the Arkansas River to the Spanish settlement of Taos. Arriving on the Arkansas River early in September, the party waited for word from Taos, or the Mexican government, until September 20; then, having received none, they divided, Sibley[15] and part of the men proceeding on to the Spanish settlements, while Reeves and Mather and part of the men, including Walker, returned to Fort Osage. On the way back they threw up mounds to mark the road until the cold weather compelled them to stop work. In the spring they returned and completed the marking of the road.[16]

Williams continued on with Sibley to Taos and parted from his old friend at that place on November 30, 1825.[17] For his services he received as compensation $132.67 at the rate of $33⅓ per month.[18] This marked a decided break in his life, and many years elapsed before he again returned to Missouri.

When Sibley arrived in Taos, there was still delay in completing the arrangements between the United States and Mexico about the marking of the road. It took, in fact, a year to work out the details and get the permission of the higher officials. Major Sibley reported later he had marked the road from Taos to the crossing of the Arkansas. He made his final report accompanied by a map

14 Treaty between the Commissioners and the Kansas (August 16, 1825), *Indian Affairs, Laws and Treaties*, II, 248. Treaty ratified by Congress (May 3, 1826). —*United States Statutes at Large*, VII, 270.

15 Major Sibley remained a short time in Santa Fe and then proceeded to Mexico City to carry on further negotiations. See George P. Morehouse, "An Historic Trail Through the American Southwest," *Journal of American History*, Vol. III, No. 3 (1909), 468.

16 Report in Library of Congress of B. H. Reeves and Thomas Mather, dated Franklin, Missouri, November 5, 1825, sent to Hon. James Barbour, Secretary of War.

17 Record of General Accounting Office, Records Division, Washington, D. C.
18 *Ibid.*

of the route. This map and report were prepared by Joseph C. Brown, the surveyor of the party, and finished on October 27, 1827.[19] It was the first map of a surveyed route lying between the frontier and any point farther west. The route marked followed generally the well known Santa Fe Trail from Fort Osage to the Arkansas River, striking it just south of the Smoky Hill of Kansas, and following it along the north side to Pawnee Rocks, the Caches, then crossing the river about twenty miles below Chouteau Island, proceeding south to Cimarron Creek, and from there, in a general westerly direction to the Point of Rocks and a route marked by natural objects to Taos—a total distance of 747 miles. A cutoff is marked from Gravel Rock, near the Caches to the Cimarron Creek, with the notation, "This road unsafe in very dry weather." In his report Brown observed that "travellers have discovered it as unsafe. It is incommodious of water & timber for fuel & wants such prominent land marks as will be a sure guide. On this route has been much suffering; in the day time dangerous."

The Brown report is complete in every detail, with the map in sections. It describes the route, the streams, watering places, grass, timber, mountains, and topography of the country traveled. Any traveler with the report and map could not have gone off the course. It apparently attracted little attention for the reason that the facts and details contained in it were common knowledge to some of that time, and with the succeeding years to large numbers who used the route.

[19] Report of Joseph C. Brown, dated October 27, 1827. MS in Old Map Files of the Chief of Engineers, United States Army, Washington, D. C.

CHAPTER EIGHT

As a Mountain Man

WE HAVE a fairly accurate record of the life of Old Bill Williams up to the time he arrived in the Spanish settlements towards the close of 1825 and from the year 1841 on to the time of his death. The intervening years of his life in the mountains and plains of the West, when he was hunting, trapping, trading, and living with the various Indian tribes, are years when we get only a glimpse of him now and then. Notwithstanding our want of detail, these were the years when he made a reputation for himself, the years in which his exploits made him famous as a mountain man. Much has been written about his doings; some of it is authentic, much is fiction. The separation of fact from fancy is quite an impossible task at this time and will not even be attempted. The brilliant young English army officer, George Frederick Ruxton, may have met Bill Williams in Santa Fe or Taos in the winter of 1846 and 1847.[1] He might well have camped and hunted with him

[1] George Frederick Ruxton, *Adventures in Mexico and the Rocky Mountains* (London, John Murry, 1847; New York, Harper & Bros., 1848), describes his trip through the Spanish settlements and hunting in the Rockies in 1846 and 1847. *Life in the Far West*, by the same author, was first published in *Blackwood's Magazine* (London, 1848), in serial form. Afterwards it was printed in book form by Harper & Bros. (New York, 1848). He describes the mountain men and particularly Williams. Ruxton says in his introduction to the book that the incidents related and the characters are "no fiction." He gives an account of the death of Williams (page 234).

in the spring of 1847. Surely Ruxton met and talked with men at Santa Fe, Taos, and Bent's Fort who knew the mountain man, who had been his companion on trapping trips, and who had seen him about the settlements. Some little doubt is cast on his accounts of Williams from the fact that he describes the death of Bill Williams, when in truth Williams was still living. Ruxton himself died in August, 1848, some months before Williams was killed.[2] Colonel Frank Triplett gives a most interesting record of the mountain man's exploits, secondhand, but from one who claimed to have been associated in many an exploit with Williams.[3] We cannot help being a bit confused when Williams is made a member of the Ashley expedition in 1823, when in fact he was in business with Ballio on the Neosho and definitely living with the Osages. Then, too, we find the Colonel closing the career of Williams at the time that another writer has him beginning his adventure in the West.[4]

There is, however, much of truth in all these accounts, and after all, what does it matter? It is undoubtedly a fact that many of these adventures, or similar exploits narrated by Ruxton, Triplett, the writer for the *Globe-Democrat*, and others, did occur in the manner related, if not in the life of Williams, then as the experiences of other mountain men. In those days truth outran fiction. The dates may be moved about because of fault in memory; names of persons may have not been set down with accuracy in the recitals, or places may have been mislocated. The life of that day and time has been correctly portrayed in the main. The wonder is not that we do not have more, but rather that we have as much as we do, when we consider that most of these men were out of touch with those who wrote down happenings. The major-

[2] Ruxton arrived in St. Louis, Missouri, in company with Captain Andrew Cathcart on August 16, 1848. They had planned a hunt in the Rockies. At the time he was quite ill, and passed away August 29, 1848.

[3] Colonel Frank Triplett, *Conquering the Wilderness*, 431–58.—Not generally considered of any great historical value.

[4] Articles in the Sunday Magazine Section of the *Globe-Democrat* (St. Louis, Missouri, December 24, 1911), purporting to give an interview with Jesús Rupert Váldez Archeleuta, a onetime comrade of Williams. There is much in the article to cast doubt on its value for biographical purposes.

ity of their comrades could not read or write. Their associates were men like themselves, or Indians, and each day had more important matters to attend to than that of keeping a reckoning of their adventures.

Williams was thirty-eight years of age when he arrived in Santa Fe. Although he may not have been considered by some as a finished mountain man when he came to Taos with Sibley, he was not long in demonstrating to the men of that calling that he could take his place with the best of them. He had started out in life from a good home; he had been well brought up, with some education and religious training. The influence of the religious training of Joseph and Sarah Williams, however, had disappeared. His ideas on religious questions had undergone a change, and he was beginning to approach that subject from an Indian point of view. He began to entertain doubts as to whether the white man's religion was the correct one, possibly because in his contact with the Indians he had seen them living happy and contented, with a religion fundamentally different from his own. His point of view had changed in regard to values. What he, as a young man, would have revolted against, now seemed second nature; and what he, as a young man, had valued, had entirely lost its attractiveness. Houses, dress, books, cleanliness, restraint, and the refinements of civilization had become irksome and of no interest to him. He was a fit candidate to enter the inner circle of trappers and hunters.

Williams' arrival in the Southwest was about the time of the beginning of the substantial trade between the United States and the Spanish settlements, coming in over the Santa Fe Trail. It was the period of the opening up of the Southwest outlet for peltries and furs passing out through Taos and the Arkansas River. Up to that time, a very small quantity of furs had come into St. Louis by way of the southern route. The great highway for fur trade had been the Missouri River and the plains. William Bent established a trading post on the Arkansas River in 1829 to take advantage of the trade going out that way, and also to have a headquarters from which he himself could operate as an Indian trader. This post became one of the rendezvous for the trappers

Frederic Remington, "I Took Ye for an Injin,"
from *The Century Magazine* (November, 1890)

"The free hunter was never more satisfied than when he made the imitation so perfect that he was taken for an Indian."

Alfred Jacob Miller, "The Trapper's Bride,"
from the Porter Collection

"The intermarriages between the trappers and the Indians were more than unions of convenience. In many cases the white men and their adopted peoples became blood brothers through these unions. Williams had kinsfolk among the Osages through his marriage. He had become a Ute through marriage and adoption."

and the most important point between the frontier and the Spanish settlements on the Santa Fe route. In fact, on account of Bent's Fort being placed where it was, the established route to Santa Fe laid out by Sibley, with Williams' help, was changed so as to pass the fort and continue over the Raton Mountains, instead of along the Cimarron cutoff. Then the furs began to flow east over the Santa Fe Trail, as well as over the northern route along the Missouri.

Williams knew furs and their value; he also knew how to deal with the Indians and those engaged in marketing furs. At least several years spent in trapping and curing furs, five years in handling, sorting, and packing furs about the posts, and three years engaged in trading on his own account with the Osages, Kansas, and Kickapoos, had completed his apprenticeship. Indeed, his education along these lines was practical and complete. One could say he was entitled to a master's degree, and when, in after years, he signed himself "Bill Williams, Master Trapper,"[5] he might well have looked back to the years prior to 1825 as the days of his schooling.

When Williams arrived on the Río Grande, there were three distinct races in that part of the Southwest. There were first the New Mexicans, the ruling class, a mixture of the Spaniards and the Indians, speaking the Spanish language. They lived in towns scattered up and down the Río Grande Valley, from Paso del Norte to Río Colorado, their chief settlements in the north being Santa Fe and San Fernando de Taos.

Then there were the native Pueblo Indian peoples, who lived in community houses, often several stories high. Each pueblo was distinct in organization and life from the other pueblos, and often spoke a different dialect; yet each traced its origin back to Montezuma.[6] Lastly, the nomadic Indians, of which there were three

[5] Private Papers of J. S. McGehee. (MSS), II, 57.

[6] This Montezuma is not the Aztec Emperor whom Cortez found in Mexico, but a mythical god-hero of the same name. He is the symbol of past glory, and the Pueblos kept a sacred fire burning in each village in the belief that he would return, descending to them on the column of smoke from that fire. See H. H. Bancroft, *Native Races*, III (*Myths and Languages*), 75–77, 80, 171–75.

chief nations, the Apaches, Navajos, and Eutaws or Utes. Many years after Williams' arrival, Bill Hamilton tells us, Williams gave him a manuscript of a history he had written of his life among the Apaches and Navajos and the Pueblos. Hamilton considered this a very accurate account of these three tribes, which delineated with preciseness their "characteristics, habits and customs."[7] The manuscript was placed in a safe at the Indian agency of the Crows on the Yellowstone River, at which time Major F. D. Pease was agent. In 1872, when Hamilton was United States marshal, while he was away from the post on the trail of some cattle thieves, a fire broke out at the agency. No effort was made to save this priceless manuscript and it was lost.[8] It indeed would have been a signal contribution to history had it been preserved.

The Pueblo Indians in the Southwest were quite distinct from the Mexicans. These people had survived the Spanish invasion and still maintained their customs, manner of living, and civilization. With the exception of one or two uprisings against oppression and cruelty, the Pueblo Indians continued in the even tenor of their ways, living in their adobe community villages, dividing into their various clans, worshiping the sun, moon, stars, and snakes, and performing their ceremonial dances, as they had done without change for hundreds of years. The changes which took place in the Southwest were not influenced in the slightest degree, one way or the other, by these Indians. A strictly agricultural and pastoral people occupying only a limited area, beyond which they never went, it might be said that the world passed them by, and they allowed it to pass. Their one wish was ever to be let alone.

Although it has been reported that during his early years in the Southwest, Williams spent some time with the inhabitants of the Zuñi Pueblo, and among the Laguna, Isleta, and Tigua Indians, this is doubtful.[9] The history of all Pueblo peoples has been that they did not welcome strangers among them. Moreover, there

[7] W. T. Hamilton, *My Sixty Years on the Plains,* 102.

[8] Hamilton gives the date as 1873, but must be mistaken as the fire occurred October 30, 1872; see *Annual Report of Commissioner of Indian Affairs for 1873,* 248.

[9] *Globe-Democrat* (December 24, 1911).

was nothing in any Pueblo Indian village to attract a man of Williams' temperament. There was practically no hunting, trapping, or trading to be carried on. Irrigation of land and tending flocks of sheep never appealed to Williams. It has even been said that children of mixed blood of these Taos Indians never grew to maturity. From the time when Esteven, the advance agent for the friar Marco de Niza, was cut into small bits in 1539 by the Zuñi Indians for attempting liberties with their women, strangers never found a welcome from them.

The Apaches at that time were one of the main tribes of Indians in the Southwest. They then occupied generally a territory lying on both sides of the Río Grande, south of what is now the route of the Santa Fe Railroad, and extending down into the present northern Mexico, with their westward excursions for foraging and hunting extending to the Colorado River, and their eastward range to the lower valley of the Pecos River. Another branch of these Indians lived in the Raton Mountains north and east of Santa Fe. Up until about 1836, the Apaches were friendly with the whites but continually at war with the Mexicans. For two hundred years the Spaniards and Mexicans could not subdue them. During that period the wily savages would make peace with the people in one direction so that they could have a place to trade what they had stolen from the others; they are the only tribe who lived "neither upon agriculture nor upon the chase";[10] yet the women carried on a little cultivation during the summer time, raising pumpkins, corn, and a few melons.

When in need of horses, they would descend on the Mexicans in northern Mexico; when in need of meat, they carried on marauding expeditions into the Río Grande Valley, bringing back mules, sheep, and cattle; they even went at far as the Great Plains for the buffalo. The Apaches were never given much to trapping and hunting for skins, and no considerable amount of trade in furs was ever carried on with them.

The second tribe of nomadic Indians referred to above was the Navajo, numbering at that time about ten thousand. Today they

[10] Chittenden, *op. cit.*, II, 883.

have a population estimated at over thirty thousand. They occupied the country north of the Apaches as far as the Colorado River. The Navajos were expert horsemen and were nomadic, except in winter when they lived in hogans built partly of earth and timber. As a race they were tall and spare of figure. They had flocks of goats, sheep, and horses, which they continually added to from time to time by descending into the Río Grande Valley and raiding the herds and bands of the Mexicans and Pueblo Indians. This tribe had a limited contact with the Mexican authorities, now and then meeting with the Mexicans, visiting their towns, and entering into treaties with them, but with no intent to keep their promises, for no sooner had the Mexicans raised a new crop of grain, than these same Indians would descend into the valley, driving off sheep and taking their toll of the new crop.

There was constant danger of this tribe's invading the Mexican settlements, a danger which continued until after the American occupation of the country, when they were soundly beaten by a force under the guidance of Kit Carson in January, 1864.[11] The Navajos did no trapping and little hunting, chiefly for the reason that their land was poor in fur-bearing animals. The women spun the coarse wool from their flocks into blankets, and these blankets were famed throughout all the western country in Williams' day for their waterproof qualities, warmth, and durability.

There was yet another tribe of nomadic Indians with whom Williams had much to do, and at whose hands he finally met his death. These were the Eutaws, or Utes. These Indians, a numerous tribe, were a branch of the Shoshones, and lived largely from hunting and trapping. They spent most of their time on horseback and were the best horsemen in the mountains. Off their horses they were anything but impressive, being smaller in stature than the Apaches and Navajos, but what they lacked in appearance, they made up in spirit. Fighting was breath to their nostrils. As a general rule, they bore excellent reputations for honesty, were less inclined to gambling, wore better clothes, and had a more uniform food supply than any of the Indians of the Southwest.

[11] Thomas Edwin Farish, *History of Arizona*, II, 170.

They did a considerable amount of trapping and gathering of furs, one of the reasons for this being that they lived in a rich, fur-bearing section of the mountains. The Utes always claimed the right to hunt buffalo on the great prairie, a right denied by the Arapahoes and Cheyennes, whose territory they usually invaded on their buffalo hunts. The result was continuous enmity and fighting between the plains Indians and the mountain Utes, and they were inveterate and mortal enemies. On the other hand, the Utes got on fairly well with their neighbors, the Apaches and Navajos. While it is true there was always some fighting among the Utes, Apaches, and Navajos, usually this was occasioned by the young bucks who wanted to make a coup,[12] or exploit themselves as warriors, but there never was the same bitter feeling among the three southwestern tribes that existed between the Utes and the plains Indians, or the neighbors of the Utes on the north.

Amidst this medley of people Williams started his real mountain life. He necessarily had to acquire the several dialects and adapt himself to the new order. This was not difficult, as languages were easy for him to learn. The remainder was applying and developing what he had already learned. He seemed always to make Taos rather than Santa Fe his headquarters for recruiting and for a place of rendezvous. This town in those days seemed more popular with the mountain men than the capital, probably because there were fewer officials there to regulate their conduct. It was just a sleepy quiet Mexican village; yet for Williams and the other American hunters it represented the metropolis of their existence.

As was not unusual with this class of men, Williams is said to have become enamoured with one of the *señoritas* of New Mexico and to have married her and had a son born of the marriage.[13] There is no record of this other than the reference given, and no trace can be found of this marriage or of the son said to have been

---

[12] Pronounced as if spelled "coo"; a French term referring to the custom of Indians to strike or touch an enemy, either living or dead. This could be done by striking the foe with a stick or anything else, and several could strike the same enemy, each one counting a coup. Sometimes the Indians carried a stick called a coup-stick, with which they struck their foes.

[13] Lewis, *op. cit.*, 191.

born. Still it may be a fact, since it was a common occurrence for an American hunter or trapper to marry one of the native women at the Spanish settlements.

Williams was of a restless disposition. He had to be moving, to be active. He spent time first with one Indian tribe then with another. The Utes seem to have been his favorites, for he spent more time with these Indians than with any others. He liked their country better than that of the others. It is said he was adopted into the Utes and "had a squaw among them."[14]

It is claimed that his first years in the mountains were spent more in wandering than in trapping. One of the early trips took him with two companions on a four months' trapping venture. After outfitting at Taos, they went over the Raton Mountains, down the Purgatoire, sometimes called the Las Animas, then north of the Spanish Peaks, up the Arkansas, into the South Park country, then out by way of the Platte. Falling in with John Smith, they went on to Bent's Fort, where they disposed of their furs. Within a year or two he was again out with his traps, intent more on discovering the nature of the country than on looking for pelts. This time he was gone more than three years. Crossing Arizona and tramping the Mogollon Plateau, along the Little Colorado, visiting the Petrified Forests and the Grand Canyon, thence to the Colorado River, living off the country all the time. Although he had intended to go on to California, his plans were changed, for, after all, what did it matter where he went? Turning north from the Colorado, probably where the stream which bears her name enters the Colorado River, he headed north. He passed the Great Salt Lake and on north into the Coeur d' Alène country. Here he is claimed to have worked for the Hudson Bay factor for a winter, netting eleven hundred dollars from the season's catch; then out of the mountains by way of the Yellowstone, and back to Bent's Fort.[15]

It was the time when there were beaver in every stream, and

14 Thomas E. Breckenridge, "The Story of a Famous Expedition as Told by Thomas E. Breckenridge," *Cosmopolitan Magazine* (August, 1896), 405.
15 *Globe-Democrat* (December 24, 1911).

beaver skins were bringing a good price. One who was skillful in trapping, could, in a few months, acquire skins and hides sufficient to barter for the articles necessary to supply his wants and the means to satisfy his craving for excitement.

Whenever Williams came into Taos, Bent's Fort, or any of the other posts, he had money to spend. That always went for strong drink or gambling. He is said to have lost one thousand dollars to Lucien Maxwell in one game of Seven Up.[16] Likely there are more stories told of his sprees and debauches than of any other activity of his life. His sprees took place at posts or settlements, with others being present, and this may account for the stories of his drinking. There were generally no eyewitnesses to his exploits when trapping or in his Indian contacts. Drinking was the usual and common practice of that day and place, and in this particular he was no different from most of his fellow trappers. Perhaps it should not be confined to that period altogether, nor to the class to which he belonged. We find this same trait of human nature displayed in others who go for long periods in a monotonous walk of life. One thing should be noted about these wild trappers and their celebrations, they never had any regrets after it was over. They could talk about these celebrations and remember them as they sat around their campfire, getting ready for the next carousal. This phase of their lives has perhaps been too much stressed. It was rather an opportunity to let off steam, helping to keep an even balance in their lives. While the settlements and the towns attracted them, any great length of stay became monotonous, and they longed for the freedom of the camp.

Bill Williams soon learned that traveling and trapping with large parties did not pay. In fact, with his ability to trap the beaver and cure the skins, he early came to the decision that the best method to carry on his excursions into the mountains was with a small party or, better still, by himself. He was confident of his own ability to ferret out the best beaver streams and to avoid dangers from the Indians. It became a rule of Williams' life to do all of his trapping in this manner. Although occasionally we find

16 *Ibid.*

him with a party, in none of these instances is there an account of any substantial amount of furs obtained.

Likewise it was his invariable rule never to allow women with him on his trapping expeditions. He could progress faster, be less liable to attack, and secure more peltries in a short time when he had only Bill Williams to look out for. Some called him "Old Solitaire," or referred to him as trapping alone and to his desire for solitude. An old Ute once pointed out on the east fork of the Gunnison River the place where Williams had trapped alone one winter. The old Indian referred to him as "a great trapper, a great hunter, took many beaver, and a great warrior—his belt full of scalps; but no friend; no squaws; always by himself."[17] That was hardly a correct estimate of Williams, for he was very companionable and those who knew him confirm this. When he did join a party, there was always a sense of security against the Indians, for no one knew better than he how to guard against attacks, or how to fight when sorely pressed.

Bill Williams, after one of his successful trapping trips, set up a store in Taos and settled down to the humdrum life of a country storekeeper. Accustomed to action, and plenty of it, the haggling with the Mexican women over small differences in price finally wore out his patience, and Williams went out of this business in a novel way. He took all of his stock of cloth goods, consisting of bolts of printed calicos, into the street and soon had a crowd of women about him. Then he said, "Here, damn you, if I can't sell you goods, I will give them to you," and taking hold of the end of the calico, he would throw the bolts out as far as he could, and let the women fight and scramble for the cloth.[18] With each bolt he thus relieved his mind with respect to his feelings toward the women of the community. Calico was then worth one dollar a yard. Of course, such action was eccentric, to say the least, and was considered by the natives as that of a crazy man.

Freed from the responsibilities of the store, Williams was again

[17] Triplett, *op. cit.*, 457.
[18] Private Papers of J. S. McGehee. (MSS), II, 218.

at liberty to follow his own inclinations, and these led him back into the mountains. Equipped with a riding horse and a pack animal, some staple supplies, powder, lead, and a few beaver traps, he never gave a second thought to the loss of the store.

CHAPTER NINE

Bill Williams, Master Trapper

IF IT WAS Bill Williams' intention to make a reputation for himself in the calling he had chosen, he succeeded. Seven years after he had arrived at Taos with Major Sibley, he had no peer as a hunter, trapper, marksman, and horseman, or in his intimate knowledge of the several Indian tribes in the mountains of the region. In appearance, ability, and achievement, he had become a marked man among his comrades, as well as an outstanding character known to the various Indian tribes, and the Mexican, English, and American company men. So far as has been discovered, there is no picture of Bill Williams in existence. We find some rough sketches among the Kern papers, which may have been intended to represent Williams, but they do not give one a real picture of the person. It is rather from the odd fragments of description by the men who knew him that the reader must make a mental picture of him.

One of the best pen sketches we have is from Albert Pike, who was with Williams for a time in the fall of 1832. The two were with a party of hunters, exploring the trapping possibilities of the country about the headwaters of the Red River, in Texas; but meeting with little success, or tiring of the manner in which the party was being conducted, Williams left with a few companions and returned to Taos. Pike left a sort of diary, which contains many interesting details of Williams' appearance and habits.[1] The description we have of the mountain man was not from one who had any extended acquaintance with the class of men Williams represented, and for that reason some of the statements cannot be taken too literally. Albert Pike himself, with a few others, arrived at Taos on November 25, 1831, "with icicles on their beards and blankets and snow knee-deep," and with the feet of every man in the party frozen except one.

To him the Governor's Palace was a "mud building fifteen feet high with mud covered portico supported by rough pine pillars," and, he noted, without "any garden, fountain, or grand staircases." He showed no enthusiasm for the adobe style of architecture, or for the life in Santa Fe, which has appealed so much to visitors in later years. To him even the daily life of the governor seemed woefully out of keeping for a chief executive. He noted that that dignitary not only raised "some red pepper in his garden, but he gets his water from the public spring," like the other inhabitants. Perhaps had the young Bostonian been more experienced in regard to the value of water in a dry country, he would rather have enlarged on the fact that Santa Fe had a spring from which there was an available year-round supply of water for everyone.

Living for a time under the conditions then existing in Santa Fe, eating the rough fare, fighting fleas, dirt, and filth, associating with the Mexican peons and coming in contact with the easy morals of the women, meeting free and company trappers, traders and rough western adventurers of all grades and classes, both educated and uncouth, who spoke a babble of dialects—all this was a novel experience for one who had been brought up in the classical atmosphere of the old elms on Cambridge Square.

Hearing in the summer of 1832 that a John Harris, of Missouri, then in Taos, was organizing a party for the purpose of entering and trapping the Comanche country, upon the heads of Red River and the Washita River, Pike went up to Taos from Santa Fe to join them. The party, as made up, consisted of some seventy or

[1] Pike, *op. cit.*

eighty men, "of whom about thirty were Americans, among whom was Bill Williams, one was a Eutaw, one an Apache, and the others Mexicans." Harris was going out under a *guía* or license from the authorities and was required to take a certain number of natives with him.

The party seems to have been financed by Harris, but Williams became one of the leaders soon after leaving Taos. From early in September until late in October, Pike saw much of Bill Williams. He described Williams as "a man about six feet one inch in height, gaunt, red-headed, with a hard, weather-beaten face, marked deeply with the small pox." He was "all muscle and sinew, and the most indefatigable hunter and trapper in the world," who had "no glory except in the woods," and "a shrewd, cute, original man, and far from illiterate."[2] Such was Bill Williams after some nine years as a preacher and missionary, twelve years on the fringe of civilization, and seven years in the mountains and on the plains.

The young Harvard graduate began to encounter new experiences in meeting men of Williams' type, all very different from his previous life; yet one can read between the lines that he very rapidly adjusted himself to the demands of the day. One noticeable adjustment was in the matter of the daily fare. He recites in his diary that on September 23 their supply of provisions was extremely low and in order to replenish it, they "killed an old mare," but on account of lack of acquaintance with horse meat or prejudice against eating it, Pike's mess "refused to be partakers, determined to starve two days longer before eating any of it." Williams and the others did not entertain the same prejudice, for they picked the bones clean.[3]

The supply of meat for the party continued to be rather meager,

---

[2] *Ibid.*, 37, 38.

[3] Alexander Ross, who had many years experience in the fur trade in the Northwest, said: "I have seen the whites, in a camp teeming with buffalo, fowl, fish, and venison, longing for horse flesh, and even purchasing a horse in order to feast upon it. Nor is it uncommon in these parts to see the voyageurs leave their good venison and eat dogs' flesh." Alexander Ross, *Fur Hunters of the Far West*, (ed., M. M. Quaife), 262

and on October 7, Pike's view in regard to the old mare was becoming modified, for when "a Comanche horse, which they had found, blind in one eye," was killed, he "partook" of the meat. Some ten days later, his taste for horse meat must have been completely cultivated, for on October 18, he left camp in the morning "after a hearty meal of horse meat." When such a change took place in less than a month, we wonder if perhaps Pike would not have become a real mountain man had he lived a few years of that life.[4] Had he had more actual experience, it might well be that some of his recitals of what took place might have explained and left a clearer understanding of what actually happened.

Williams seems to have done most of the hunting for the party. Almost daily reference is made to his ability to shoot and to get game. At one place the party came across some cranes on a lake; Pike sought to get a specimen, but without success until "Bill Williams succeeded toward night in bringing one to camp." Williams was always reputed to be "a dead shot with his rifle, though he always shot with a double wobble, for he never could hold his gun still; yet his ball went always to the spot."[5]

This method of sighting was not just one of his eccentricities. Sergeant Harry A. Fulmer, one of the Training Division of the Chicago Police Department, after almost twenty years of instructing in revolver, shotgun, and rifle shooting, tells us that many of the best marksmen are unable to hold their guns steady, but permit them to weave across the target. Apparently these men train themselves to put the final pressure on the trigger at the time the line of sight is crossing the bull's eye.

In this matter of marksmanship, Williams was opinionated, to say the least. He knew he was a better shot than any of his comrades and was ever ready to back his skill by betting as high as one hundred dollars on a shot.[6]

---

[4] Pike adopted one of the characteristics of the mountain man, for in later life, when a distinguished citizen, he wore his hair long, reaching to his shoulders. —See picture in H. L. Stillson (ed.), *History of Free Masonry*, 794.

[5] Narrative of Micajah McGehee, in Private Papers of J. S. McGehee. (MSS), II, 58.

[6] *Ibid.*

There was a story told that on one occasion in the Panhandle country about twenty soldiers and a few trappers, including Williams, were penned up in an old adobe building by a large band of Indians. One of the Indians mounted a rock and by sign and gesture showed his contempt for the whites. Williams carefully loaded his long rifle, took aim, and dropped the brave. Terrified by such marksmanship, it is said, the natives gave up the siege and left. When measured, the distance was extraordinary for a rifle shot.[7]

Being an expert shot was not an unusual accomplishment of the frontier man; rather it was a sort of preliminary requisite if a mountain man was to continue to live and keep his scalp lock. At this time the muzzle-loading, flintlock, long-barreled rifles were in use and one of the most famous gun makers of the period was Jake Hawkins, of Missouri. His guns were considered the best by the hunters, and unless a trapper carried a Hawkins, he did not feel he was properly armed. The expression "a regular Hawkins," when applied to anything, came to mean that the article was of superior merit. The mountain man's greatest pride was in his marksmanship and his dearest possession was his rifle. Sometimes fantastic names, like "Kicking Betsy," "Go-and-Seekum," or "Knock-Him-Stiff," were bestowed on that possession. His very life depended on the skill with which his one shot was sent home. If that shot missed, it might mean his life, or a hand-to-hand conflict in which he must depend on his tomahawk for defense.

With a single load, and with his life perhaps depending on the accuracy with which he drew his bead and shot his gun, it is not remarkable that most of the mountain men were almost uncanny marksmen. Then, too, shooting was as common to the education of the youth and the grown man of that time as the three *R*'s are today. Whenever the hunters and mountain men gathered at rendezvous or in the settlements, shooting matches were the order of the day.

Instances are many of these trappers shooting through a cup of whisky on the head of a comrade, as is related of Jim Bridger.

[7] Frank Evarts Wells, *Story of Old Bill Williams*, 13.

94

Mike Fink deliberately murdered his friend Carpenter in a rage while engaged in such an exhibition of skill.

Not only was Williams confident of his ability to shoot more accurately than the other mountaineers, but in trapping he considered himself the greatest trapper and hunter of the West. He was, as we have said, accustomed to sign his name and his peltries "Bill Williams, Master Trapper." His sole ambition in life seemed to be to kill more game and catch more beaver than any other trapper. He was sure of his ability, and that, considered with his other eccentricities, made many believe he was crazy.

Bill Williams was a man of tremendous energy and physical endurance; he could travel great distances, even, as Pike noted, "running all day with six traps on his back," and a beaver trap weighed five pounds. When Williams was well past middle age, McGehee pointed him out as being a "most indefatigable walker." His gait was distinctly peculiar, for he did not "walk on a straight line, but went staggering along, first on one side and then the other."

Williams was of that spare, lean type, usually found among this class, but he seemed to be tougher and more rugged than the average.

The mountain man was an excellent horseman. His years of experience with horses had made him a finished rider. To be sure, all mountain men were horsemen, but his reputation as a horseman was about equal to his fame as a trapper, for there was no horse or mule that he could not ride. He may have acquired this skill while with the Osage Indians, noted as a nation for the number of their horses and for their daring riding. In riding, as in other things he did, he developed eccentricities which gave him a distinctive appearance. He used a short stirrup and rode leaning forward, which gave him the appearance almost of a hunchback.

Pike and others have charged that Old Bill became utterly regardless of human life and developed into a ruthless killer, especially of the Indians. With all mountain men of that day, including Bill Williams, the first instinct was self-preservation. One could well say it was the most marked and prominent characteristic in his daily life. The life of a trapper was a constant struggle with nature to get food to eat, wood with which to cook it, and water to drink, but more important, to guard against the Indians. One trapper stated when he had water, food, and fuel, "I was in town, plenty of wood, plenty of water and plenty of nice fat venison, nothing to do but cook and eat."[8] But more important than food and water, as the trapper's experience over the years had taught him, was constant watchfulness, when among hostiles, to avoid an attack and prevent the savages from getting the upper hand.

Bill Williams was not a killer by instinct; rather he was a killer when necessary to preserve life. He had been in many a fight with the Indians and one who knew him said he "bore the mark of balls and arrows."[9] Craig, a comrade who had hunted and trapped with Williams, says that Bill Williams "was the bravest and most fearless mountaineer of all."[10]

The mountain man not only knew most of the principal Indian dialects, but was proficient in the universal sign language common to all Indians of the old West. At one time, when it was storming, one of the members of his camp was laid up with rheumatism, and Williams started out to procure shelter from near-by Indians. He shortly returned, accompanied by two women carrying lodge poles and covers, and he soon had protection from the inclement weather; all of this was done by sign language. On another occasion, he brought some Indians in from a distance by "riding four or five times round on a circle of about ten feet in diameter," which meant that he was calling to them to come and hold a talk.[11]

The trappers and mountain men, as a class, were little given to cleanliness, always wearing their buckskins until shiny with grease and discolored by smoke and dirt. Williams seems to have outdone his contemporaries in this particular respect. All the accounts we have of him stress his dirty and greasy appearance. Some years later, when on a visit to Missouri, he called on his daughter Mary, who in the meantime had married and had a small daughter of

[8] "James Clyman, His Diaries and Reminiscences," *Quarterly of the California Historical Society*, IV, 117.
[9] Narrative of Micajah McGehee, *loc. cit.*, 57.
[10] *Lewiston* (Idaho) *Tribune* (March 3, 1919).
[11] Pike, *op. cit.*, 54–55.

her own. Williams' appearance must have been most startling; he wore a buckskin shirt and his trousers were worn, shrunken, and dirty from use. His beard was long, and his hair, slightly tinged with gray, also worn long, trapper fashion, hung down to his shoulders. The impression he gave was that of alertness, not unlike one who is on constant guard against some unforeseen object or enemy. He was quick of movement, and in stature slightly stooped. He spoke in a high-pitched voice, giving his words a peculiar emphasis; this was the result of his years of speaking the several Indian dialects. It was little wonder that the small girl was so badly frightened that she hid under the bed and could not be induced to make up with him. She had no occasion, however to be frightened by the old trapper, for "he was a warm-hearted, brave and generous man."[12] The life he had led over the years had indelibly left its stamp on him, thus giving him the appearance of being more ruthless than he was at heart.

It was a common practice among these men to eat choice parts of game killed at the time the butchering was being carried on. If one were hungry, cooking was not a necessity; in fact, the buffalo liver, flavored with the contents of the gall bladder, was a delicacy which cooking spoiled. Again Williams seemed to have outstripped his comrades in this respect, for we find he would eat, with great relish, without cooking, the legs of a fetal calf.[13] This was an Indian custom and he had acquired the taste from his association with the ones who practiced it.

One of the most noticeable changes which had taken place was in his religious beliefs. During his early manhood, he had been accustomed to think on religious and spiritual subjects, but now he seemed to have confused and mixed the white man's religion with that of the Indian. He came to believe in the doctrine of the transmigration of the soul, and went even farther and thought he knew the particular animal into which his soul would pass after he was dead. He knew he would become a buck elk, and even described to his comrades on several occasions the kind of

[12] H. L. Conard, *op. cit.*, 202.
[13] Narrative of Micajah McGehee, *loc. cit.*, 58.

elk he would be and the place in the Bayou Salado that buck elk would range. Williams solemnly warned them if they saw an elk with certain peculiar markings, not to shoot that elk, because that would be their old comrade in a new form.[14]

Notwithstanding these notions, he remembered the days of his early religious training and often referred to the time when he was a circuit-riding preacher; he carried with him into the mountains the remembrance of the services that were associated with that preaching. Once on a trapping expedition on the Yellowstone with Bill Gordon,[15] a Snake chief named Pim died; this Indian had come into contact with the whites, was friendly to them, and had been impressed with their medicine when he had seen one of their white comrades buried with a religious service. He wanted to be buried with that same white man's medicine and had left that as one of his dying requests.

Williams did not have a Bible with him, but he remembered the funeral service and conducted the ritual with all due solemnity. It was a strange service, a white man and former preacher, no longer believing in the efficacy of the Holy Book, conducting the funeral service over the remains of a red man, who no longer trusted the religion of his own forebears. We can still hear Bill Gordon's contagious laugh as he related the incident to his comrades at the campfires.[16]

The truth of the Pim incident cannot be vouched for, but the desire of an Indian to inquire into the white man's religion was not uncommon. In 1820 a delegation of Osages went to St. Louis and requested Bishop du Bourg to "send Catholic missionaries among them to teach them the way of God."[17] The Nez Percés[18] and Flatheads, having heard of the power of the Christian religion,

---

[14] Conard, *op. cit.*, 201, 202.

[15] William Gordon was with Major Joshua Pilcher and employed by the Missouri Fur Company at the time Colonel Leavenworth led the expeditionary force against the Arickaree Village in 1825. Gordon set fire to the village after the Indians had left.—Chittenden, *op. cit.*, II, 605.

[16] Tripplett, *op. cit.*, 415.

[17] W. W. Graves, *Rev. Father John Schoenmaker, S. J.*, 17.

[18] The Nez Percés Indians sent four of their number to St. Louis in 1832 to get religious men to come among them.—W. F. Wagner, *op. cit.*, 110n.

on three separate occasions, in 1831, 1835, and 1839, sent deputations to St. Louis to have men sent to them that they might be instructed in the white man's religion.[19] It can be said that the Indians were truly religious in feeling and usually faithful to the doctrine of their tribal beliefs in these matters.

On another occasion, while Bill Williams was at Bent's Fort, a Mexican woman died, and the members of her family were considerably distressed that the poor woman should be buried without the benefits of a religious ceremony. Old Bill rose to the occasion and conducted the service in a manner quite satisfactory to the mourners and consoling to the members of the family. Even Williams himself took considerable satisfaction in the manner in which he performed the burial service.[20]

Living as he did among the Indians, he naturally acquired many of their concepts, firmly believing that dreams portrayed future happenings and that each man had his good and bad medicine. On occasion he and the others of his class wore turquoise earrings and gayly ornamented clothing; they emulated the Indians in dress, deportment, manner of speech, and conduct toward each other. Francis Parkman, some years later, met a party of mountain men on their way east, and they had painted their faces with vermilion, plaited their hair with mud and put on gay decorated buffalo robes; on seeing Parkman, they began to strut and show off, just as the Indians often did with white men around.[21] "The free hunter was never more satisfied than when he made the imitation so perfect that he was taken for an Indian."[22]

The mountain man took each day as it came; if he were successful in his gathering of peltries, he enjoyed life while he had the means; if unsuccessful, he enjoyed life just the same. Free from responsibilities, unrestrained by conventions of society, with health and a few good companions, the mountain man was always ready for a new adventure, especially if there were prospects of beaver and fat buffalo.

[19] Chittenden, *op. cit.*, II, 643.
[20] Memorandum of Micajah McGehee, *loc. cit.*, 218.
[21] Francis Parkman, *The Oregon Trail*, 60.
[22] Chittenden, *op. cit.*, II, 842–43.

CHAPTER TEN

Piracy on Land

HORSES WERE ONE of the important factors in the lives of the western Indians. From a social and economic point of view, one could say the horse exerted greater influence in the daily lives of the red men than did any other single force. Upon their mounts they depended for getting food, transportation, and protection from their enemies. The Indians with a goodly supply of horse flesh were the strong tribes. Where they had few or no horses, they were of little consequence and usually inferior, both mentally and physically. If it is true that the horse was introduced into North America by the Spanish *Conquistadores*, the native inhabitants of the country had, by the middle of the eighteenth century, adapted their lives to dependence upon this animal.

What was true of the use the Indian made of the horse was even more true of the whites who roamed over the plains and mountains. The horse was an absolute necessity to the mountain men. They would rather be left without arms and food than deprived of their horses and left afoot. If the Indians contemplated an attack on a band of traders or trappers, the first move was to try to sneak up on their horses and drive or stampede them, for without their horses the whites were at the mercy of the red men. Every young Indian boy was brought up to steal horses and instructed in the technique of that art, for being successful in stealing horses carried with it about the same distinction as being a great fighter.

Horse stealing early developed into a common practice; the Indians preyed on the whites; the mountain men stole from the Indians and Californians; the Comanches, Apaches, and Navajos stole from the Mexicans; the Utes stole from the Arapahoes; the Pawnees preyed on the Santa Fe traders; and the Comanches ran off the horses of the Mexicans, the trappers, and their Indian neighbors. Ownership of livestock was coexistent with the power and ability to retain possession against the efforts of others to get away with this important property.

Horse-stealing excursions were a business which the trapper looked upon as "perfectly legitimate in its character when properly directed,"[1] according to the code of the mountain man of this period. This meant that the plans must be carefully laid and successfully carried out, the horses secured even if some of the owners might be killed. To be sure, one mountain man must not steal from another or from friendly Indians; such taking was considered as a grave offense, and if caught the thief would pay the penalty, which was often death. The taking must be from the Californians or Mexicans, or from an unfriendly tribe of Indians. Since the former had vast herds of horses, and were not trained to defend themselves against raids of this character, the mountain men and even the Indians made a business of going into California and Mexico on horse thieving parties. In fact, the going out on these excursions, spying out the country, rounding up the horses, and getting them out, came to have a sort of fixed routine, which was usually followed.

One day in the early thirties, a *cavayard*[2] of some three hundred mules and horses was being driven toward Bent's Fort on the Arkansas. Out in front, leading the band, was a buckskin-clad trapper, with long hair and whiskers worn mountain-man fashion, mounted on an Indian pony. He was riding with noticeably short stirrups, which gave him a hunched-up appearance; across his lap

[1] Narrative of Micajah McGehee, *loc. cit.*, 59.
[2] A term used as applying to a band of horses. It is a corruption of the Spanish word, *caballada*, often used colloquially by the Mexicans as *cabayada*.

he carried a long rifle. On each side of the main band of horses was a rider, not unlike the leader in dress and general appearance, who occasionally turned back into the band a stray horse which had broken out. Bringing up the rear were some half-dozen riders with a couple of pack mules. It was quite evident that both men and horses had covered much ground, for although the horses were unbroken for the most part, they had become accustomed to being driven in a band. All the horses and mules were footsore and jaded and the men in charge were grimy with dirt, their clothes ragged and worn. This was not a trapping party, for there were no signs of furs or traps, and their baggage consisted of a few cooking utensils and blankets. In sight of the fort, an air of excitement and expectancy became manifest among the men; even the horses seemed to raise their heads and travel at a livelier gait. From the adobe fort there were signs of life, and the roof of the lookout began to be occupied.

Charles Bent,[3] one of the proprietors, had no doubt been awaiting the approaching party, for on their arrival he had mounted a horse and went outside to greet them. The man riding the lead horse was Bill Williams. The greeting was brief: "Wagh, old hoss," on one side, and "How, Bill," on the other. They shook hands leaning out of their saddles and conversing for a short time. "Bent," said Williams, "take all these horses and roll out that old barrel of whisky that's been in the storeroom so long. I'll kill it, or it shall kill me."

Bent looked over the band of horses indicated. He didn't have to ask any questions. They were California horses. Possession meant ownership, although they carried various brands and some had their ears split. It was a fair offer and the trade was soon made.[4]

[3] Charles Bent was one of the famous Bent brothers. His father, a native of Massachusetts, came to St. Louis in 1804 and was prominent in the affairs of that city. There were seven sons. Charles was early engaged in the fur trade in the southwest. He was the first governor of New Mexico; was killed and scalped in the massacre at Taos on January 19, 1847.

[4] Captain James Hobbs says in his *Wild Life in the Far West*, 49, that in 1842, "Old Wolf," a Comanche chief told Bent he could supply him with all the mules and horses he needed. He says, "Bent offered to give him the market prices for all such stock and had no conscientious scruples about the way the Indians obtained them."

Bent ordered the gate to the fort opened and *cavayard* soon was corralled inside the post. The barrel of whisky was rolled out of the storeroom, the head was knocked in by Bill Williams, and "every one about the fort got on a glorious big bust together, which continued until the barrel was empty."[5]

On this particular expedition the Californians had resisted the summary appropriation of their livestock by this wild band of foreigners, and some fighting had taken place. The well-known marksmanship of the trappers had rendered the Californians cautious, and the fighting was not pressed on either side at the time of the raid.

The mountain men had planned their thievery well and had executed it with equal skill; they were soon through familiar passes and over the mountains onto the desert. The owners of the livestock gathered together their friends and neighbors, determined to avenge this raid and get back their lost horses. This stealing of their horses had been carried on too much. The thieves must be killed and the horses recovered. Enthusiasm ran high as they planned what they would do to the Americans when caught. The thieves would be roped and dragged until life was gone, then left for the wolves to eat. They shortly picked up the trail; it could be easily followed, and being less encumbered than the mountain men, they came, before long, within sight of the cloud of dust raised by the horses driven by Williams and his companions. There the singing ceased; not so many threats were heard; enthusiasm began to diminish; they didn't urge their horses on as before; they seemed in no hurry to attack the *Americanos*. They made camp within sight and out of gun range of the land pirates who had been aware of their approach before they had come into sight.

That night the mountain men took the offensive. Employing Indian tactics, after the Californians were asleep, they crawled up on their pursuers' riding horses, evading the night guard, and cut the hobbles and riatas and with yells and noise stampeded every horse, driving them into their own herd, leaving the Californians

[5] Narrative of Micajah McGehee, *loc. cit.* 60.

to make their way back afoot as best they could. These were the horses Williams was now trading to Bent for whisky at the fort. From our present-day point of view, it is difficult to understand the motives of men who would carry through such a venture, enduring hardship and taking the risks they did to acquire horses, only to throw them away in one wild orgy. Was it the love of adventure, the Indian traits they had developed, or was it just part of their life as mountain men? Whatever it was, this stealing of horses on large scale happened not once but innumerable times during the period prior to the Mexican War.

The Californians were not only preyed on from the Southwest, but in the North the Indians got their horses from this same source. The Nez Percés, Yakimas, and Cayuses very early made up a strong war party, and crossed through the hunting grounds of the Indians to the south of them, and into the Sacramento Valley of California. This party, having reconnoitered the country thoroughly, then rounded up a large band of native horses and succeeded in getting away with the spoils, driving them back north to the Walla Walla Valley. These tribes always had plenty of horses and carried on considerable trade in horses in later years with the immigrants passing through their country.

In the late fall of 1832, Bill Williams and half a dozen companions were some 325 miles southeast of Taos. They were on foot and headed back to the Spanish settlements.[6] How long they remained without mounts or where they wintered is not known. Williams fades out of sight in the Southwest, only to turn up in the Green River country the following July as a member of the famous Joe Walker expedition into California. Captain Bonneville had equipped and sent out a party of free trappers, as he supposed, on a lawful purpose, but the expedition in reality developed into a lawless excursion, extending over a year. Williams and Walker were friends dating back to the time they went on the Sibley expedition together. Then they were novices; now they were mountain men. If this party was not the most famous of its kind, it was the one about which the most has been written.

[6] Pike, *op. cit.*, 80.

In order to get a proper appreciation of this expedition, it is necessary to review briefly the events leading up to the sending out of the party.

Captain Benjamin Louis Eulalie de Bonneville[7] procured a leave of absence as an officer in the United States Regular Army, to extend from August, 1831, to October, 1833, in order to undertake a combined exploring, trapping, and trading trip to the Rockies. From this trip he expected to make his fortune. The staff officers of the Regular Army, hoping to derive benefit from the excursion, suggested to Captain Bonneville that on this leave he ascertain the "nature and character of the several tribes of Indians inhabiting those regions; the trade which might be profitably carried on with them; the quality of the soil, the production, the minerals, the natural history, the climate, the geography and topography, as well as geology, of the various parts of the country within the limits of the territories belonging to the United States, between our frontier and the Pacific."[8] It was rather a good-sized program if the staff expected the Captain to follow literally their instructions.

Captain Bonneville had no difficulty in getting Alfred Seton and his New York friends to finance the trading venture. From New York, Captain Bonneville proceeded to Fort Osage, the "jumping-off" place at the time. For guides he hired Captain Joe

[7] Benjamin Louis Eulalie de Bonneville was born in France, April 14, 1796. His father was a man of parts but got into trouble through his writings. Young Bonneville and his mother left France and in company with Thomas Paine came to New York. Through Paine's influence, he got an appointment to West Point, entering April 14, 1813. He was commissioned December 11, 1815, and served until General Lafayette visited this country. He was assigned to accompany the General on his visit; returning to France with the visitor, he remained abroad for a time. On return, he was assigned to a post in the West and there conceived the idea of a trading company. After his return from the mountains, 1835, he sought reinstatement, which was granted by President Jackson, who thought he had been of service to his country through his explorations. He served in the Seminole, Mexican, and Civil wars, was retired Brevet Brigadier General. Died at Fort Smith, Arkansas, June 12, 1878. He was married twice, first to Ann Lewis and later to Susan Neis.

[8] Letter of Major General Macomb, in Washington Irving, *Adventures of Captain Bonneville*, 427, 428.

Walker and M. S. Cerré,[9] who were both competent and experienced. He soon had 110 for his party; and quite likely, had he wanted, he could have had many times that number, for it was one of the best-provisioned and equipped trading parties to leave for the mountains.

The expedition, from the standpoint of its backers, was an absolute failure; from the army side, little could be reported of the information he was directed to obtain. Whatever Bonneville may have lacked in ability to make money out of such a trip, or however gullible he was, to the sorrow of his backers, he made up in a claim to fame won by the treatment he accorded to all those with whom he came in contact. Surely the mountain men greatly profited by his coming.

The inevitable happened with Bonneville: he did not know the trading business and had no experience in trapping; he was wanting in almost every essential quality. His trading stock and finances gradually slipped away, with nothing to show for them.

After a series of losses in his ventures, the first year out, Bonneville planned in 1833 to recoup his failures by sending Captain Joe Walker on a combined trapping and exploring expedition into the country about the Great Salt Lake. He was ordered to "keep along the shore of the lake, and trap in all the streams on his route; also to keep a journal, and minutely to record all events of his journey, and everything curious or interesting, making maps or charts of his route, and of the surrounding country."[10] The clerk of the party understood the instructions to be to "steer through an unknown country toward the Pacific, and if he did not find beaver" to return to the Great Salt Lake in the ensuing summer.[11] One of the members of the party some years afterward said, that

[9] Michel Sylvestre Cerré, often called Lami Cerré, was born in St. Louis, April 17, 1803, of French descent. Family engaged in the fur trade. Young Cerré was engaged in Santa Fe trade; conducted a post on the Missouri for a time; worked for Bonneville; later in employ of American Fur Company; elected to Missouri legislature 1848; clerk of the circuit court, 1849, and sheriff of St. Louis County, 1858. Married a relative of the Chouteaus; died January 5, 1860; left a family.

[10] Irving, *op. cit.*, 187.

[11] Wagner, *op. cit.*, 147.

while the mountaineers were organized "for the purpose, ostensibly, of trapping for furs on the waters flowing from the Sierra Nevada Mountains into the Pacific Ocean, in fact, the chief object was to steal horses from the Spaniards residing in California."[12]

In the light of subsequent events, one is led to believe that the latter purpose was the idea of the members of the party, even if Captain Bonneville had other plans. Walker experienced no difficulty in getting together a band of about forty, most of whom were real denizens of the mountains. In this group were Bill Williams, Joe Meek,[13] Joe Gale,[14] Mark Hind, Bill Mitchell,[15] Alexis Godey,[16] Antoine Janise, Bill Craig,[17] George Nidever, John

[12] Beall, *op. cit.*

[13] Joseph L. Meek, called Joe or Major Meek, born in Virginia, 1810; started his career at age of eighteen; first employed by Rocky Mountain Fur Company and followed hunting and trapping for about ten years; settled in Oregon, held various political offices, and was sent as a delegate to Washington to work for statehood; made a record trip crossing the mountains in winter and created a stir by appearing in Washington in his trapper's habiliments; had an Indian wife and left children.

[14] Joseph Gale was a native of the city of Washington. He was a member of a party of trappers under Ewing Young in 1831, going to California. After his return from the California trip with Walker, he was employed for a time as the leader of a trapping party by Nathaniel J. Wyeth. He was in Oregon between 1842 and 1843, associated with Ewing Young in his enterprises, and stayed on in Oregon after the latter's death.—J. J. Hill, "Ewing Young and the Fur Trade in the Far Southwest," *Oregon Historical Society Quarterly*, Vol. XXIV, No. 1, 29; F. G. Young, "Ewing Young and His Estate," *Oregon Historical Society Quarterly*, Vol. XXI, No. 3, 196, 200, 203; Osborne Russell, *Journal of a Trapper*, 1.

[15] Bill Mitchell was a well-known trapper. He made several hunts with Williams; made his headquarters in the Southwest; served as a scout for Major Reynolds in summer of 1848 in campaign against Apaches.

[16] Alexis Godey was of French parentage, born in St. Louis. If he was with the Walker party he was very young. He served under Frémont in the second, third, and fourth expeditions and was appointed an officer by the Colonel in the California campaign. He usually hired as a hunter. He settled in Bakersfield, California, and engaged in the real estate business. Attending a circus he got too close to a lion and was scratched severely, dying from blood poisoning on January 19, 1889. He had a succession of Indian wives and left a widow on his death. Godey left an estate of some ten thousand dollars.

[17] William Craig was born in Virginia about 1800. While still a youth he became involved in a quarrel and killed his adversary. This was the occasion for his entering the life of a trapper. He was in the mountains as early as 1829. He was very friendly with the Nez Percés who only knew him by the name of William. He married one of the tribe. After the fur trade passed he settled in the northwest; was for a time a subagent among the Nez Percés, and acted as inter-

Price,[18] and Zenas Leonard.[19] In order to equip the party properly for a year's trading and trapping, Captain Bonneville used up all of the supplies and merchandise. Each man had four horses and blankets, buffalo robes, provisions, and every article necessary for the comfort of men engaged in an expedition of this kind. Joe Walker was a natural leader of men, perhaps because he was less boastful and pretentious than most of his comrades, which made him the more forceful. It should be added, however, that whatever leadership he assumed was rather limited, for most of the men he commanded were "free trappers." They traveled in a party only for adventure and self-protection. This expedition, under Walker and the forty mountain men, started on July 24, 1833, and proceeded to Bear River, where they hunted for a few days. They laid in a stock of meat and then went on toward the Great Salt Lake. Finding no streams of consequence flowing into the lake and very few beaver signs, the trappers then turned back and pursued a westerly direction into the mountains and again did a little trapping. From this point on they gave up any attempt to trap or to follow out their instructions in regard to investigating the fur possibilities of the country; as for trading with the Indians no effort was made, and their only contact with the natives was of a hostile nature. The party at about this time seems to have become possessed with a lawless spirit, if, indeed, it had not already laid its own plans well. After parting with Captain Bonneville, he and his orders were literally out of the minds of the mountain men. Whether originally they intended to go on a marauding and law-

---

preter in 1855 when treaties were made with the Nez Percé, Flathead, and Black-feet Indians. Craig Mountain, Idaho, is named after him. Died September, 1868.

18 George Nidever and John Price both settled in California and did not return with Walker.—See H. E. Bolton, *New Spain and the West*, II, for more about Nidever.

19 Zenas Leonard was born March 19, 1809, at Clearfield Creek, Pennsylvania. Upon arriving at age of twenty-one, he notified his father, a farmer, that he thought he could make a living easier than picking rocks. He went to St. Louis and hired out to Gant and Blackwell as clerk of a trapping party. After five and a half years in the mountains, he returned to his home and wrote his narrative in 1839. Later he returned West and settled and carried on a merchandising business in Jackson County, Missouri.

less trip into California, or whether that became their purpose as time went by, is not quite evident. In any event the expedition intended for lawful purposes took on quite a different color. Zenas Leonard, the clerk of the party, left an account of the trip, wherein he explained why they had killed the Indians, but made no mention of the horse stealing or excesses in other directions. This account was written by him after he had returned to the East and was first published in the local paper in his home town.[20] Undoubtedly he did not care to enlarge on phases of his adventures which, if told, might not be understood by his Pennsylvania friends and neighbors.

One afternoon while they were encamped on the Humboldt River, which had a milky cast, Bill Craig, one of the party, stripped and started for the swimming hole. He was just about to plunge into what appeared to be deep water, when he stopped to investigate, and found that just beneath the water, well out toward the center of the stream, there was deep mud. Wading to where there was a current in the river, he found the water there a little more than waist deep. On looking towards the camp he espied Joe Walker coming towards the river, and he was "jumping like a buck deer." When he arrived at the bank he said, "How is it?" and Craig replied, "Joe, it is just splendid." With that Walker plunged head first from the bank into the stream where the mud was deepest. Craig, knowing what would follow, got out of the water and into the bushes on the opposite side. After Walker had extricated himself from the mud, he got his gun and started out to kill Craig, but fortunately the matter was patched up between them. This place on the Humboldt River was afterward known as "Walker's Plunge" or "Hole."[21]

The attitude of the members of this expedition toward the natives is shown by their utter disregard for the rights or the lives of the Indians. One trapper, having lost a trap, said he would kill the first Indian he met. Not long afterward, seeing two Digger

[20] The original narrative of Zenas Leonard was published in 1839, a portion appearing in the Clearfield *Republican*, of Clearfield, Pennsylvania, his native town. Copy in the Huntington Library, San Marino, California.

[21] Beall, *op. cit.*

Indians fishing on a stream, he deliberately killed one, the other escaping. Again, when the mountain men ran across a large body of Digger Indians, presuming them to be hostile they wantonly killed twenty-five, although the facts are that the Indians had apparently gathered merely out of curiosity to see the white men, the like of whom they had perhaps never beheld before, or, in any event, only at very rare intervals on their hunting grounds.

The party reached and crossed the Sierras in the late fall of the year, meeting with considerable snow and much hardship. Coming down the Sierras, they passed through the Yosemite Valley on the way, being the first whites to discover this place. Afterward Walker had inscribed on his tombstone, "Camped at Yosemite, November 13, 1833."[22] When they reached the plains of California, game was plentiful, feed for their horses abundant, and the climate mild. They progressed toward the coast in a leisurely manner. The party stopped at the ranch of John Gilroy about where the town of that name is situated, and where they were hospitably received by the owner.

They fell in with a Yankee sea captain named John Bradshaw, who invited the whole company on board his ship, the *Lagoda*, where a feast was given with much drinking. It was kept up all night. They made their way to Monterey, arriving about Christmas time, and there wintered. From all accounts, they were cordially received by the natives. Governor Figueroa gave them permission to remain in the country during the approaching winter, to hunt as they wished and to trade as much with the natives as they pleased. Such supplies as Captain Bonneville had provided for the party were soon "squandered away" and, in a word, they "revelled in a perfect fool's paradise."[23]

The life in Monterey for a time appealed to these hardened citizens of the plains. Williams and many others could speak Spanish fluently, and were not unaccustomed to the manner of living in Monterey, which was very similar to that of Santa Fe and Taos,

---

22 H. H. Bancroft, *The History of California*, III, 391. It is likely the date is wrong.
23 Irving, *op. cit.*, 337.

where they had often wintered. They also knew how to deal with the Californians and the native Indians. Tiring after a time of this life in California, with fiestas, bull fights, cock fighting, horse racing, but no beaver trapping or Indian fights, Walker, Williams, and the others, decided they had had enough of settled life and longed for the mountains. Walker reported that many of the men were offered fancy wages if they would stay, particularly those who had had any mechanical skill. At least two of the party, George Nidever and John Price, we know, actually settled there, and probably four others remained.[24]

Captain Walker did not return by the way he had gone in, but sought new adventures by passing up the San Joaquin Valley, in a southeasterly direction, and out into the desert through a pass, since known as Walker's Pass, north of the Tehachapi where the route of the Santa Fe cuts off from Barstow to Bakersfield. On their way out through the San Joaquin country they rounded up a likely bunch of "five or six hundred head of the Spaniards' horses and they drove them through what is now known as Walker's Basin and Walker's Pass of the Sierra Nevada."[25] Leonard, the clerk of the party, says they returned with 52 men, 315 horses, 47 beef, and 30 dogs. He does not mention the taking of any horses, except to say, "Stealing horses is practiced more than any other kind of theft, and it is not recognized as a crime, owing, probably, to the cheapness of these animals."[26]

As soon as the party had crossed the Sierras, they turned north and followed the east side of the mountain range, and then attempted to cross through central Nevada. After much hardship they finally succeeded in getting across the desert and into the Green River country. The accounts of the trip leave some gaps; all we know is that in June, 1834, Walker and some of his men had rejoined Bonneville at the place agreed upon. We know that the expedition had little to report in the way of journals kept, charts made, the character of the country about the Great Salt

[24] H. E. Bolton, *The Spanish Borderlands*, II, 45.
[25] Beall, *op. cit.*
[26] Wagner, *op. cit.*, 219.

Lake; they had no peltries to turn over to Bonneville; in fact, it is doubtful if many of the horses got as far as the rendezvous. For the goods he had given them to trade with, they had nothing to show.

It is needless to say Captain Bonneville was disgusted and disappointed; he had been ill-advised and apparently deceived. "The horror and indignation felt by Captain Bonneville at the excesses of the California adventurers, were not participated in by his men; on the contrary, the events of that expedition were favorite themes in the camp. The heroes of Monterey bore the palm in all the gossipings among the hunters. Their glowing descriptions of Spanish bear-baits and bull fights especially, were listened to with intense delight; and had another expedition to California been proposed, the difficulty would have been to restrain a general eagerness to volunteer."[27] In summing up the net results of this exploit, one writer has said that Walker, with his men, "pursued a career toward California, which emulated the Forty Thieves of the stirring story of Ali Baba."[28]

In the meantime the Great Salt Lake remained unexplored and Captain Bonneville's supplies and goods were gone, and he was past the period he should have reported for duty in the army. The account of this trip into California was passed on from one campfire to another and likely lost little in each retelling. Williams may have left the main party at some place after crossing the Sierras, with a part of the spoils, and proceeded on to the Arkansas River, for that is the report that Ruxton left of the Walker party.[29]

Joe Meek, who told the story of this same expedition some years later, says that after getting out of the San Joaquin Valley, they passed by Lake Tulare, crossed the desert in a southeasterly direction to the Mohave villages on the Colorado. From the river villages, which were about where Needles, California, is now situated, the party proceeded down the Colorado River to the mouth

27 Irving, *op. cit.*, 342.
28 Frederick S. Dellenbaugh, *Breaking the Wilderness*, 277.
29 George Frederick Ruxton, *In the Old West* (reprint 1916), 221–81.

of the Gila; they then doubled back as far as the fork of the Bill Williams River. Here they met "Frapp and Jervais,"[30] partners in the Rocky Mountain Fur Company, with about sixty trappers. The two parties then united and proceeded up the river, across country to the Little Colorado, then to the Moqui villages. Here, Meek relates, they helped themselves to the fruit and melons. The Indians resisted and some "fifteen or twenty were killed." However, he says of himself, "I didn't belong to that crowd, I sat on the fence and saw it through. It was a shameful thing." Some doubt can be entertained as to this story, since melons among the Moquis are hardly planted at the time Meek went through the country in late spring. But he never failed to tell a good story when he was so engaged. From the Moqui village, he says they proceeded northeasterly to the Río Grande.[31]

Joe Meek does not mention the horses taken; he describes rather what would be the trip of a band of hunters. It would have been impossible to have taken any number of horses over the route he claims to have traveled. If Meek covered the country in that year, the party out of California must have divided, those with the horses going up the old Spanish trail and the others going southeast to the Colorado.

We have another account of Bill Williams going into California on one of these thieving parties, but the result in this case was not so satisfactory as the others. In one of the periods between trapping seasons be organized a party and descended on the coast of lower California, where they succeeded in rounding up some fifteen hundred head of mules and horses and driving them out of the country, up through the mountains and onto the Mohave Desert. The Californians pursued them across the desert and it is said that some two-thirds of the stolen horses died from fatigue,

[30] Henry Fraeb and Jean Baptiste Gervais were partners of Thomas Fitzpatrick, James Bridger, and Milton G. Sublette, and these formed the Rocky Mountain Fur Company. They bought out in 1830, Smith, Jackson and Sublette. Meek must have been confused as to the trip to the Colorado, as Fraeb and Gervais were back on Green River on June 20, 1834, and the Rocky Mountain Fur Company, of which they were partners, was dissolved.

[31] Frances Fuller Victor, *The River of the West*, 152, 153.

overdriving, and lack of water and food. It was indeed a *Jornada del Muerto*,[32] in the true meaning of that expression. The Williams party finally outwitted their pursuers and reached the mountains, but were not able to profit much by their effort. The Indians of southern Utah, through whose country they were traveling, succeeded in evading the watchfulness of the night guard and in stampeding the entire band. Williams and his comrades were obliged to return to the Spanish settlement on foot. The mountains had meted out a sort of even handed justice to their children. For a number of years, the trail which the Williams party followed across the Mohave Desert was marked by the skeletons of the horses which they lost on the way.[33]

In 1839, in the Southwest, the Apaches and Navajos, led by Jim Kirker,[34] became such a menace in their horse stealing and preying on the settlements that the Mexican authorities in Chihuahua offered nine thousand dollars' bounty on Jim Kirker's head. Kirker had been trying to keep on good terms with both the Indians and the authorities. With this offer made, he decided he had better cast in his lot with the Mexicans.[35] He sent word that he had been a captive among the Indians and if the government would employ him he would undertake to clean the Indians out of horses. A truce was patched up and Governor Trías issued him a *guía* or sort of letter of marque to proceed against the Apaches and Navajos on the agreement that he and his associates could keep the horses they could steal and a bounty of fifty dollars for each scalp.[36] Kirker organized his party in and about Santa Fe from the Americans there at the time, with some Shawnees, Cherokees, and Delawares, getting together about seventy in the

[32] Means literally "dead man's journey."

[33] Report of a trip by Lieutenant George Douglas Brewerton in 1848 from Los Angeles to Santa Fe in John C. Van Tramp, *Prairie and Rocky Mountain Adventures*, 183, 184.

[34] James Kirker, an Irishman by birth, was known to the Mexicans and Indians as Santiago Querquer. In 1835 he received a license to trap and trade for a year with the Apaches, from Governor Abino Pérez of Santa Fe. He spent most of his time in the Southwest and in later years was called Captain Kirker by reason of services rendered the military as guide and scout.

[35] Hobbs, *op. cit.*, 81.

[36] *Ibid.*, 97.

party, The venture was most successful from their view. The spoils they took from the Indians were 1,000 horses, 300 sheep and goats, 183 scalps, and 18 women, besides recovering the goods stolen from a trader. Upon their return to Chihuahua, the Mexicans decided that since the horses brought back had been stolen from them by the Apaches and could be identified by marks and brands, they would not allow the Kirker party to keep them. The Governor balked at paying for the scalps because of the large number and refused to count the eighteen Apache women, since they were not scalps. This was the last straw, and one of the leaders of the party, Shawnee Spiebuck, said he could remedy this objection. Drawing his butcher knife he grabbed one of the women with the evident intention of killing her and taking her scalp. This was too much for the officers and they agreed to count the women as scalps.

Induced by threats, the governor finally did pay for forty scalps, leaving the mountain men in a rather hostile mood. They held a council and Spiebuck and most of the hunters decided to take their horses and leave that city. Daring the soldiers and the authorities to stop them, the mountain men divided the horses and drove them out of the city to Santa Fe, where part were sold and the remainder driven on to Bent's Fort. Kirker stayed in Chihuahua, leaving his share in the corral, thinking he could settle with the government. He never got a cent for his share of the scalps, nor was he allowed to take any horses.[37]

Bill Williams was only one of many who had engaged in horse stealing from the California missions and *ranchos*. Thomas L. Smith, reported to have been with Ashley in 1823 in the fight with the Arickaras, was a master horse thief. He trapped in the Southwest with Ewing Young as early as 1826. Later, while trapping in the Green River country with Jim Cockrell, he broke his leg, shattering the bone so that a portion protruded. Smith himself decided on an amputation. With a file, a saw was made out of a butcher knife. Then, cutting away the flesh, with the help of Cockrell, he tied up the arteries, sawed the bone, seared it with a

[37] *Ibid.*, 99.

red hot iron and sewed up the stump. The operation was a success.[38] When his limb was healed, he made himself a wooden leg and became known as "Peg Leg" Smith. He was a famous horseman and spent most of his time in the saddle, the wooden leg apparently not inconveniencing him to any extent. He was probably the most successful horse thief on a large scale that we know of. In fact, "Peg Leg" Smith spent most of his time organizing expeditions into California to steal horses. He holds the record, along with Jim Beckwourth, as they are reported to have gone into California by the southerly route and succeeded in getting out with three thousand head on one foray. It is said, however, that after the country passed from the Californians to the United States, "Peg Leg" discontinued his activities because he had no desire to operate against his own countrymen. It may be that his fear of what might happen to him if he was caught by the American authorities had full as much influence in causing this decision as did his patriotism. Strong drink was his downfall, and he ended his days in San Francisco, a victim of that curse, in 1866.[39]

With the decline of the fur trade, many of these wild characters of the mountains turned to horse stealing as an outlet for their activities. Joe Meek relates how a party of these renegades, under the leadership of a trapper named Thompson, became active as horse thieves. In 1839 they raided the Snake Indians and got away with a large number of their horses, but ran afoul of Joe Walker, who made them return the horses to the Indians. Two years later this same Thompson, with a few chosen companions, descended into California and succeeded in getting away with a large number of horses. These they drove over the mountains, across the desert, and headed for the Missouri settlements. It was hard going and a rough trail, and when they had reached the Platte River the band they had started with had been reduced in number by one-half.[40]

These thieving excursions into California by Bill Williams and

---

[38] C. G. Coutant, *History of Wyoming*, 201.

[39] *Ibid.*, 201.—Captain James Hobbs says Smith died in 1868 in Calaveras County, California, as a result of a drunken fit. See Hobbs, *op. cit.*, 46.

[40] Rufus B. Sage, *Rocky Mountain Life*, 51.

the trappers were not wholly devoid of good. In going and coming on these marauding trips, trails were discovered which later became routes for lawful commerce, trade, and immigration. Colonel Frémont tells of meeting in 1834 an emigrant train at Fort Hall on the way to California "under the guidance of Mr. Joseph Walker, who had engaged to conduct them, by a long sweep to the southward, around what is called the Point of the Mountains; and crossing through a pass known only to himself, gain the banks of the Sacramento by the Valley of the San Joaquin."[41] This is the same Captain Joe Walker, who with his forty land pirates ten years before had first gone through that pass driving horses appropriated from the Californians.

Besides the horses and mules taken, these lawless adventurers brought back information concerning the country beyond the Sierras, the people who inhabited the Pacific slope, and the resources of the country beyond the desert and of the Sierras. The stories of this country filtered back across the plains and influenced migration. The rights of the parties involved, the morals or the ethics of taking others' property, were never considered by the trappers and mountain men, nor did they consider they were doing anything reprehensible. Horse stealing was just a phase of life in the mountains and plains.

41 Van Tramp, *op. cit.*, 408.

CHAPTER ELEVEN

Passing of the Fur Trade

WILLIAMS SPENT THE YEARS from 1825 to 1846 in the mountains. These were the years when the fur trade reached its high mark and also began its decline. They were years when the free trapper came to the fore, new methods of trade were adopted, and the flint-lock gun gave way to the percussion cap. There developed among the mountain men during this period a technique and a code. A man was rated on his ability to trap and take care of himself.

The several Indian tribes had each become quite distinctive to the trappers, almost as much so as the peoples of the world seem different from each other. Some tribes had continued to be friendly, while others had remained unapproachable. Further-more, some of the tribes were friendly to certain trappers and trad-ers, and unfriendly to others. A fur company could not make con-tacts of itself, but the individual employee could, particularly the free trapper and trader who had no company policy to follow. The intermarriages between the trappers and the Indians were more than unions of convenience. In many cases the white men and their adopted peoples became blood brothers through these unions. Williams had kinsfolk among the Osages through his mar-riage. He had become a Ute through marriage and adoption.

To enumerate all trappers who identified themselves with the Indians would include most of the mountain men. Edward Rose and Jim Beckwourth,[1] mulattoes, had become chiefs among the Crows; John Smith[2] lived with the Cheyennes and had considerable influence over them. Scores of instances could be cited where a white man had gained the confidence and friendship of some Indian tribe. "It was a common thing among all the Indians to adopt white men into the tribes and occasionally to make them chiefs. They were sensible of the superiority of the white man's intellectual knowledge and the advantage which his knowledge gave him, and when they found one who would enter with true spirit into their own manner of living, they were always ready to honor him with authority."[3] It naturally came about that as trade with the Indians was controlled more by these personal contacts, the company traders correspondingly lost their influence and trade.

For both the whites and the Indians, there were two main trapping seasons in the year. In the spring, as soon as the ice broke up in the streams, the trappers would begin their work and continue until along in June. Then for a period of two months there was no trapping, and the time was usually spent at some rendezvous. The fall season began in September and lasted until the streams froze again. The winter was the off time for the trappers. Sometimes, if places could be found where there was wood, game, and little danger from the Indians, they would stay in the mountains, but more often they retired to one of the frontier trading posts and wintered. We find many of them in the Río Grande settlements or at places like the Pueblo, Fort Bent, or Fort Laramie.

The custom of carrying on trade at a place of rendezvous had

[1] Edward Rose's father was a trader among the Cherokees, his mother was half-Indian and half-Negro. Rose was with Hunt on his trip across the country in 1811 and served General Ashley as interpreter at the time of the fight with the Arickarees in 1823. He was a man of powerful physique and great courage. He married into the Crow Nation and came to be a chief among them. He was not highly regarded by his fellow trappers, being considered a renegade; said to have met his death at the hands of the Crows through jealousy of the medicine men. See also Chittenden, *op. cit.*, II, 684.

[2] Sometimes known as Jack Smith; was from Missouri and acquired a wide influence over the Indians and Mexicans; at times traded out of Bent's Fort; married and left a number of half-blood Cheyenne children. Much is told of Smith in L. H. Garrard, *Wah-To-Yah and the Taos Trail.*

[3] Chittenden, *op. cit.*, II, 684.

been instituted first by the early Canadian traders. The Hudson's Bay Company in the Northwest had sent out their traders to meet with the Indians as early as the beginning of the century. In the mountains General Ashley adopted this method the very first year he was out, in 1822, for Beckwourth tells that "after caching our peltries and goods by burying them in safe places, we received instructions from our general to rendezvous at the 'Suck' by the first of July following."[4] Word would be passed out by the companies that at a certain time and place the traders would be on hand with their goods. When the appointed time came, there was usually gathered large numbers of Indians, free trappers, and other persons who were interested in trading.

Brown's Hole in northeastern Utah on the Green River was a famous place to rendezvous. There was plenty of feed and forage for the horses, wood and game were handy, and it could be reached from almost any direction. The place took its name from an old mountain man named Baptiste Brown. Lying west of this was another famous site for rendezvous—"Pierre's Hole" or "Pierre's Hole under the Three Tetons," named after an Iroquois chief killed there in 1827. Sometimes it was referred to as "Teton Basin." There was a valley extending southeast and northwest fully thirty miles in length and in breadth from five to fifteen miles. A clear stream flowed through it from the Teton range. It was an ideal place to congregate.[5] East of the Teton Range and south of Pierre's Hole, from which it was separated by a narrow precipitous pass, was another place for rendezvous known as "Jackson's Hole," named for David Jackson of the firm of Smith, Jackson and Sublette. Where the city of Ogden, Utah, now stands was the meeting place of the Hudson's Bay Company, named after Peter Skene Ogden. Other places where rendezvous were held were Jackson's Little Hole, Gardner's Hole, Bayou Salado, Wind River, and a score of others less frequented.

A rendezvous of this kind was a sort of annual fair or outdoor

---

4 T. D. Bonner, *The Life and Adventures of James P. Beckwourth*, 62.
5 Chittenden, *op. cit.*, II, 657, 747–49.

market, affording an opportunity for the mountain men to meet, gossip, trade and find out the latest news from back home or the States, and to drink, carouse, and let off excess energy. The accepted practice at rendezvous was that there should be no fighting between the Indians and the traders. Unfriendly tribes would even come in, bring their villages with them, and carry on trade and dealings with the trappers. But when the meeting was over and they started away from the rendezvous, all truces were at an end. There were times when feelings could not be held back, as in the case of the Battle of Pierre's Hole in 1832, between the Blackfeet and the trappers. At the time this fight took place, there were gathered at the rendezvous some hundred lodges of Indians, many trappers employed by the American Fur Company, one hundred men of the Rocky Mountain Fur Company, some twenty belonging to Wyeth's party, as well as numerous free trappers. The companies were always well represented, either by their heads or agents.

Free trappers and their parties found a reday market when they came in with their furs. Such occasions were marked by a period of excesses; whisky and other strong drinks were always in demand; there were brawls and fighting, often resulting in serious consequences to the combatants. At the first rendezvous attended by Joe Meek in the summer of 1829, the year he began his mountain life, he says that he was "shocked to see four trappers at a game of cards with the dead body of a comrade for a card table."[6]

Dancing, singing, shooting, horse racing, and other games and sports were carried on until the trapper had spent all his earnings, and often he continued his spree as long as his friends had anything left. The young Indian women would dress in all their finery and parade up and down to attract the trappers. Many a mountain man thus fell before the wiles of the dusky maidens. Usually a satisfactory trade was made with the parents of the girl and the trapper started on his next hunt with a helpmate. It was also during these rendezvous that most of the plans were made for trapping

6 Victor, *op. cit.*, 51.

and hunting parties in the fall. Groups were organized, trappers hired out or organized their own parties, and by the end of August the rendezvous was over and the place deserted.

Furs and robes gathered at the rendezvous from the free trappers, from the Indians, and from the parties sent out by the fur companies themselves were nearly all shipped or carried by various means back to the city of St. Louis or through Montreal in Canada. The English companies had established posts in the Northwest and north of the Missouri River, and the American companies had their posts along the Missouri, at Fort Bent on the Arkansas, and at several posts along the east slope of the Rockies.

Money played no part in the economic structure and life of the area during these years. Furs were the medium of exchange and were passed for the staple article of the day. One beaver skin represented so much lead, powder, sugar, or coffee. Money was not needed. Since the coming of the whites into the country, the Indians had developed needs, and they found, as time went on, that guns, powder, lead, knives, awls, beads, vermilion and other paints, tea cups, and kettles were essentials of life. Thus, with the furs going east and the inhabitants demanding more and different commodities, a continual stream of commerce was kept up with the civilization of the East, and more and more men became interested in the West. The permanent post or fort for trading was found more serviceable. The Rocky Mountain Fur Company had its last rendezvous in the summer of 1838 at the forks of the Wind River,[7] and the American Fur Company rendezvous was held for the last time the next year, on the Green River.[8] The custom of meeting for trade at the designated place was kept up for a time by some. In 1842 a meeting was held at Brown's Hole, which was much like the old rendezvous.[9] But the regularly established trading posts had taken their place.

The period, in addition to the changes wrought in the fur trade, marked the passing of the flintlock gun and the introduction of

[7] Russell, *op. cit.*, 93, 94.
[8] Victor, *op. cit.*, 255.
[9] Hamilton, *op. cit.*, 97.

the percussion cap. The effect of this invention on the final conquest of the West was as far reaching as that of any other single event. In the years when the flintlock gun was used and before the gun firing the percussion cap was perfected, the Indians, although using a few flintlock guns, continued the use of bow and arrows. Contrary to the usual notion, the Indian did not make the most of firearms; he rarely was a good shot, and having little experience with mechanisms, did not always keep his gun in serviceable condition. In many ways bows and arrows were more dependable; they could be used in all seasons of the year and in all kinds of weather—could be shot instantly and repeatedly.

The old flintlock carried only one shot, and the flint did not always strike fire; the powder had to be kept dry or it was useless. In a gale of wind the powder would blow out of the pan and it was reprimed with difficulty. The Indians could shoot their arrows with accuracy and killing force. The flintlock, as compared with the bow and arrow, had only the advantage that it reached farther in fighting, for at close range the arrow was equally deadly. In buffalo hunting many mountain men preferred the bow and arrow and the lance to the flintlock. In group fighting full advantage could not be taken by the whites, since all did not dare to discharge their guns at the same time.

If the one shot in the old flintlock failed to reach its mark, the mountain man would reload, provided he had the time; but at bay, where seconds counted, he had to resort to his knife or tomahawk. With the percussion cap invented and perfected, the situation was entirely changed. Weather no longer had to be reckoned with, and the trappers could reload and cap and shoot their guns with greater rapidity and fewer misfires. Those who were most expert with their guns could load and shoot four times a minute. In 1835, when Samuel Colt invented the six-shooter, with its revolving chamber of six loads, the Indians, with their bows and arrows, were doomed. One can well say that Colt's invention and perfection of the six-shooter marked the end of the Indians' supremacy.

The mountain men as a class always kept up with any new invention in guns, fully realizing its importance. This was illustrated when in 1842 Williams went on his trading venture with Perkins and Hamilton: each man in the party had a rifle, two pistols, a tomahawk, and a large knife. The pistol was not only used by the trader, but was used with deadly accuracy. At the summer rendezvous at Brown's Hole in 1842, Hamilton tells us that with three posts, each squared to about twelve inches at the top, set to project some six feet from the surface, and spaced about twenty-five feet apart, many trappers, riding at full speed, could put two bullets in each post from a distance of ten feet with their Colt six-shooters, and most of them could put at least one bullet in each post.[10] It early became evident that the pistol with its six shots was the weapon to use in close fighting.

With the aid of a gun which was mechanically designed to fire one shot after another, without the necessity of stopping to reload, the whites were given an advantage which was the deciding factor. A few men, each of them with seven bullets—the one in his rifle and the six in his pistol—could stand off any number of Indians. If he should possess two revolvers, a mountain man would become almost a walking arsenal, and filled with confidence he acted the part.

The Indian, however, although courageous and unmindful of danger or death, invariably became confused and bewildered in a fight when fellow warriors began to fall about him. This was not due to his lack of courage, but rather to his inability to carry on after reverses had come. Further, as is common with primitive peoples, the Indian tribes, made up of clans or blood brotherhoods, were bound in a spiritual manner to their chief and to fellow warriors. The annihilation or general depletion of a clan's membership in battle was recognized as a very evil omen. Likewise, the death of a chief had a deep spiritual, perhaps even a religious meaning.

The Indians planned on fighting with odds in their favor, taking their enemies by surprise and overwhelming them with superior numbers. Colonel Henry Dodge knew that watchfulness and a display of courage were essential in dealing with the red

[10] *Ibid.*

men. In 1834 he went through the Indian country west of Fort Gibson, knowing "the influence of dauntless boldness over Indians, who dread every loss, and seek the attainment of their ends by cunning and management."[11] They never seemed to be prepared for loss or figured on a certain proportion of their number being killed in a battle. Let any one of a dozen things happen and they were at the mercy of the party they had attacked. This again was caused by the fact that they, as is the case even in partly civilized society, were governed by taboos. That is to say, many happenings or circumstances were taken as evil omens, and to violate established rules of conduct in the face of such omens, though it meant victory at the time, would in their belief mean also that some terrible recompense would have to be made later on. The accounts are numerous of a large force of Indians attacking a small group of mountain men, starting out with every apparent intent to overwhelm and carry through their charge; yet, when met with fire and when their comrades began to fall, the chargers hesitated, wavered, broke, and retreated.

During the years, Williams and his contemporaries had traveled here and there, over plains and mountains, and had become acquainted with practically all the ranges, the valleys, the streams, and the water holes. They recognized natural objects from a distance as old friends, and knew the places to avoid as well as those where the best hunting and trapping grounds were available. Their network of trails and paths and their knowledge of the country extended from the Río Grande settlements to Oregon and from California back to the Missouri frontier. The one definite record which has been preserved of Old Bill's visit to Arizona is in the statement of Antoine Leroux, who in 1837 met Williams, all alone, on the river in Arizona which afterwards was named for him.[12] Old Bill had traveled westward from the Río Grande settlements, across "Apachería,"[13] or land of the Apaches, to the

---

[11] Chittenden, *op. cit.*, II, 632.

[12] Diary of R. H. Kern, with Captain Sitgreaves, in 1851, on an expedition down the Zuñi and Colorado rivers. MS in Huntington Library, San Marino, California.

[13] J. Disturnell, *Map of the Republic of Mexico 1848*. Apachería was the

stream now called Bill Williams' Fork, had done some trapping there for beaver, and then had traveled downstream for three days, but towards the mouth there was little or no beaver on account of the dryness of the country and the periodical floods. Williams had then left the river and had gone in a northerly direction across to the Colorado River and at that point was swallowed up in the mountains.

The next year he bobbed up in Wyoming, a thousand miles from Arizona.[14] From the Green River rendezvous that summer, Captain William Stewart,[15] an English army officer seeking adventure on the plains, made up a party to hunt buffalo. Accompanying Captain Stewart was a young man also seeking adventure, Isaac P. Rose. They had with them as hunters the veterans Kit Carson, Tom Biggs,[16] Bill Doty, Lucien Fontenelle,[17] and Bill Williams.

The party crossed over the plains toward the buffalo country, and almost at the outset the Crows succeeded in running off their horses. Williams reported the loss and plans were immediately

---

name commonly used by the Mexicans when referring to the area south of the Navajos and Hopis in Arizona and New Mexico.

[14] J. B. Marsh, *Four Years in the Rockies,* 222.

[15] Sir William Drummond Stewart, Bart., was born in Scotland in 1795. He fought in the Battle of Waterloo under Wellington and was wounded. In 1832 he came to the United States, and with letters to Governor Clark of Missouri, and Generals Atkinson and Ashley, he arranged for a hunting trip in the mountains. He spent three and a half years in the Rockies, then returned to New York. Instead of returning to England, he went back into the Rockies with a well-outfitted expedition and stayed for a year and a half. He returned again in 1842 taking with him an artist named Miller to sketch and paint scenes they visited. He wrote two works: *Altowan,* edited by J. Watson Webb and published by Harper & Bros., in 1846, and *Edward Warren,* published in 1854 in London by G. Walker. His name is not attached to either.

[16] Thomas Biggs was a mountain man; he had charge of a company of trappers working for L. B. Fontenelle in 1837, when the latter was employed by the American Fur Company.—Russell, *op. cit.,* 81, 82. He was wintering at Bent's Fort when Frémont came on his Fourth Expedition. Biggs has been confused with Thomas O. Boggs, son of Governor Boggs of Missouri, who settled in New Mexico in 1844, and was the executor of Kit Carson's estate.

[17] Lucien Fontenelle was with the American Fur Company for some time and acted as guide for Rev. Samuel Parker and Dr. Marcus Whitman on their first trip to Oregon in 1836. He was a member of the firm of Fontenelle, Drips & Vanderburg.—Dellenbaugh, *op. cit.,* 287.

made for action. Kit Carson took young Rose with him and, picking up the Indian trail, followed it. Williams returned to the rendezvous to get horses and incidentally any trappers who cared to go. There was no trouble in getting men to go after Indians, with Carson and Williams in the party. Following the Indians, the mountain men soon overtook them. Rose says that "not wishing to be recognized by his old enemies," he held back. Williams and Carson, it is evident, did not feel the same way, and they maneuvered until they had the Indians rounded up and their horses back.

Williams' return to the rendezvous to get trappers may have been due to the fact that he did not want to be encumbered with Captain Stewart and Rose in the event of conflict with the Indians. He perhaps felt as Colonel King S. Woolsey[18] did at one time in the late sixties. The Indians had been committing depredations for some time in northern Arizona and the authorities requested Woolsey to see what he could do toward subduing them. He and a companion prepared to take after the Indians. A captain and a company of soldiers stationed at Fort Whipple tendered their aid to the two old Indian fighters. Woolsey tried to discourage him, but the military man was persistent and went along with his company of soldiers. The party proceeded southwest of Prescott and finally met up with the Indians at Date Creek among some rocks, and the shooting began. The captain kept close to Woolsey and continually sought directions as to what he should do. Finally Woolsey's patience became exhausted and he asked the captain to order his soldiers back and to go with them, for, as he said, "I can't fight these Indians and look after you and your soldiers at the same time."

The next time we run across Williams is in the mountains north of Taos. This time he was in company with Dick Wootton and a

---

[18] Colonel King S. Woolsey was a native of Alabama and settled in Arizona before territorial government was formed; he engaged in farming, mining, stock raising. He was one of the organizers of the Atlantic Pacific Railroad; helped build the first irrigation ditch; after coming of the whites, was a member of early legislatures and leader of the local forces in a number of Indian campaigns. Died June 29, 1879, Phoenix, Arizona.

trapper named Walters, out on a trading venture with the Indians of that section. But they met with misfortune, for the three men were ambushed while traveling in a canyon. Walters was not very seriously hurt. The bullet had entered his left side and had passed under the skin almost half way around his body, but he was able to retain his saddle. The three men made a break out of the canyon and got away. They gave up the idea of trading and took Walters to Bent's Fort, where he stayed and recovered. He was through with the mountains, but not so Williams and Wootton; they headed back into the Indian country.[19] From the stories related by the other trappers, we find Bill Williams during this period on the Columbia River, on the Yellowstone, the Missouri, and in the Salt Lake country.

The years went by. Williams had gained a reputation as a mountain man, based on accomplishments. He always brought in more beaver skins, better prepared, than those of the other trappers. He had and spent more money than the others. The average price of beaver was four dollars per pound and it took almost eighty skins to make one hundred pounds. All the streams swarmed with these animals; thus "a mine of wealth here lay open to the industry of the trader and trapper."[20] Williams was conspicuous in his celebrations at times of rendezvous. He seemed to have a charmed life in his many conflicts with the Indians. His custom of traveling alone and then turning up at unexpected places after an absence gave a certain air of mystery to the man. All of these facts made him a subject of gossip among the men in the West, and his goings and comings were often told and retold, his eccentricities were enlarged upon, and his peculiarities emphasized. Yet these years were hard on his physical reserve; he was aging, and the old machine was being worn down.

With the wealth he had acquired during the most profitable period of the fur trade, he had developed and was able to satisfy an ever greater desire for drink, but it was telling upon him. Old in the ways of the mountain and plains, he had become old in

19 Conard, *op. cit.*, 147, 148.
20 Chittenden, *op. cit.*, 818.

Alfred Jacob Miller, "Interior of Fort Laramie,"
from the Walters Art Gallery Collection

"The winter was the off time for the trappers. Sometimes they would stay in the mountains, but more often they retired to one of the frontier trading posts and wintered. We find many of them . . . at places like the Pueblo, Fort Bent, or Fort Laramie."

Charles Bodmer, "Blackfeet Indians on Horseback,"
from *Travels in the Interior of North America*

"Varmit air bad now en then, but Blackfeet is the ornariest, them
Injuns air . . . . Blackfeet air worser'n ary cats en panthers en Grizzlys.
Don't yer never ferget Blackfeet."

appearance. He came to be known as "Old Bill" Williams to all who had occasion to mention his name. With the attainment of the affectionate prefix "Old" to his name, for that is what it amounted to, Bill Williams was recognized as a sort of daddy to them all, and with the changing times described above, he began to play, to an even greater extent, the part of a pathfinder for other men.

In the fall of 1840, a party of old, experienced trappers, made up of Old Bill, Kit Carson, Bill New,[21] Bill Mitchell,[22] and a Frenchman named Frederick, set out from the Green River. That fall they trapped the Green River country and wintered at Brown's Hole. In the spring they went back into the Utah area and Middle Park, hunting and trapping. They then returned to Roubidoux's Fort in the summer.

Beaver was getting scarce, their catch was not so large as usual, and the prices had fallen off considerably. It began to look as if they must turn elsewhere for a living. When fall came, they headed for the Arkansas, looking for something to turn up. When they reached that river, Mitchell and New decided they would stay and do some hunting. Williams and the others went on to Bent's Fort. In a week or so their two comrades turned up much the worse for their hunting trip, for they had been caught off their guard by the Indians and had been robbed of even their clothing. In that destitute condition they had been turned loose. Two such old-timers did not give up, but made their way with much suffering to the fort.[23]

Carson and Williams stayed a time at Bent's Fort, and then decided to make a visit back to their early surroundings in Mis-

[21] Bill New was a mountain man during Williams' time. He was killed at Rayado, New Mexico, about 1850, by the Jicarilla Apaches. He was living peacefully on a ranch at the time, and was killed only after desperate resistance against the Indians who attacked him, when he was at work in his fields.—DeW. C. Peters, *Kit Carson*, 354.

[22] Bill Mitchell during his years as a trapper joined the Comanches and lived with them. His object was to find out the location of a gold mine in Texas he thought the Indians knew of. Failing to learn anything about it, he returned to trapping.

[23] Blanch P. Grant (ed.) *Kit Carson's Own Story of His Life*, 48; Peters, *op. cit.*, 158–62.

souri. Mounted on their Indian ponies, with a buffalo robe or two and with few belongings besides their arms, they had indeed little to show for the years they had spent in the mountains. First Williams visited his older daughter, Mary, who was living in Kansas not far from the place they were when he left. She was married to a man named John Mathews, and they had a small daughter named Sue.

Old Bill could not get used to the surroundings. The country was not the same. When he had gone west in 1825, there was not a single house in that part of the country beyond Independence, but at the time of this visit, the region was being rapidly settled. He stopped in Kansas only a short time, however, and then continued on into Missouri. Finding that his brother John was then living on a farm, he located the place and went out to visit.[24] He created a stir in the neighborhood. No one recognized him, not even his brother. This is not altogether surprising, since they had not seen each other since about 1825, when Bill set out for the West under Sibley.

"H'ye, John!" shouted Bill as he rode up that evening.

John turned and replied just as lustily and cordially, but without knowing to whom he spoke. The tall, long-haired, bewhiskered creature, who looked much too big for his horse as he rode along with knees cocked up under his chin, was no one from the neighborhood.

"Wagh! Don't ye know yer own brother, ye old hoss?" queried Bill, dismounting and shaking the kinks out of his long legs.

"I would if I seed him, but ye're no kin o' mine, that I know of."

Old Bill exhausted all arguments. Finally, becoming exasperated, he pulled off his buckskin hunting shirt, extended his long hairy arm, and pointed to the tattooed initials of his name. "Thyar, ye old mule, I'll prove it to ye. Recollect the day I got them put thyar when we war boys back in old St. Louis County?"

His brother John did remember the day his older brother had come home, pushed back his sleeve, and proudly showed them

[24] The farm is now in Maries County, Missouri, occupied by Perry and Josie Williams, the great-grandnephew and niece of W. S. Williams.

his initials tattooed on his arm. He examined the stranger's arm. This creature was none other than his brother, Bill, then known in the family as Wild Bill.

Habits which Old Bill had formed over the years showed here on his stay with his brother in the Ozarks, as well as later in Gasconade County, where he visited his mother. The mountain man could not be induced to sleep indoors or on a bed, but insisted on going outdoors and rolling up in his robes and blanket, even with snow on the ground. He vowed he would strangle if he stayed inside and that a bed was the work of the devil. This aversion to couches and buildings was noticeable among all mountain men. In 1865 when the old trapper, Pauline Weaver, was attached to Fort Whipple, Arizona, as a guide, he never stayed at the post at night, but had a camp on Granite Creek and there slept on the ground, rather than in the quarters provided for him inside the fort. Professor Bolton refers to the effect of outdoor life on men of that class and those unaccustomed to the habiliments of civilization. He tells us that Álvar Núñez Cabeza de Vaca and his companions, after some eight years of wandering among the Indians, at last reached Mexico and were given clothing to wear and quarters with beds. The wanderers found they could not wear the clothing with any comfort, "nor could [they] sleep anywhere else but on the ground."[25] Eight years of sleeping on the ground had weaned them from beds for good.

During the visit of the old trapper, his brother John killed a calf on one occasion and did some hog killing on another, to provide meat for the family. Old Bill shocked them at both butcherings by squeezing out the contents of the intestines, and devouring those choice morsels on the spot, Indian fashion.[26] He had in truth become more Indian than white man.

Among the contents of the sack he brought with him, which he called his "possibles," were gold nuggets from the Rockies; he showed these to John.

[25] Bolton, *The Spanish Borderlands,* 44.
[26] The incidents of his visit at the butchering and relative to finding gold, as told by Mrs. Ashley G. Williams, Waynesville, Missouri.

"Why don't ye come back to the mountains with me in the spring? Thar's plenty gold where this is had, enough to make us both rich," he said.

"I'd sure go, but a man cain't walk off and leave his family, ye know," John responded reluctantly. He always felt that had he gone, he would have become rich. Bill's youngest brother, Benjamin, did go out west for a time, as did the nephew, Micajah, when he got older, his memory fired, no doubt, by the many stories which Old Bill had told during his visit.[27]

One evening after supper, the John Williams family was gathered about the fireplace with Old Bill the center of interest.[28] That day Old Bill had killed a wildcat, which the men folks thought had been the cause for the loss of a large number of the hens. He had dropped the running cat by a long shot across a gully, on the far side of the opposite hill. The conversation turned to the events of the afternoon and John Williams said: "That war a mighty likely shot o' yourn, Bill. Them cat beasts had been a-killin' them hens till we war nigh out of 'em. Derned if a wild cat ain't about the cussedest critter on airth."

"Yar plum wrong, John," said Bill. "Varmit air bad now en then, but Blackfeet is the orneriest, them Injuns air. Yessir, fer jus plain bad medicine, give me Blackfeet. Them is alluz a-lookin' fer har en a-stealin' en a-skulkin' like a hell cat. Them Injuns go afoot mos' tha time en yer ain't safe when that thar pison is near yer. When a child air in thar diggins, yer scalp lock ain't too tight. No, John, Blackfeet air worser'n ary cats en panthers en Grizzlys. Don't yer never ferget Blackfeet."

Old Bill filled his pipe with tobacco cut from a plug, went over to the fire, lighted a splinter, and then lighted his pipe, and was back squatting again. He puffed his pipe a short time in silence and then resumed.

"Onct I war a-trappin' on the heads o' Yellowstone. Spring it war, en beaver a-runnin' and me a-makin' em come. Most three

---

[27] *History of Cole, Moniteau, (etc.) Counties, Missouri*, 1129.

[28] As told by Walter Williams of Maries County, Missouri. He is a descendant of John Williams, brother of Bill Williams.

plews I'd a-taken. With nary a Injun sign thyar about and no trapper t' bother. I got sort o' keerless in my doin's en onct when I war out two days en when I fetched camp arter dark I was powerful gant, en hungry as a wolf in winter. First off I keered for ol' Flopear, that war my mule, and Santyfee, that war my hoss; then I builded me a fire. I knowed I hadn't orter, I knowed it right then. I war a-cookin' beaver tails. Jest as I'd a-blistered one en war a-retchin' fer it out o' th' fire I heered a noise, en then mos't about to run over me en tramp me war three Injuns. I could feel my har being lifted and war nigh to goin' under, jest like yer kill a fat buffalo. Them war Blackfeet en mor'n likely had been a-spyin' me fer days. Thyar I war and nary time to git my shootin' iron, Fetchem, en no chanct ter fight them varmints. Thar was a piece o' brush alongside th' river about a rifle shot distance, en this child tuk fer them willows. All I had war my har en my possibles en my toothpicker here."

Old Bill drew his long butcher knife from his belt and ran his thumb along the blade. Then he took a small stone from the pouch he always carried, knocked the ashes from his pipe, put it away, and began to whet the knife, already as keen as a razor.

"Them Injuns jes' kep' comin', en this old hoss only touched the ground a time or two, fer I didn't aim ter let them Injuns rub me out. Them bucks fetched me twict, onct in the shoulder and onct in the thigh, but I made them willows. Injuns air all the same some ways; they don't hanker ter take no chances and alluz aim ter jump yer without yer lookin'. Them dogs didn't foller me fur, cuz they aimed to get me by spyin'. It sure would a taken mor'n them Injuns ter get me in them willows with th' dark all settled down. John, I cached, I did. Them arrers hadn't o' done no great sight o' harm 'cept in the meat o' my leg en I butched it out. Th' t'other only cut my shirt a little—th' buckskin stopped her. I slipt a'past 'em en tuk to th' hills afore mornin'. Then I war safe. I laid up two days and nights. It was a long piece from rendezvoo and I sez, 'Bill, them consarned Injuns hain't any call on them three plews o' beaver.' I callated my hoss and mule would be treated Injun fashion. The more I thunk about it, the madder

I got at them consarned Injuns. Why, that mule an hoss knowed mor'n a white man. Then one o' them bucks had my Fetchem—that gun war the out-shootest gun ary a man ever drew a bead on. 'Wagh, Bill,' sez I, 'mix yer medicine, mix it powerful, make her good en strong.' I tuk them Injuns' trail and follered th' sign. It was plenty easy. Cage hyar could o' follered Old Flopear's track. Yer could see it plain as ther brush along th' water. Them Injuns had all my peltries en things, en didn't travel no great country ary day. I warn't in no hurry cuz my leg war swelled. I tell ya, John, it war poor eatin' with no meat en nuthin ter make it come, only berries, en I kilt a snake and getched a few birds' aigs. With thet arrer hole in my leg en a gant belly I tell yer I war all set fer them Injuns en I aimed to make 'em go under. In four days I spied 'em. They never knowed it fer I kep' cached th' hul time. Long the next arternoon they kilt a fat buffalo cow in a park en turned to en et near all of it. 'That,' sez I, 'air powerful good medicine fer yer old timer.' Injuns sleep right smart arter eatin' fat buffalo, en all that fleece, en rump en good cow, I knowed comin' good doin's fer me. John, I had ter be keerful, cuz old Flop-ear war worser'n a passel o' dogs when it come ter knowin I wuz around. I didn't let her git th' wind o' me. She'd a spoilt it ef she had a smelt me. She could smell better'n a wolf. I tuk my time en spied out th' lay. Arter dark I eazed up on them Injuns, every consarned one o' em, sound asleep, with their feet ter th' dead fire."

Here the old mountain man raised up from a squatting position on the floor, put his whetstone away in his sack, and with his butcher knife in his hand, took on a crouching position. He looked as lithe as the wild animal they had killed that afternoon. Every muscle was tense, and his eyes shone like a cat's eyes in the semidarkness of the room. The light from the logs burning on the hearth cast their long shadows on the wall, and the red of the flaming embers flashed and reflected from the long shining blade of the knife he carried in his hand. The group about the room was tense with excitement.

"Thar they war, like snakes full o' prairie dog—meaner than any snakes thet I had ever heerd tell of."

Old Bill took two short steps forward, and then knelt and with his knife made a sharp cut, and with the other hand a movement as if covering something.

"I cut his throat and stopped the grunt." Here he dropped his voice, as if muttering to himself. "Then I sez, 'Thyar one Blackfoot that'll nary steal no more peltries from ye.' "

Stealthily rising again to a crouching position, Old Bill moved across the room about three feet to one side; he raised his long knife in the air, and plunged it down towards the floor, at the same time almost hissing.

" 'Nother rubbed out, en a clean cut twixt th' ribs. Nary Blackfoot buck can shoot an arrer into me and set me afoot. Not this child."

Old Bill, then apparently looking toward the third Indian, twice went through the quick round motion with his hand and knife, as if cutting the scalp and then yanking it off.

"I sculped 'em, I did, en that air Injun never knowed what had come o' the other two." Old Bill rose up and then resumed his narrative. "I steered the coals in the' fire ter get a little light, then I kicks that air buck square in th' belly. I fetched 'im a powerful kick.

Old Bill drew back and made a vicious kick: he went through the pantomime of shaking his knife and the scalps in the face of the imaginary savage, standing over him like a grim messenger of death.

"When that air buck seen this yar toothpicker, all bloody, en them sculps, en then seen them Injuns sculped en gone under, en me a-standing there a-shakin' blood in his face en a-pintin' at 'im en a-wavin' them sculps at 'im, he let out a yell worser'n a painter. Yer could o' heerd 'im clean to Middl' Park, en he war up en gone quicker'n an antelope on the dead run."

Old Bill resumed his squatting position, replaced his butcher knife in his belt, and began to refill his pipe. Immediately a flood of questions followed. His brother John said, "What did you do then, Bill?"

"Well, John," said Old Bill, "I war a powerful gant, en I finished up that cow en flung the bones at them two good Injuns. Then I got old Flopear en Santyfee, packed up my peltries, gave Old Fetchem a bear hug, en left that air country."

"But, Uncle Bill," chimed in little Cage, "Why did you let that Injun go, why didn't yer kill 'im?"

Old Bill looked first surprised at the asking of such a foolish question, and then recognizing the immature years of Cage, said, "Ef I'd a kilt that Injun, Cage, thyar wouldn't a been nobody left ter tell them Blackfeet how them bucks had gone under nor who'd a rubbed 'em out."

It is small wonder that although little Cage had the measles at the time, they could not keep him in bed when Old Bill sat about the fireplace narrating his adventures or describing life in the far West. Later on in life, when Cage had attained the age of twenty-three, he captained a party of forty across the plains to California and was for a time engaged in mining in the West, but he eventually returned to the Ozarks. His brother, Bill, never left the old farm and lived there until he died.

Old Bill soon traveled on up into Gasconade County, where his mother was living with his youngest sister, Arabella. His mother was then eighty-six years of age, and had seven years of life still left. Although most of his family had ceased to be proud of the reputation which had drifted back across the plains, his mother had never lost faith in her son Will, as she called him. When he appeared clad in his greasy buckskin suit, with his whiskers and long hair and queer manner of expression, he was nevertheless her missing boy. She ran to him and attempted to embrace him when he entered the house. Old Bill would have none of it. He put her away almost gruffly, expressing himself in Indian language, which seemed to come easier. Likewise, when his sisters tried to show their affections toward him, he told them it was unnecessary. He had changed, at least partially, into a man of a different race from that of his own kinsfolk.

He visited for a time with his family, and then continued on into St. Louis. They never saw him again. He stayed in St. Louis for a short time and loafed among those of his kind who had come back for a taste of civilization after varying periods of life out West.

The record of the doings of Old Bill typifies the life of the average mountain man. Without any realization of it, these men were performing a genuine service to the United States and were preparing for even greater service when in later years the call came to them for help. The preparation, it is true, was not a purposeful one; these men had no end in view, but just the same, as time went on and they learned to take care of themselves and acquired a knowledge of the country and came to have a thorough understanding of the Indians, such skill, familiarity, and understanding were the instruments by which the final conquest of the country was accomplished. Hunters and trappers from the ranks of the mountain men were the interpreters and guides of the army—were the eyes and ears and props of every government expedition; their achievements were the background of all claims made to disputed territory. And, finally, a mountain man, or a group of these denizens, usually led the emigrant trains across the plains and through the mountains to their new homes in the West.

One need only take the experience of the United States Army in the Southwest to prove the statement. The New Mexico country had been a foreign country and not open to the official penetration of our agents. When the Americans came, they found the trader and the trapper of the Rockies to be the only dependable source of information available to them. A map of the Southwest, made in 1851 under the direction of Colonel John Monroe of the Ninth Military Department, perhaps best illustrates the situation. This map, made within a few years of the American occupation, covers Arizona, New Mexico, parts of Colorado, Nevada, and Utah, all there making up the territory of New Mexico.

No survey had been made of a large part of this country, yet a map was drawn, showing most of the streams, mountains, and passes with surprising accuracy, based upon information furnished in large part by the mountain men. The gracious acknowledgment in the legend clearly states their part in its making: "The Río del Norte from its head to Taos, Sierras de San Juan and Chow Atch, and the region as far as the mouth of the Huerfano, are from a may by 'Old Bill Williams,' and from additional data furnished by Dr. H. R. Wirtz,[29] U.S.A., Messrs. R. H. Kern and E. M. Kern, San Vrain, [30] LeRoux,[31] Hatcher,[32] and others."[33] The last three named, along with Old Bill, were mountain men. The others first visited the country under the guidance of mountain men.

[29] Horace R. Wirtz was born in Pennsylvania and appointed to the army from that state. He became assistant surgeon December 5, 1846; stationed at Taos with army when Frémont went through in 1849; promoted to surgeon April 16, 1862; brevetted lieutenant colonel for faithful and meritorious service during Civil War; was later stationed at Fort Whipple in Arizona; died January 24, 1874.—Records of the Office of the Surgeon General, War Department, Washington, D. C.

[30] Colonel Ceran St. Vrain, born in St. Louis, of French parentage was engaged principally in Indian and Mexican trade from 1824 to 1850, most of the time as a partner in the firm of Bent, St. Vrain & Co., and part owner of Bent's Fort. He early settled in New Mexico and married Miss Branch of Taos. His trading activities took him over the country as perhaps no other man, and he had a wide acquaintance among all classes. His home was at Mora, where he died in 1870.

[31] Antoine Leroux, also known as Watkins Leroux or Joaquin Leroux, came to the Southwest during Mexican rule, and was a trapper and hunter; was rather well educated; early became familiar with Arizona; trapped the Bill Williams River as early as 1837; was guide for Col. P. St. G. Cooke from Santa Fe to California in 1847, on the march of Mormon Battalion; served under Lieutenant J. H. Whittlesey in punitive campaign against the Utes in 1849; was guide to Captain L. Sitgreaves on survey for road from Zuñi to Colorado River in 1851; and was guide to Captain J. Gunnison in his survey for railroad across Colorado and Utah in 1853.

[32] John L. Hatcher, sometimes called "Hatch," was born in Wapakneta, Ohio; he was a small man, full of humor and good stories and on several occasions displayed unusual nerve and daring. He worked for Bent as an Indian trader, and was considered one of the best; also served in various other capacities; was for time a partner of Bent in farming and stock raising; served as guide to soldiers going between Bent's Fort and Santa Fe.

[33] Original map on file with the United States Topographical Engineers in the War Department, Washington, D. C. Copy is Map No. 3 in *The Official Correspondence of James S. Calhoun*, compiled by Annie H. Abel.

CHAPTER TWELVE

Fur Trading with the Indians

THE RULE SEEMS TO BE, once a mountain man, always a mountain man. With few exceptions, the men who followed that life for any length of time found they could not be content in any other. If Williams had any thoughts of settling down when he headed for Missouri, a few months there settled the doubt. He must get back to the mountains. The only questions were where to go, with whom to go, whether to trade or trap.

During his visit to St. Louis, and while making the rounds of the resorts where the mountain men congregated, he ran across an old friend, George Perkins, a mountain man of fifteen years' experience. Perkins thought a trading trip across the plains, ending up at the old summer rendezvous ground on Green River, would be the very thing and would be much more profitable than trapping.

The idea suited Old Bill. The Hamiltons, relatives by marriage, had a son of slight build and not in the best of health. They thought a trip to the mountains might improve the son's health and make him more rugged. In return for taking the lad into partnership, the mountain men could get the family to back them in a trading venture among the Indians. The senior Hamilton arranged the credits as his part, Bill Williams and George Perkins contributing their experience as their part of the venture, and each was to have

139

an equal share of the returns.[1] People in St. Louis were willing to gamble in the fur trade. It was no trouble to finance a fur trading or trapping expedition. Greater returns could be made in such ventures than in any other speculation, provided, of course, all went well.

Williams and Perkins selected goods which they knew would suit the Indian trade. They picked up eight free trappers to accompany them under the usual agreement, they to keep all the furs they trapped, but to have no interest in the trading. At the outset Bill Williams assumed the leadership. The party loaded their goods on wagons, left St. Louis early in the year 1842, and proceeded to Fort Independence. There they traded their wagons for a pack outfit, since, considering the country they expected to travel, this would better serve their purpose. With all details arranged to Williams' satisfaction, they struck out across the plains on March 15, 1842, heading for the Platte River. Little did the Hamilton family realize that once started across the plains, their son, William T. Hamilton, would never turn back to life in the city, but would remain and become one of the well-known scouts and western characters whose life on the plains would stretch out over a period of more than half a century.[2]

[1] *My Sixty Years on the Plains,* by W. T. Hamilton, is referred to in this chapter unless otherwise indicated.

[2] William T. Hamilton, also known as Bill Hamilton, was born December 6, 1822, at River Till, in North England, a son of Alexander and Margaret Hamilton. His parents emigrated to America and settled in St. Louis when he was a small baby. In all he had five years schooling. After six years spent in the mountains, trading and trapping, he went to Hangtown, California, in 1848. There he married and had one child, but both mother and child died in 1851. Hamilton joined the Buckskin Rangers, serving to protect the miners against the Indians. He was active in Nevada in 1853 and in the Modoc Indian War in 1856. Continuing in government service, he served with distinction in campaigns against the Klamath, Tule Lake and Pitt River Indians. For a time was a trader at Fort Benton, the sheriff of Chouteau County, and United States Marshal in 1869; he worked for the government among the Blackfeet in 1873 and was with General Crook in 1876 in the Sioux campaign. Hamilton died at Billings, Montana, May 25, 1908. He was considered the best-versed scout in Indian sign language in the West. He was known to some Indians as "Sign Man"; he also had wide reputation among them as a healer and medicine man.—*Contributions to the Historical Society of Montana,* III, 33–37; James U. Sander (ed.), *Register of the Society of Montana Pioneers,* 246–47.

On this trip the party came in contact with the Kiowas, Cheyennes, Sioux, Pawnees, Arapahoes, Crows, Blackfeet, Shoshones, Utes, and Navajos, and with all of them Williams was acquainted, if not personally, at least sufficiently to know how to treat with them. Many of these tribes he had spent time with or had actually lived with, and he was on more than friendly terms with some of their chiefs. We get from the trip, furthermore, another side of the mountain man which is not generally stressed. That was his native shrewdness and keen appreciation of human nature, particularly of the red man.

They were hardly well started on the plains before they sighted a party of Kiowa Indians out buffalo hunting. Williams at once gave orders to round up their stock, coralling it in an enclosure made by their packs. These Indians gave up their chase and made for the traders' camp. Riding up, they demanded presents from Williams for traveling through their country. The old man looked them over, conversed with them in sign language for a time, and then gave them some tobacco, which did not seem altogether to satisfy them. This did not disturb the old scout, who explained to young Hamilton that they were "only a small thieving party led by a young brave who had two feathers stuck in his scalp lock." Williams had, nevertheless, prepared for action if the Indians had showed any hostility. This incident illustrates one of his outstanding characteristics—the foresight of the man in his dealing with the Indians—explaining perhaps the uniform success of his Indian contacts.

Arriving at the North Platte River, they met up with a small scouting band of Cheyennes, a nation with which he had been on friendly terms for a number of years. The wily old mountain man prepared food for these Indians, in order that during their feasting he might find out what their village needed most and what they had to trade. Getting all the information he wanted, after smoking a pipe with them, he sent them back to their chief, White Antelope, with presents and a message that the traders would arrive at their village the following day. Arriving at the Cheyenne village, Williams seemed in no hurry to trade. Placing his goods in the chief's care, to insure them against theft, he began to get the Indians in the proper frame of mind for trading.

Presents played a large part in all dealings with the Indians. Manuel Lisa, as astute a trader as ever traveled the plains, is said to have realized fully "the indispensable functions of presents." Williams learned it back in his early life with the Osages and demonstrated its use when he gave away three hundred dollars' worth of goods to them before he began talking trade on the Sibley survey, with the result that it cost him only five hundred dollars more to satisfy them. Falling back on the proper practice, Old Bill gave the women coffee, hardtack, and molasses for a big feast. This was done "off hand and with generous impulse" to impress the Indians with the idea that he would be likewise liberal in his trading.

After the feast was over, a pipe was lighted and passed; then Bill Williams was ready for trading. He laid out in piles his stock of goods, consisting of powder, beads, paint, blue and scarlet cloth, blankets, calico, and knives. A fixed price was established for the different skins and no deviation was allowed from that price, even if there was a difference in the quality of the furs. This was an essential principal in trading; otherwise jealousy and hard feeling would arise among the Indians on account of the condition and quality of their pelts, and trouble would be inevitable. The trading was successful from the viewpoints of both Williams and the Indians, the Williams party getting a goodly number of first-class furs. After the trading, we find Old Bill was again in no hurry, for he stayed and visited. He and the Indians put on a buffalo hunt the next day, the trappers joined with about fifty braves. Some twenty squaws went along to do the butchering. A number of buffalo were killed, and feasting followed in the regular Indian fashion. Then, trading for some horses, they packed their peltries and left, being assured of a warm welcome should they ever come in contact with these Indians again.

The next Indians they fell in with were a village of Sioux, with Big Thunder, an old friend of Williams, as their chief. The Indians had some furs, and trading was carried on for a time, Williams adhering strictly to the usual formalities. While the traders were with this band of Sioux, the Pawnees, old enemies of the tribe, one night succeeded in running off a part of the Indians' stock, including the mules and horses of the traders. The white and red men joined forces in taking after the raiders, followed their trail night and day and, overtaking them, recovered their stock and succeeded in getting two scalps. Here again the old friendship between Williams and the band of Sioux was recemented. The Sioux were numerous. Word traveled to the other villages, and he would be doubly welcomed when he arrived at any of their villages.

Arriving at the Laramie River, they stopped at another Sioux village, headed by Chief Black Moon. The report of the part played by the traders in the skirmish with the Pawnees had reached that village. What the Indians had in furs soon passed to Williams. In the meantime he had sorted out, classified, and repacked all the beaver, small furs, and robes, for in this manner he could get a better price for the finer furs from the company buyers than if they were indiscriminately packed.

Soon after they met a company trader, Louis Vásquez.[3] He had ox teams and wagons loaded with goods, which he expected to trade with the very tribe already visited by Williams. Vásquez was not in good humor, because Williams had got in ahead of him, but he wanted the furs and offered to trade.

Old Bill was a hard trader, with all the advantages in his favor, and Vásquez was a trader of no mean ability. The maneuvering, dickering, and trading carried on that day by those two old masters would likely have been highly entertaining if it could have been recorded by picture and sound. That day his partner, Hamilton, was so impressed with the old mountain man's ability that he thought Williams should have been engaged by the gov-

[3] Vásquez is the usual spelling of the name although it is sometimes spelled Vásques. Coutant, in his *History of Wyoming*, 205, said that Louis Vásquez established a trading post on Clear Creek, Colorado, and from the post sent numerous expeditions into Wyoming for the purpose of trading with the Indians. He was at one time a partner of Jim Bridger. Louis Vásquez is often confused with Auguste Vásquez.

ernment as a diplomat, for he made a most favorable trade with the company man.

Finally Vásquez met terms which were acceptable to Old Bill, but with very bad grace. He even threatened to make it impossible for free traders like Williams to operate in the future, to which Williams replied, "Good, Mr. Vásquez, remember I will be on hand to take an active part in the matter when it occurs." The old trapper got for their furs $750 in cash and a quantity of goods suitable for the Indian trade.

The party now moved into the Arapaho country. Although this tribe had furs to trade, they were not to be fully trusted. They were the foes of his friends, the Utes, and undoubtedly each had good grounds for distrusting the other. Yet on this venture business was business; Old Bill let bygones be bygones and got in touch with some of them. Negotiations were conducted through their chief, Yellow Bear. The traders got from the barter some hundred robes and a quantity of other good furs. After the Arapaho trading, the trappers headed for the Green River, which was reached by way of Sweetwater, through the Crow country. Since he knew what to expect from this nation, Williams left nothing to chance, but took the utmost precaution to prevent being taken by surprise. Each camp was selected and arranged with the view to defending it, guards were kept during the night, and care was taken in the daytime. A small band of Crows came to the camp, and Williams halted them outside and carried on a talk. They demanded a feast, said the traders should exchange good horses for their poor ones, that presents of blankets and furs must be made, and the traders' goods must be shown. They were insulting and showed plainly they had come with the intention of cleaning out the party. Old Bill knew they had nothing to trade, and by presenting them with some tobacco, got rid of them for the time. They left with the declaration that the party were "mean white men," but this did not cause him any alarm.

In the Wind River country, they ran across one of the English company's traders named Pomeroy. Williams, under the excuse of "diplomacy," led Pomeroy to believe that the season's catch

Frederic Remington, "A Fur Trader in the Council Tepee,"
from *Harper's Monthly* (February, 1892)

"After the feast was over a pipe was lighted and passed; then Bill
Williams was ready for trading."

Frederic Remington, "A Brush with the Redskins,"
from *The Century Magazine* (March, 1891)

"The trappers withheld their fire until the Indians were within easy
killing distance, then turned loose; the onslaught was completely
checked."

Frederic Remington, "Couriers,"
from *The Century Magazine* (July, 1891)

"Old Bill Williams again engaged as a scout, this time with the Missouri Volunteers against the Apaches."

Frederic Remington sketch,
from *The Cosmopolitan* (July, 1896)

"On Christmas Day, the Colonel decided to dispatch a party down the Río Grande for supplies. . . . Frémont picked King, Breckenridge, Creutzfeldt, and Bill Williams for this trip, and although they were 160 miles from the settlements they started on foot with 'one blanket apiece, a few pounds of frozen mule meat, about one pound of sugar, a little macaroni, and a few candles.' "

of furs and robes had all been traded by the Indians, and that Williams' furs were his only chance to do any trading, because the Indians were leaving for the spring buffalo hunt. A most favorable deal for cash and goods was made with the company's agent. The Williams party now moved into the country of the Blackfeet, Bloods, Piegans, and Crows, and extra precautions was taken to guard against an attack, either by day or by night. From trading, they turned to trapping, desiring to take advantage of the season before it was too late. Coming across a number of moccasin tracks, Williams said they were those of Blackfoot Indians, out marauding, for they usually go "to war on foot."

The prediction proved true, for early one morning a number of Blackfeet attacked the party. The trappers were forewarned and ready, and the Indians received a warm reception; two were killed and several wounded, with no damage to the trappers. Old Bill even restrained some of the younger men from following up the Indians who had been repulsed, for "he considered it dangerous, charging an unknown number of Indians at night, although he had concluded that there were not more than a dozen in number." In the early gray of the morning another Indian was shot while trying to crawl through the grass, presumably to recover the bodies of his dead comrades. With that the Blackfeet gave up the attack and withdrew.

On checking up after the Indians had left, it was discovered the horses had suffered the most damage from the attack, and Old Bill's ire rose. From the diplomatic trader he reverted to the mountain man and white savage. He would have revenge on these Blackfeet. No difficulty was experienced in following the Indians' trail, since they had never expected that the whites would take the offensive. After following for several miles, Williams got in view of the Indians, without being discovered, and by a circuitous route cut them off from a patch of wood toward which they apparently were heading. There were eleven Indians to contend with, but Old Bill was in charge of about an equal number of trappers. The raiders were afoot, armed with bows and arrows and old flintlocks, and were retreating, encumbered with two wounded comrades. The whites were mounted and armed with good guns and deadly Colt six-shooters, which gave them a decided advantage. Williams divided his force, directing one part to engage the Indians, and the other he led around a hill in order to get between them and some trees towards which they were traveling. There followed a fight in which there was never the slightest doubt of the outcome. It was Williams' motto, "Never, if possible, let an Indian escape who has once attacked you." Once started in a fight, he never let up until it was finished. Soon only five of the Indians were left, and they succeeded in reaching a small clump of willows, but it was not long before the battle was over and not one remained to carry back to their village the story of the disaster which had overcome the marauding band. They scalped the Indians, as was the custom, gathered up their effects, and returned to camp. Among the articles taken were several which apparently belonged to white trappers, indicating, as they afterwards learned, that this band had killed the owners and made away with their goods.

Williams had been for some time on the lookout for his friends, the Shoshones, and from time to time would spy out the country with his glass. One day he saw at a considerable distance a band of Indians whom he knew to be the Shoshones "by the way they acted." Riding towards these Indians, he fired a gun, indicating that he was a friend. Old Bill was right, for the Indians did prove to be Shoshones. Word of their arrival in the neighborhood, accompanied by the scalps of the Blackfeet, which the Williams party had lately taken, was sent to the old chief, Washakee, a personal friend of Bill. They were assured thereby of a friendly and enthusiastic reception upon entry into the village. Williams had lived with this tribe, and it was like coming back home when he met Washakee. "Long-lost brothers could not have been more affectionate." A feast was prepared for the trappers with the best the Indians could offer, followed by a period of unrestrained celebration and dancing, the scalps of the Blackfeet providing in small part the inspiration. The old chief gave orders to his tribe to bring in all furs and robes and "give a good trade to their friends."

During the stay of the Williams party with Washakee, three surviving members of the trappers attacked by the Blackfeet came into the village. It appeared that a party of five were trapping when attacked by these Indians. Two of the group were killed and all of their horses run off. The offenders were the band that had run afoul of Bill Williams and had been cleaned up. The three survivors had a considerable quantity of beaver, and they joined the Williams and Perkins party. Reports came in that there were a large number of Blackfeet in the vicinity, and a council was held between the Indians and the whites to devise some plan to get rid of these enemies. "Williams was the leading spirit in the council." Various plans were discussed, until finally it was decided to take the offensive with their combined forces, Old Bill urging that a raid be made. In view of the manner in which he conducted himself in their war council, it is little wonder the Indians had come to hold him in awe and reverence. Dividing their forces, Washakee and Williams sought out and located the Blackfeet and outwitted them in their maneuvering; after some fighting, the enemy retreated. The Shoshones for a time were rid of their enemies and another tie bound the friendship between the Indian chief and the white man. Friendships of this kind—and there were many—had made deep inroads in the fur companies' trade.

When they completed their visit and their trading, Washakee agreed to take the traders' furs, as well as those of the three trappers, to Fort Bridger. Thus relieved of the encumbrance of the robes and pelts, without the necessity of caching them, the party was free to trap for the month which remained before the end of the season. They ran across a party of seven free trappers, two of whom had been wounded in a fight with Indians. It was a chance meeting of old mountain men, most of whom were acquainted with the Williams outfit. They joined forces and traveled to Fort Bridger, where the companies' representatives were gathered. In the fur trading the post had by this time taken the place of the annual summer rendezvous. Williams did the trading of the furs for the party, but "it took three days before the trade was consummated" to his satisfaction. They were paid partly in goods, partly in cash, and partly in St. Louis exchange. The company traders would have preferred not to have done business with Williams, but since he had the furs, there was not much escape; they had to dispose of their goods and get furs in return. Williams was not well liked by the company men, perhaps because they saw in him the force which was breaking their control of the Indian trade, or was depriving them of their monopoly. After staying at Fort Bridger for a period, "drinking, gambling, racing horses, and taking part in shooting matches," they moved over to Brown's Hole, sixty miles away, and spent the remainder of the season there. A trading tent was set up and they disposed of the remainder of their goods to Utes and Navajos, who had come in to the old gathering ground.

About September 1, the season being over, trading was also brought to a close and a reckoning was had with Perkins and Hamilton and the other members of the party. Old Bill divided the returns with his partners and gave the men their share, taking his own part in cash. Bidding them good-bye, he headed for the Río Grande settlements, telling them he had business to attend to in Santa Fe, but he promised Perkins and Hamilton that he would be back in the spring. He had had a most prosperous season and had been associated with loyal and competent partners. Now, with plenty of money, he could drop back into his old surroundings in Taos and enjoy that life for a spell. Old friends would surely be there, and the happenings of the outside world could be learned. After the excitement of the past six months in trading, Indian fighting, and hunting, he would partake of the comparatively peaceful life of the Spanish village of Taos.

The average mountain man's life was usually one of enigmas, contrasts, and contradictions. There are some phases of their lives we never have understood, nor can we explain. After spending the winter in Taos, Williams went over the Sangre de Cristo Mountains in the spring and stopped for a time with his old friends at the Pueblo. He then went on to Bent's Fort. There in March, 1843, he fitted out for his spring hunt. His credit was good with Bent, St. Vrain & Company as evidenced by his note and undertaking:

Ft. Williams, Ark. R
Mch 13, 1843

$300

On or before the first day of September next, I promise to pay
to the order of Bent, St Vrain & Co., the just and full sum of Three
Hundred Dollars, without defalcation, for value received payable
in good merchantable beaver at the rate of four dollars per pound.
Test.

Wm. S. Williams.

Wm. A. Train.

"I have four Beaver Traps belonging to Bent, St Vrain & Co
for the use of which for my present hunt I am to pay them one
pound good Beaver each, and if they are not returned, I am to
pay them Eight Dollars each for them or thirty-two dollars.

Wm. S. Williams.

Ft. William Arkansas R.
  Mch 13th 1843
Test.   *Wm. A. Train*

The note and undertaking carries the following endorsements:

Aug. 31, 1843   Wm S. Williams   Dr.   Cr.
  " ", "   By 1 Beaver Trap ret'd
                 by Jos. Brown
  " ", "   To hire of above Trap
                 1 lb. Beaver or $4.00

Rec'd August 31st, 1843 by hands of Joseph Brown, on a/c
of the within Note, 10¾ lb. Beaver.

Wm A. Train
for Bent St Vrain & Co.

Rec'd Sept 23, 1843 by charge to a/c of Wm. Garcia Seventeen
Dollars

Wm. A. Train for
Bent St Vrain & Co.[4]

[4] *The Colorado Magazine*, VII, 197. The original note was given to the Colorado Historical Society by Mrs. H. L. Lubers, the granddaughter of William
Bent.

Old Bill sent back one of the traps and some Beaver skins by Joseph Brown from some place in the mountains. The credit through William Garcia was money due him from dealings he had had with Garcia. We do not have evidence of the final discharge of the note.

The borrowing of this money was typical of the mountain man, indicating the way his finances usually stood. Here was Williams, trading only a few months before, with business ability worthy of a great merchant, acquiring worldly wealth in abundance, then traveling to Taos. We can judge of the results, for in a few months he was stone broke, reduced even to the point where he had to use credit to get beaver traps and supplies to start out on another hunt. All the proceeds of the preceding summer were gone. He had given his word that he would return in the spring to Perkins and Hamilton, and he was on his way back. Likely Williams had no regrets. He had a grand time while it lasted; maybe he would do better the coming year. He may also have reasoned that life is jut a one-way road, with no return trip, and that a shroud has no pockets.

CHAPTER THIRTEEN

Trapping and Indian Fighting

KEEPING THE PROMISE made to Perkins and Hamilton at the end of the trading trip in the preceding fall, Old Bill rejoined them on March 23, 1843. He found his partners and a number of trappers camped on the Green River, planning a trip into the Northwest. One of their number, named Durango, had trapped in the Walla Walla country for the Hudson's Bay Company. He told wonderful tales of the beaver to be had in the streams flowing from the Blue Mountains. Old Bill readily agreed with the suggestions for a trip there. He had never trapped the country they planned to visit, but had always intended to do so. By common consent Williams became the leader, remaining chief until the party was broken up some two years later.

The gain to be had from their prospective venture was probably not the thought uppermost in the minds of the trappers. The trip was, instead, an opportunity to visit new places; to roam, to hunt and trap—merely to go on living the lives they had in the past. The route for the trip was decided upon; agreement was reached as to the share each was to have from the proceeds; in short, all arrangements were made.

Forty-three men made up the party. All were capable, dependable veterans except Bill Hamilton and George Howard, a younger brother of one of the trappers. It is doubtful if in the history of the mountains there were ever gathered in one trapping party more men qualified to meet and surmount all obstacles which might arise. Hamilton said it was a group, any one of whom "would have been able to command an army" had the occasion arisen.[1] The men were divided into four messes, one group consisting of Williams, Perkins, Hamilton, and eight men; the others, of about an equal number. In the area they expected to hunt and trap, the Indians had the reputation of objecting to and resisting any trespass. Yet, if we compare the final results of this party with those of other trapping parties, we learn they lost only five men during the trip, and that they had their furs and horses at the end—indeed an exceptional record.

It was agreed that all furs or robes taken were to be owned in common, and that the profit would be divided equally. Williams, Perkins, and Hamilton, however, on their own account and independent of the others, took along some five pack horses laden with goods to trade with the Indians. They started in a northerly direction from the Green River in the latter part of March, 1843, and visited the territory from which later came Wyoming, Idaho, Washington, and Oregon.

The first task undertaken was to "made some meat" for the trip. To do this, they proceeded over into the buffalo country, where a number of buffalo were killed and a supply of "jerky" was prepared.[2] Along with this they put up a goodly amount of depuyler or *depouille*,[3] and pemmican.[4] Jerky, depuyler, and

---

[1] Hamilton, *op cit.*, 172.

[2] Jerky is made by cutting the meat into strips or sheets, and then placing it in the sun for a few days to dry. Meat thus cured will keep indefinitely. It can be eaten without cooking, or, if in camp, may be pounded and then boiled with water and salt. Jerky is a common way of keeping meat, both in the West and Mexico. Meat thus cured will be reduced to less than 7 per cent of its former weight or, it takes fifteen pounds of fresh meat to make one pound of jerky.

[3] Depuyler is the layer of fat which runs from the shoulder to the last ribs of the buffalo, near the backbone, and ranges from five to eleven pounds per animal. It was stripped off in a layer and dipped in hot grease, and then dried and smoked for a time, and usually eaten with lean or dried meat.—Hamilton, *op. cit.*, 33.

[4] Pemmican was made by powdering the jerky made from the choice cuts, then mixing it with a tallow or marrow and packing it into skin bags. It was a common food among the Indians, who often mixed it with berries (especially

pemmican were concentrated foods, easily carried. A small amount would sustain life for a long period if no other food were available.[5]

They wintered the first year in the Klamath Lake country, and in the spring of 1844 proceeded south through what is now northern California, then crossed the mountains near Tule Lake, Honey Lake, and Pyramid Lake, and traveled along the east slope of the Sierra to the Truckee River. From this point they again turned north, so that the second winter found them in northern Nevada. In the spring of 1845 they proceeded in a northeasterly direction, trapped Bear River, crossed Green River, went up into the center of what is now the state of Wyoming, visited the Hot Springs, then turned back, and broke up at the head of the Laramie River, after the spring trapping season was over.[6]

While the Williams party were in the Blackfoot country during the first spring of the trip, they met a band of Bannock Indians. Since some of the trappers had known and were friendly with Tygee, the chief of this particular band, a little trading was done. On the Boise River, they stopped at a Hudson's Bay Company post and traded. Such an act would not have been countenanced by the English a few years earlier.

At that time the influence of the Hudson's Bay Company, through its trading posts and the parties it sent out, was still felt to a certain degree in all sections they traversed. This control, however, was on the decline. The company was no longer the dominant factor in the fur trade. The trapping parties still working for the company were, for the most part, poorly equipped and the men themselves were far from equals of the free trappers of the period. On two occasions the Williams party came across such groups and had to provide them with the necessities of life because of the desperate conditions in which they were found.

From the Boise River post they went north to the Grande

service beries) and other foods, or seasoned it to suit particular tastes. It is known as *tasajo* among the Mexican and Argentinean cattle growers, and is a staple of their diet.

[5] Chittenden, *op. cit.*, II, 811.

[6] Hamilton, *My Sixty Years on the Plains*, has a full description of the trip.

Ronde Valley, then called the Camas Prairie, where they stopped for a time to trap. There they came in contact with a band of unfriendly Bannocks, led by a chief named Hawlack, who had "stripped and robbed many small trapping outfits." Size did not count, however, with these Indians. They ordered the trappers to unpack their goods and to surrender some of their horses. In reply, the Indians were given to understand that if they wanted to be friendly and smoke the pipe of peace, there would be no objection, but if it was fighting they wanted, that too was satisfactory.

The savages withdrew, but the white men were too well acquainted with the Indian nature to be fooled. The utmost precaution was taken to guard against a surprise attack. Early the next morning the horse guard caught several Indians, concealed beneath wolf skins, attempting to crawl up on them. The trick was too well known, and two of the would-be wolves were killed Since their ruse had failed, the main band of the Indians, numbering some three hundred braves, attempted to overwhelm the trappers, attacking the camp from two directions. The trappers withheld their fire until the Indians were within easy killing distance, then turned loose; the onslaught was completely checked. The Indians were not prepared for such coolness on the part of the white men, nor were they in the least ready for what immediately followed. Before they had a chance to reorganize, the Williams party mounted their ponies and charged in turn, bringing their Colt six-shooters into use with deadly effect. It was in this charge that Albert Smith, a Virginian, was killed. After the Indians had retreated, it was found that some forty of them had been killed, about sixty of their ponies had been captured, and a considerable number of their flintlock guns, bows and arrows, lances, and spears had been taken. Besides the trappers' loss of one in the death of Smith, four of their men were seriously but not mortally wounded, a number received minor wounds, and eleven pack animals were killed or wounded so badly that they had to be killed. The injured trappers were placed on a travois,[7] and the

[7] A travois was made by lashing poles to the sides of two horses and tying

party moved on to the Umatilla River. Hamilton said of the charge led by Old Bill that day, "I have never been in one which was so savagely executed."[8]

The practical effect of the superiority of the multiple-firing pistol was again clearly demonstrated in that engagement. The trappers were convinced that the Indians had received such a lesson that it would be some time before they would attack a similar party of travelers. News traveled fast even in the mountains. The report of the fight and the decisive results spread rapidly over all that country. The expedition received thereby a reputation which undoubtedly saved them much trouble with other tribes. When they came to the territory of the Umatilla Indians, who lived along the river of the same name, they were doubly welcomed because they could show the scalps recently taken from their enemies, the Bannocks.

The spring trapping season being over, they could take things easy. With plenty of leisure, they spent a delightful summer moving from place to place in the Umatilla country, hunting and fishing just enough to keep their larder supplied. That summer they also went across the Tygh Valley, explored about the John Day and Des Chutes rivers, and engaged in salmon fishing for a time with the Indians. There Old Bill told his comrades that "the time is not far distant when this country will teem with life and the Indian will pass away."[9]

They then made their way to the Hudson's Bay Company's trading post on the Columbia River, where they found Dr. McLoughlin, the venerable factor and part owner of the company, in charge. They traded their furs for cash and goods, stopping three days while Dr. McLoughlin sent a runner to Vancouver for the cash. During that visit Old Bill and the Doctor had long conversations on various subjects relating to the mountains, past history, the Indians, and the future of the region. Williams told the

a blanket between them; not an easy means of transportation for a man badly wounded, especially if the country where they were traveling was rough.

[8] Hamilton, *op. cit.*, 132.

[9] *Ibid.*, 137.

factor that the monopoly theretofore enjoyed by the Hudson's Bay Company was gone, that the territory would become a part of the United States, and that shortly immigrants would come in great numbers across the plains. Dr. McLoughlin expressed himself as "surprised when Williams gave him the whole history of the country, and said he had not expected so much information from a trapper."[10] Old Bill was as well informed as the factor on the rights and standings of the two nations in the Northwest.

In September, when the furs were beginning to be at their best, the trappers went south to the Rush River. There they began trapping with a vengeance, and after forty days were able to report that the river was the best beaver country they had found. They also added that they had trapped it clean. It was such methods of wanton destruction of the beaver which caused the almost utter extinction of the species during the years the trappers held sway. The party wintered in 1843 in the Klamath Lake country, during which period friendly relations were established between them and the Indians thereabouts, so that Williams, Perkins, and Hamilton were able to carry on some little trade.

They went down Lost River to Tule Lake in the spring of 1844, and then into the Modoc country. There the Indians displayed a hostile attitude and refused all overtures, saying, when offered a pipe, that they did not smoke with white dogs. The Modocs were known to use poisoned arrows, and to be savage fighters as well. The trappers here took extra precaution about their camp; they dug rifle pits and piled their baggage, logs, and dirt on the outside. A corral was made for the horses, and in it they put their mounts with pack mules on the outside to protect them. Because an arrow could not penetrate wet leather, or rather because wetness made it much harder to pierce, their buckskin clothing was soaked in water. The night guard was doubled.

The first nights passed without attack, but one morning the Indians sent a few braves toward the camp to reconnoiter. Old Bill went out to meet them and carried on a conversation for a long time in sign language. The Indians demanded that they be

10 *Ibid.*, 140.

given horses, guns, and other belongings of the trappers. They threatened that if the demands were not complied with, they would annihilate the trappers, indicating this by rubbing the palm of one hand over the other. Old Bill, diplomatic and forceful, told them they would get nothing, that they could be friends with him and his party, or they could fight; either would be good. The council, therefore, broke up without any progress being made. It was evident that the trappers would be attacked.

The charge was not long in coming. Dividing their forces into several attacking parties, about two hundred Modocs attacked the forty-two mountain men. Their charge was met with a devastating fire from the trappers. Confused by the falling of a number of their braves, most of the Indians hesitated, but a few kept up the charge. They were living up to their reputation as savage and courageous fighters. The mountain men then brought into use their shotguns which had been loaded with slugs and reserved for the proper moment. Nevertheless, a few of the Indians got within their barricade, and hand-to-hand fighting ensued, during which the Colt six-shooter and the trapping hatchet were brought into play to dispatch the few invaders.[11] Some hand-to-hand fighting also took place about the corral with the same results as inside the barricade.

All the bravery of the Modocs could not stand up against such a reception as they had received. They were defeated and withdrew. The fighting was over. In this fight, the trappers lost three veterans and a number were wounded. The Indians' loss was large; there were fifteen dead braves inside the rifle pits in addition to those on the outside and about the corral.

George Howard, one of the party, described the daily life of these trappers very graphically when he said, "The people back in the states have no conception of the life of a trapper. One day it is all peace and harmony, with the trappers enjoying life as few could ever in civilization. The next day just the reverse among hostile Indians."[12] With the Indians showing such hostility, there

[11] The hatchet was one of about two pounds in weight and served as a most formidable weapon in the hands of a powerful man.
[12] Hamilton, *op. cit.*, 140.

was no chance to do any trapping; so after a council, the party concluded to move south and east, out of the Modoc country. In the latter part of the season they reached the Honey Lake country, where they got on better with the natives and did considerable trading. They then traveled south along the east slope of the Sierra Nevada to the Truckee and Carson rivers, and from there turned back to Humboldt Lake, where they spent the summer.

Old Bill and his trappers spent the spring of 1845 hunting northern Nevada, where they again had hostile Indians to contend with, this time the Pah-Utes. The old mountain man did the best he could to gain their confidence, but it was no use. The Pah-Utes would neither allow the hunters to trap in peace nor to remain in the country. Traps had to be set with utmost precaution in order to guard against ambushes and surprise attacks. But, notwithstanding all safeguards, Frederick Crawford, one of the younger members of the party, failed to come in one day. Following up his trail, they came to where his horse had stood, and where he had been ambushed. Continuing still farther, they came to Crawford's body lying on the river bank. He was scalped, his eyes had been gouged out, and his body outrageously mutilated. The poor chap had met a horrible death. Crawford was a native of Texas, was well educated, had an attractive personality, and had been very popular among his comrades. Not much was said by the trappers— a sort of silence prevailed among them. It seemed as if by unanimous consent and without discussion of the matter, they agreed that their comrade's death would have to be wiped out.

Encouraged by their killing of Crawford, a party of the Indians made an attack on the trappers. Each man felt responsible personally for Crawford's death. While the red men were still some distance off, the trappers heard a shot, which, it was concluded, must have been fired from Crawford's gun, in the hands of one of his slayers, for no Indian had a gun which would shoot like that. That shot was the signal for action. Leaving a small guard at the camp, and with old Bill at their head, they charged the band of Pah-Utes. The natives tried to fight back, but being armed with bows and arrows, they could not defend themselves, let alone do any damage to the trappers. Several were killed and others became confused. Then the comrades of the late Crawford had them at their mercy. No quarter was given: they must pay for killing the white man's friend; the Indian law would be executed to the letter. The net result of that charge was that the trappers did not lose a man, only a few were wounded, and only two of their horses were killed. On the other hand, twenty-five of the Pah-Utes were killed, forty-three horses were taken, and the trappers recovered Crawford's horse, rifle, and pistols. Crawford's death was wiped out according to the mountain man's code.

The country having again proved uncomfortable, they went on to Raft River, meeting on the way a party of seven Hudson's Bay men in destitute condition. These men had been out hunting, poorly equipped with Hudson's Bay flintlocks and with little or no provisions. Williams and his companions relieved their wants by supplying them with food and horses. After trapping Bear River, Williams' party crossed over to Green River and spent a few days at the Hot Springs in the Big Windy River Valley, where they met another group of four company trappers. The latter had lost one companion and all their horses in a conflict with the Blackfeet. In what is now Wyoming they met an emigrant train going to Oregon. Old Bill's prophecy was coming to pass.

After the close of the spring trapping season of 1845, the thirty-eight remaining members of the party reached Laramie River, and after settling accounts they broke up. Twenty-five of the men took furs they had coming to them and went on to St. Louis. Old Bill Williams, George Perkins, and Bill Hamilton sold their furs to buyers who were there at the time and divided the proceeds, Old Bill taking his share in money. Then in company with Perkins and six of the others, he set out for Santa Fe.

The success of the expedition from the standpoint of the trappers was, in a large part, due to their leader. Old Bill was at all times prepared for every emergency. For whatever events might come to pass, he was ready. The Bannocks found him alert. When the Modocs attacked the camp, matters were so arranged that the

Indians could not overwhelm them by superior numbers or their fierce attacks. The Pah-Utes found it unprofitable to molest them. The events of this two-year adventure prove without fear of contradiction the right of Old Bill to the reputation of being the greatest of mountain men.

It is probable that Williams set out for Santa Fe with the object of visiting Bent's Fort where he might settle his obligation, now of more than two years' standing, to Bent, St. Vrain, & Company. We do not know, however, if he reached the fort, what happened to his money, or how long it lasted. But knowing his improvident habits and knowing that only a few weeks later he was again working, it would seem it did not last long.

Early in August, 1845, Captain John C. Frémont's Third Expedition had passed through Bent's Fort and on August 20 had reached the Pueblo. There the party stayed but a few days before proceeding up to Arkansas River. They arrived at the Grand River on the twenty-sixth. Either at the Pueblo, or on the way, Frémont engaged Williams as a guide. He went to work on August 28. The expedition was one of the military and geographical surveys west of the Mississippi by the Corps of Topographical Engineers of the United States Army, for which Congress had appropriated $30,000 that year.[13] Here was a well-organized, fully provisioned military party with good prospects for adventure which may have attracted Old Bill. He was offered the job of guide and accepted, but stayed only until he reached the Salt Lake country.

The expedition followed up the Arkansas River to its head, crossed the divide between there and the Grand. On September 22, Captain Joe Walker joined the party and relieved Williams of the work he was doing. The expedition here divided into two parties, and Frémont, with the smaller number, proceeded towards the Sierra Nevada. The other party, under Lieutenant Talbot, with Walker as guide, turned south.[14] Williams stayed

[13] See "War Department Appropriation Bill," *United States Statutes at Large,* V, 745–47, for fiscal year ending June 30, 1846.

[14] Narrative of Thomas S. Martin, 9–10. MS in Bancroft Library, Berkeley, California.

on as guide until October 27, 1845, and was paid for his services for a period of sixty-one days at one dollar per day.[15] Later, in March, 1848, Captain Joe Walker left Frémont in California, when he discovered the real purpose of the expedition, and after Frémont had declared his intention of disregarding the orders of the California authorities.[16]

In the meantime, changes had been taking place in Old Taos and the other New Mexican settlements. Williams learned enough while with the Frémont party to know that war between the United States and Mexico was about to be declared, and that California would probably revolt. Mexican rule in the Southwest could hardly withstand attacks from the stronger nation. A new order seemed inevitable.

There were many men like Bill Williams with family ties, business connections, and friends in the Mexican territory. Even though they were American in origin, ideas, training, and thoughts, contacts with the New Mexicans counted. Many, no doubt, felt the opportunity was at hand to introduce a proper government; yet there were those who did not particularly care to see the old life changed.[17]

After leaving the Frémont party near the Salt Lake, Williams turned back towards the Pueblo, ready for new adventures. All mountain men, including Williams, had a very slight regard for the military, especially the soldiers. Either because of his love for fun, his lack of respect for the military, or as a result of a drunken spree, Old Bill decided to have some fun with a patrol of soldiers he saw after he had reached the plains. Attracting their attention, he proceeded to act the part of an Indian, riding towards them in a threatening manner, and then away, until they gave chase. Finally overtaken, or allowing himself to be taken, he was brought

[15] United States General Accounting Office, Records Division, Washington, D. C.

[16] The records of General Accounting Office, Washington, D. C., show that Walker terminated his employment March 4, 1846. See also Allan Nevins, *Frémont*, I, 262.

[17] A large number of mountain men joined the Missouri Mounted Regiment under Col. A. W. Doniphan.

before Captain Philip St. George Cooke. The Captain could not see much humor in the escapade. He ordered Old Bill returned under arrest to Fort Leavenworth.[18]

It was not an affair which reflected any credit on the old trapper, nor did the military regard it as a very grave offense, for so far as can be found, there was no record made of the arrest or of his being brought back to the military post. As soon as he was released, he visited his daughters, but he did not look up any of his kinsfolk, and soon turned back toward the mountains.

Inasmuch as he had no cash, he passed up Bent's Fort and the Río Grande settlements and turned to his old friends, the Utes, with whom he had not been for several years. He continued to live with these Indians, until after Kearny had taken Santa Fe and the Americans were in full possession and control. A year or so spent with the Utes was long enough, and he began to feel the urge to visit his own people again. He wondered what was happening in the Río Grande settlements under the new order, what the government in Taos was like, and what his old comrades were doing. The urge to get back there became more and more pronounced. Finally, early in 1848, the Indians were in need of supplies and had peltries to trade. Williams agreed to take these furs to a trading post and get the needed supplies. He went down to Taos. Once there, a few drinks, and Old Bill was lost. His old thirst was too much; he traded in the furs and went on a spree.[19]

Up to that point Old Bill had borne an excellent reputation for square dealing, but in this instance he failed to live up to his word with his red brothers. When he was over the effect of his debauch, there was not much left for him to do except to stay on at Taos. He could not well return to the Utes empty-handed and tell them he had been on a drunk; better to stay away until it would be possible to smooth things over. If this had happened a few years before, it would have made little difference because he could no

[18] Narrative of Micajah McGehee, in Private Papers of J. S. McGehee, II, 60, 61.

[19] Breckenridge, *op. cit.*, *Cosmopolitan Magazine* (August, 1896).

doubt have satisfied his fellow tribesmen in one way or another. Now conditions had changed. The Indians understood the white men. Williams was getting older. The lines for him were closing in. He had seen immigrant trains crossing into Oregon three years before, and since then the Santa Fe Trail and the routes to Utah had become almost crowded with one caravan after another. New Mexico, now a part of the United States, was practically as settled as Missouri when he had left there. Furthermore, he surely did not want to go east again. His utterance to Dr. McLoughlin concerning the future of the Northwest was prophetic; his insight of what would come about in the Southwest must have been even more so.

Several months later, in the early summer of 1848, Old Bill again engaged as a scout, this time with the Missouri Volunteers against the Apaches. During the Mexican War, the Utes and the Jicarilla Apaches had been raiding the New Mexican settlements, committing depredations and stealing. They continued just the same policy toward the Americans, who were engaged in establishing civil order, as they had toward the New Mexicans. Now that civil affairs were quiet, the authorities turned their attention to subduing the hostile Indians. A large band of the Apaches living in the Raton Mountains had been particularly troublesome. It seemed to the army that this band must be controlled or the military would have no influence over the Indians as a whole. A punitive expedition against them was decided upon as the proper measure.

On June 14, Captain S. A. Boake, of the Missouri Mounted Regiment, with fifty men, took the field. The company struck the trail of the Indians shortly after entering the mountains, followed up, and overtook them. A few shots were fired by the troops and returned by the Indians without any casualties. The latter got away, but left with the soldiers some thirty head of horses which had been stolen from the Mexican settlement. Captain Boake and his soldiers pursued the Indians for a time but were forced to give up the chase because the Captain became quite ill. Captain Boake, on his return to Taos, had only a few horses to show for the two weeks' expedition against the hostiles.[20]

Since it was still quite evident that, if these as yet unsubdued Indians were to have any respect for the American government, they would have to be taught a real lesson, another expedition was decided upon. Major W. W. Reynolds, of the same command as Captain Boake, therefore organized an expedition against them on a more extensive scale. He employed Old Bill Williams, Old Jim Kirker, Bill Mitchell, and a man named Fisher[21] to act as guides and spies, and with some 150 soldiers left Taos on July 8, 1848. Once in the Raton Mountains, his guide picked up the trail at the point where Captain Boake had been forced to return. The Indians headed west, crossing the Río Grande Valley and into the San Juan Mountains, north of the Chama River. The soldiers, led by the scouts, had no difficulty in following their trail, finally catching up with them in the mountains, where the Indians decided to stand their ground. There the soldiers split into three divisions. Major Reynolds took charge of one division, Captain Salmon of a second, and Captain Stockton of the third. A band of Utes had joined with the Apaches so that altogether the hostiles numbered about four hundred braves. On July 16, some fighting took place, and it continued with intermittent skirmishes for about a week.

By July 23, the Indians had taken a strong position at the "Pass of St. Johne Mountain," now known as Cumbres Pass, with the apparent intention of engaging the soldiers in battle. The mountains there form a horseshoe, with a pass or gap directly in the center, and this the Indians occupied. They had selected a strong position from which, it was plain, they could not easily be driven.

[20] The Santa Fe (New Mex.) *Republican* (August 1, 1848), files in the New Mexico Museum, Santa Fe. Also Report of Major W. W. Reynolds to Lieutenant W. E. Prince (August 11, 1848). MS in War Department, Washington, D. C.

[21] Fisher was an American, known among the Cheyenne Indians as *No-Ma-Ni* (Fish). He was employed as an Indian trader by William Bent in 1846; married a Mexican woman and made headquarters at Taos during the later years of his life. Fisher's Hole, a valley on the headwaters of the San Carlos, was named after him, as was a village near Pueblo, Colorado, and Fisher's Peak in the Raton Mountains.—Garrard, *op. cit.*, 114, 119.

The soldiers began their attack from three fronts. The encounter lasted "two or three hours, the Indians fighting like a set of desperadoes, and the Americans with equal spirit." Old Bill Williams was the hero of the battle, and although he was "shot in the arm, shattering it most horribly, he managed to use it so as to keep his rifle hot during the engagement."[22] The Indians could not withstand the fire of the soldiers, were dislodged, and retreated. In the course of the fight, Captain Salmon was dangerously wounded, two soldiers were killed, two severely wounded, and one slightly wounded. The Indians' loss was thirty-six killed and several dangerously wounded. Major Reynolds in his report to the Adjutant General, under date of August 11, wrote to his superior officer that "Williams, a celebrated mountaineer, who behaved himself gallantly in the engagement, was wounded badly."[23]

With that battle and the part he had taken in it, returning to live with the Utes was now definitely out of the question for Old Bill. Every Ute and every Apache brave had recognized him. They might have been able to excuse his failure to get the supplies, for they had themselves often fallen victims to the firewater of the whites, but leading the soldiers against his adopted tribe was something Williams knew that he could not explain. In the meantime, he returned to the post with the soldiers and continued under the care and attention of Dr. McNeil, the army doctor. Major Reynolds reported that all the wounded, including Williams, were "improving under the judicious care and attention of the surgeon."[24]

While still at the post, he concluded that a northern trading venture might afford a solution for his predicament. Acting on the thought, Williams wrote a letter to his friend, William T. Hamilton. It was sent by George Perkins, who was going back to the Green River country, and suggested a trading partnership. He had found Hamilton an agreeable partner and one in whom he had confidence. The letter was delivered to Hamilton, but the

[22] The Santa Fe *Republican* (August 1, 1848).
[23] Report of Major W. W. Reynolds (August 11, 1848). MS in War Department, Washington, D. C.
[24] *Ibid.*

latter never answered it, because he left soon afterward, with other gold seekers, for California. Late that fall, after he had recovered from his injury, and since he had not heard from Hamilton, Williams left Taos and went over the mountains to spend the winter with old comrades at the Pueblo, thinking that perhaps something would turn up by the following spring to mend his affairs.

CHAPTER FOURTEEN

The Frémont Expedition of 1848

OLD BILL WILLIAMS crossed the Sangre de Cristo Mountains for the last time in the dead of winter in 1848, guiding Colonel John C. Frémont and his party on their way to California, but he came to grief in the La Garita Mountains and made his way into Taos after much hardship. Going back to bring out the baggage left by the Frémont party, Old Bill was killed by a band of southern Utes. He thus met his death at the hands of the very tribe into which he had been adopted as a younger man. Finally, two years later, as a result of the mountain trip and Williams' death, Richard H. Kern, acting on information received from Antoine Leroux, a mountaineer, named a river and mountain in Arizona after the old trapper. In order to get a full understanding of the reasons and causes in this sequence of events, it is necessary to go back over the career of Colonel John C. Frémont.

By the year 1840, there was already formed in Congress the group of so-called westerners, led by Senator Thomas H. Benton of Missouri, with Senator Lewis F. Linn of Missouri, Richard M. Young of Illinois, and A. H. Sevier of Arkansas, ably assisting when needed. This group or bloc, if it might be called such, determined to fight for every inch of the Louisiana Purchase and the Oregon country. They sensed the importance to the West of a steady flow of emigration to the Oregon country and of that section's being settled by Americans, if the United States were to be assured in their claim to the territory. One way to accomplish this purpose was by bringing the importance of this great expanse to the attention of their countrymen. What better way of advertising than through a charted highway?

As a result of their activities, and to placate these noisy western men, Congress voted an appropriation to finance exploration for such a purpose. With Senator Benton's influence, it was an easy matter to have his son-in-law, who during the preceding four years had served under Jean Nicholas Nicollet and was at the time in the Topographical Corps of the army, placed at the head of the expedition.

Thus it came about that on May 2, 1842, young Frémont, then twenty-nine years of age, leaving his bride, the brilliant and talented Jessie Benton, started with a government-sponsored party to accomplish in the unexplored plains and Rockies, in a certain measure, what Nicollet had done for the Minnesota and Dakota country. The purpose was to chart the best route to the South Pass and thereby to aid emigrants in travel over a practicable way into the Northwest. True, this country had been traveled over, crossed and recrossed many times since the Lewis and Clarke trip, thirty-eight years before, but there were no exact scientific data on the regions to be crossed by such a highway, at least not sufficient to select and lay out such a through route.

Frémont recruited and fitted out his party in St. Louis. He sought to engage Andrew Dripps as the guide for the expedition, but was unable to arrange matters. By chance he fell in with Kit Carson, a young man of about his own age, then on a visit to St. Louis and described as the "Paragon of Mountaineers." Kit Carson had gone to Missouri in the late fall with Williams, had stayed over the winter, and was not then employed. Frémont and Carson were not long in completing arrangements for the latter to serve as chief guide. It was indeed a fortunate choice that Frémont made in him. It was the beginning of a friendship between them which lasted during their lives.

To Carson's ability as a scout, as much as to anything else, Frémont owed the success of his several expeditions. The fame given Kit Carson through his connection with those expeditions brought him before the public and made him a national figure. Among his comrades, where he was known, he did not need any press agent to rank him as a leader. Lucien Maxwell was hunter for the expedition and Mr. Charles Preuss was topographer. The remainder of the party, consisting of twenty-one men, was made up of Creoles and French trappers, among whom the most noted was Basil Lajeunesse.

On this trip Frémont made the acquaintance of Thomas Fitzpatrick, Céran St. Vrain, Jim Bridger, Jim Beckwourth, and other mountaineers.[1] He also came in contact with the various tribes of Indians of the plains and, in short, was initiated into the wild and free life of the trader and trapper. His route was up the Platte over a more or less well-known trail, across Nebraska, past Fort Laramie, then Independence Rock, and finally to the South Pass, which he found to be 950 miles from Kansas City. He climbed the peak named after him, observed its height,[2] and then he returned to St. Louis, where he arrived in October of the same year. Although Frémont was not the first to discover the South Pass, he was the first to gather exact data of the location and elevation. His report, written and published at government expense, accomplished all that the sponsors of the venture had expected. The young leader became a national figure. There was some grumbling in the army because an officer who was not a Regular Army man had gained distinction through political influence, shoving out of line others who had spent their lives in the service. The criticism, however, was drowned out in the popular praise of the young explorer.

Succeeding beyond expectations, the western group immediately planned a second expedition to go on from the point Frémont left off and to chart the country on the other side of the Rockies. Little or no difficulty was encountered in obtaining a second appropriation. Who should be the leader was never questioned.

[1] Frederick S. Dellenbaugh, *Frémont and '49*, 63–70.
[2] Mt. Frémont, which he found to be 13,570 feet high.—*Ibid.*, 86.

Frémont again outfitted at St. Louis and was on the plains in May, 1843. This time his chief guide was Thomas Fitzpatrick, known as "White Head," whose snow-white hair was due to an Indian encounter in Blackfoot country, when all of the party except himself had been killed.[3] Fitzpatrick was one of the best trappers and guides ever in the West, and like Carson he bore an excellent reputation. Preuss was again the chief topographer. Alexis Godey, a competent mountain man, was the hunter of the party, and Basil Lajeunesse, as well as five of the others who had gone on the first expedition, was again serving. Kit Carson joined the party when it reached the plains and really became the chief guide. The men the leader selected indicated that he had come to know mountain men.

This time Frémont followed a slightly more southern route than on the first expedition: after crossing South Pass, he proceeded on the Oregon Trail across western Wyoming and then northwesterly across Idaho to the Columbia, going down the river to its mouth. He then retraced his route and traveled south on the east side of the Sierras, until the beginning of 1844 found him on the Carson River. At this place the expedition took a strange turn. He made up his mind he would cross the mountains into California although that was then foreign country. His instructions did not include exploring any territory except that which belonged to the United States. His mind made up, he plunged into the snows of the high Sierras headed for California. It was a strange determination, and it would seem that its successful outcome grafted into his mentality a feeling that no mountain existed which he could not cross, no matter what obstacles or what climatic conditions he should encounter. All the reports the mountain men had of the crossings would indicate that these mountains could not be crossed in the winter time. The chances were against his getting the party through in the middle of the winter. Notwithstanding the odds against him, because of his courage, stamina, and luck, Frémont

[3] Thomas Fitzpatrick was also known as "Bad Hand," or "Withered Hand" because of a shattered hand. Note to diary of James Kennerly, *Missouri Historical Society Collections*, Vol. VI, No. 1 (1928), 78. An excellent life of Thomas Fitzpatrick has been written by LeRoy R. Hafen and W. J. Ghent, entitled *Broken Hand.*

got through to Sutter's Fort without the loss of a single man, although all were in a starving condition at the end of the journey.

At Fort Sutter he recruited for a short time. Then he left by the southerly route, passing up the San Joaquin Valley and out through the Walker Pass. Frémont then traveled northwest over the Spanish Trail, across to Utah and the Great Salt Lake country, picking up Joe Walker on the way, and crossed the plains by way of Bent's Fort.

Frémont was back in St. Louis in August, 1844, after an absence of fourteen months. The young explorer was now called "The Pathfinder." His exploration was reported to Congress and printed as a public document.[4] Information about the country he had traveled brought the West forcibly to the attention of the nation, and Frémont's reports of California and the conditions there undoubtedly encouraged the western group in Congress in its determination to add that part of the continent to the nation. The basis was laid for the next year's expedition, the third of the series. As for Frémont, he was brevetted a captain by General Winfield Scott and feted and dined in the national capital, even by the President. At the same time, there still existed an undercurrent of feeling against him among the personnel of the army.

Captain Frémont was not allowed to remain inactive for long. The western group, now joined by the expansionists in Congress, looked with longing eyes at California and southward to accomplish what Senator Benton had termed "Manifest Destiny," by extending the dominion of the United States from the Atlantic to the Pacific. Already Congress had passed a resolution for the annexation of Texas. There was but one step more. The western bloc had no trouble in getting an appropriation for an expedition to explore the central Rockies, examine the Great Salt Lake, the Sierras in California, and "passes through them to the Pacific."[5] The term "passes through them to the Pacific" was significant, for there is little doubt but that the real purpose was to send an armed party into California to be on hand to help wrest that country from

[4] *Congressional Globe* (March 5, 1845).
[5] Nevins, *op. cit.*, I, 235.

Mexico when the war, which then seemed imminent, should come.

The third expedition left St. Louis in the early summer of 1845. It consisted of sixty men, including Alexis Godey, Basil Lajeunesse, and twelve Delaware Indians, all fully and well equipped for any emergency—actually an army in itself, and yet ostensibly a party out to obtain scientific data. Preuss's place was taken by Edward M. Kern, a young man from Philadelphia. Kit Carson and Dick Owens joined the party on word from Frémont, who later said of Carson, Owens, and Godey, "they might have become marshals under Napoleon."

They traveled up the Arkansas River, crossed the Rockies through central Colorado and tarried a while in the Salt Lake country. Bill Williams joined the party for a time and continued with them until they left for California, some time in November.[6] With army officers in charge, the party didn't turn out just the way, perhaps, that Williams had expected when he started. When Frémont ran across Old Bill at the Pueblo a few years later, he was not meeting a stranger but a mountaineer he had known in camp, on the trail, and in the mountains.

Whatever scientific investigations and explorations Frémont intended to carry on in the Great Salt Lake country, he soon completed, for the party rushed on to California, where it arrived in the early part of the winter. The real purpose of the expedition now became apparent, for the party stayed in California, collaborating with the navy station on the coast—an armed force on the soil of a foreign nation. Frémont became involved in local politics, was a principal in the Bear Revolution, fought against the Californians, and was there when the country was taken over by the American forces. The old animosity between Regular Army officers and Frémont came to a head in a difference of opinion between him and General Stephen W. Kearny. Charges of a grave character were made, Frémont's authority was taken away, and he was ordered home. He was returned with Kearny, and upon

[6] Narrative of Thomas S. Martin, 44. MS in Bancroft Library, Berkeley, California.

arriving at Fort Leavenworth in August, 1864, was placed under technical arrest and a court-martial was ordered.

The trial, which was held in Washington, stirred men's passions. Senator Benton and his supporters came to Frémont's aid. Generally speaking, the army officers were not averse to seeing him set down. The result of the trial was a verdict of technical guilt and a sustaining of Kearny's charges. The President affirmed the verdict but refused to punish him. Frémont declined to continue in the service and resigned. Any careful student of Frémont must feel that the charges, court-martial, and verdict had a tremendous effect on him, for he never was the same man thereafter. It may have been the shock, the hurting of his pride, or the end of his career in the army, but from that time he was a changed man. This change showed in his conduct towards men and affairs, and was not always to his credit. He had risen from a lieutenant in 1842, when he was but twenty-nine years of age, to the rank of lieutenant colonel in the topographical division of the army in the short space of five years. As rapid as his advance had been, was his fall, and in 1847 he was again a private citizen.

For a time he was discouraged and disheartened. Yet a man of Frémont's temperament could not remain inactive, nor could he long resist the call of the plains and the mountains. His travels across the country had made him a firm believer in the feasibility of a transcontinental railroad, linking Californina to the East, and now that California was a part of the United States, the need of the railroad became more pressing than ever. The members of the western group in Congress were working hard for government aid for a transcontinental railroad. Here appeared Frémont's opportunity, and into the carrying out of such a project he threw all of his tremendous energy. The question to be decided by its sponsors was what route such a road should follow. Frémont determined to learn this by personal investigations. He began to think in terms of private enterprise, and with the assistance of Colonel Robert Campbell, O. D. Filley, and Thornton Grimsley, St. Louis friends, and with some contributions from Senator Benton, he

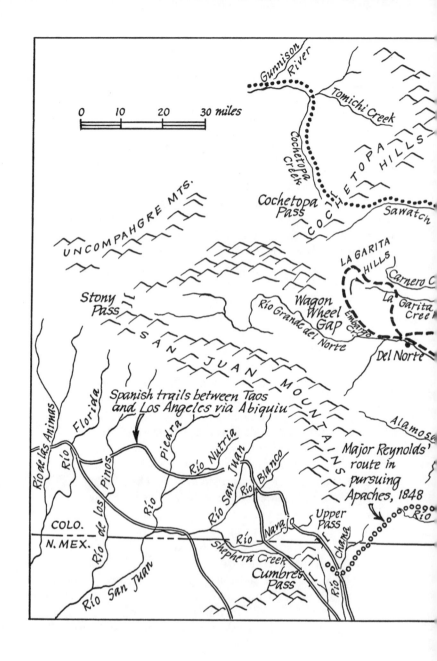

0   10   20   30 *miles*

Gunnison River

Tomichi Creek

Cochetopa Creek

C O C H E T O P A   H I L L S

Cochetopa Pass

Sawatch

UNCOMPAHGRE MTS.

LA GARITA HILLS

Carnero C.

La Garita Cree[k]

Stony Pass

Wagon Wheel Gap

Río Grande del Norte

La Embargo Cr.

S A N   J U A N   M O U N T A I N S

Del Norte

Alamosa

Spanish trails between Taos and Los Angeles via Abiquiu

Río de las Animas

Río Florida

Río de los Pinos

Piedra

Río

Río Nutria

Río San Juan

Río Blanco

Major Reynolds' route in pursuing Apaches, 1848

Upper Pass

Río

COLO.

N. MEX.

Río   Navajo

Río Chama

Río

Shepherd Creek

Cumbres Pass

Río San Juan

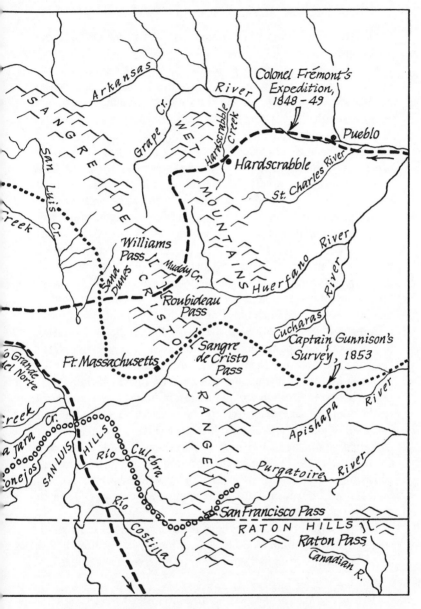

Sketch map of areas in Colorado and New Mexico in which there occurred important events in Bill Williams' career as guide.

proposed to lay out a suitable route for a railroad across the Rocky Mountains.[7]

His experience in past expeditions had led him to believe a railroad should go farther south, he judged in a line with the Arkansas River to the Spanish Trail, and thence to California. He planned to go through the Rockies in the dead of winter to establish the fact that a railroad, when built, might operate the year round. The published object of this trip was to finish certain details of his other expeditions, particularly "of the Great Interior Basin," and to discover a direct, practicable, traveling route, "if possible, a railway route from the Mississippi Valley to the Pacific on the thirty-eighth degree of latitude."[8] Even with the railroad in mind, Frémont could not altogether dissociate himself from the old life of a government explorer. He may have had in mind a plan of turning his findings, the result of this trip, over to the government, for one of the men he hired said that the men were not paid any wages, although he told them that when the work was finished, the government would pay them.[9] The route he had in mind was approximately along the line of the old Santa Fe Trail to Bent's Fort, then to Pueblo across the mountains of southern Colorado and Utah, and thence by the old Spanish Trail and Walker's Pass into California. The theory of the plan was correct, provided there was a practicable trail through the mountains, but if no such trail existed on the route he intended traveling, he would find himself and his party snowbound in the Rocky Mountains. Basing his plans on his past experiences, he went forward with them. Thus it was that on October 3, 1848, Frémont had recruited his party in St. Louis, consisting of thirty-three men, many of whom had served with him on other expeditions, and some young men who joined just for the adventure the trip would afford.

The personnel of this party is of interest. Alexis Godey, an old friend and companion of other expeditions, went as hunter. Edward M. Kern,[10] who had served the Colonel so faithfully at Fort

---

[7] Chas. W. Upham, *Life of Frémont*, 273.
[8] Narrative of Micajah McGehee, in Private Papers of J. S. McGehee, II, 1.
[9] Narrative of Thomas S. Martin, 43.

Sutter, again was with Frémont as artist. Others who had been with him before were Charles Preuss as topographer, Captain Charles Taplin,[11] and Captain Henry King,[12] besides the three mountain men, Thomas S. Martin, Thomas E. Breckenridge, and John Scott. Three experienced Frenchmen were hired, Joseph Moran, Vincent Sorel, and Longe. There was McDowell, a veteran of the Mexican War, who left the party shortly after passing Westport; L. D. Vincenthaler, sometimes called Vincent Haler; Amos Andrews, and his son Midshipman Elijah T. Andrews;[13] F. Creutzfeldt, as botanist; Edward M. Kern's two brothers, Richard H. Kern as artist and Doctor Benjamin J. Kern as the medico of the party. The other members were William Bacon, Josiah Ferguson, Henry Wise, Benjamin Beadle, Henry Rohrer, J. E. Ducatel, George A. Hibbard, J. L. Steppenfeldt, Raphael Proue, Carver, Micajah McGehee; three California Indians, Manuel, Joaquin, and Gregorio; Sanders Jackson, a free Negro who was the Colonel's servant; and Theodore McNabb, a youth of fourteen years, who was a nephew of Godey. Accompanying the party was an Englishman, Captain A. Cathcart of the Eleventh Prince Albert Hussars,

10 Edward M. Kern was a native of Philadelphia; he went out with Frémont on his third expedition; served as lieutenant of California Volunteers during the war with Mexico, and was in charge of Fort Sutter. After returning to Taos, he assisted the Army Engineers in their explorations in the Southwest; then returned East; went out with Commander Cadwalader Ringgold in 1854 on the North Pacific Exploring Expedition, as master's mate, "to take charge of the photographic apparatus."

11 Charles Van Linneus Taplin was born December, 1819, in New York; is said to have served in Texas War for independence; was with Frémont on third expedition and California Campaign; commissioned first lieutenant April 9, 1847, giving residence as Westport, Missouri; brevetted captain for gallant and meritorious service in Mexican War; resigned May 23, 1848; went with Frémont fourth expedition going through to California; went with Captain Gunnison as wagon master on expedition of 1853. Died March 14, 1855, San Antonio, Texas.

12 Henry King, native of Georgetown, D. C.; was captain of Mounted Riflemen in California Campaign from July 7, 1846, to February 25, 1847, serving under Colonel Frémont.

13 Elijah T. Andrews was appointed midshipman October 19, 1841, and continued in the service until July 26, 1848, when he was detached and obtained permission to travel in California. Andrews was at the time suffering from tuberculosis and should never have attempted the trip.

seeking hunting and adventure and destined to have his wish more than gratified.[14]

The party gathered in St. Louis, took a steamer on the river, going as far as Kansas, and then traveled three miles overland to Westport, where they organized, getting the outfit together. They left for the mountains on October 21, 1848.[15] The party was well balanced and fully provisioned for any ordinary circumstances. In the light of subsequent events, two important considerations seem to have been overlooked by Frémont in his plans: where he expected to cross the mountains and under whose guidance. Among those in the party, there was no one qualified to act as guide over the mountains to California along the route chosen. On October 29, a Delaware Indian, whom they had hired after leaving Westport to guide them, turned back, and they "proceeded on their journey without guide or trail."[16] Near Bent's Fort, Frémont called on Thomas Fitzpatrick, then in the Indian Service. It may be that he hoped to get him as guide, but Fitzpatrick was then in the employ of the government as an Indian agent, apparently contented with his work.

While the party was at Bent's Fort, several men acquainted with the country he hoped to explore attempted to dissuade Frémont from attempting the crossing because of the weather conditions, but their advice was disregarded and the party proceeded on its way.[17] Bent's Fort was as far as Andrews, Senior, could go and he gave up and remained. At the post, Frémont succeeded in getting Dick Wootton, who was entirely familiar with the mountains they

[14] Captain Andrew Cathcart was the brother of a baronet, Sir John A. Cathcart; became 2nd lieutenant in the 23rd Foot regiment, January 29, 1836; lieutenant in the 10th Dragoons, April 12, 1839; captain, November 11, 1842; transferred to the 11th Hussars, September, 1844, and retired November 3, 1846. He came to America with George Frederick Ruxton, arriving in St. Louis on August 16, 1848.–See *St. Louis Daily Union* of that date. Ruxton and Cathcart had planned a hunting trip. After Ruxton's death Cathcart joined Frémont. Later he returned to England and fought in the Crimean War, in which struggle he received the local rank of major while in Turkey, December 21, 1855.

[15] Diary of E. M. Kern, MS in Huntington Library, San Marino, California.

[16] Narrative of Micajah McGehee, in Private Papers of J. S. McGehee, 11, 17.

[17] Fort Sutter Papers (MSS in Huntington Library, San Marino, California), Vol. XXXI, No. 126.

planned to cross, to go with them. He stayed with Frémont until he saw the snow on the Sangre de Cristo Range, then quit and turned back, saying, "There is too much snow ahead for me."[18] Since it was not Frémont's usual method to leave such an important thing as chief guide of his party to chance, it has been suggested he hoped to get Kit Carson, then at Taos, to join the party in that capacity.[19] At any rate, on this trip he neglected to complete the arrangements for a guide.

That year the snows had begun much earlier than usual and had been of considerable volume. On the fourth of November the party had encountered a blizzard while crossing the plains—the same storm in which the government lost a large number of stock between Santa Fe and Bent's Fort.[20] When the party crossed the Arkansas near Chouteau's Island, the river was full of ice. It was snowing on November 6, when they reached Bent's Fort, with a foot of snow on the ground. There they could see the mountains about one hundred miles away all covered with snow. The diaries of the members of the party reported freezing temperatures beginning with the twentieth of October, and snow most of the way from Bent's Fort to Pueblo.[21] The outlook for a crossing was not propitious. Finally, on November 21, they reached Pueblo, which was an old fort near the mouth of Boiling Spring River (*Fontaine-Qui-Bouit*) inhabited then by a few old mountain men who were wintering or who had settled there with their Indian wives. The old Pueblo had been a place of considerable activity in the day when fur trading was at its zenith, but by that year the fur trade was almost a thing of the past. There was some semblance of husbandry, for the inhabitants had milk cows, and farther up the river they had raised a crop of corn that season.[22] When the party arrived, Old Bill Williams was settled there for the winter. Colonel

[18] Breckenridge, *op. cit.*, 400.
[19] Article by Professor Frank C. Spencer in the *Colorado Magazine*, Vol. VI, No. 4, 142.
[20] Narrative of Micajah McGehee, in Private Papers of J. S. McGehee, II, 33.
[21] Diaries of R. H. Kern and B. J. Kern, MSS in Huntington Library, San Marino, California.
[22] Diary of B. J. Kern, MS in Huntington Library, San Marino, California.

Frémont discussed with the mountain men present the possibility of getting through the Rockies, and sought their aid. The Colonel insisted on going forward and urged Old Bill to undertake to guide them through the mountains. Finally the old scout agreed to undertake the task, "but it was not without some hesitation that he consented to go, for most of the old trappers at the Pueblo declared that it was impossible to cross the mountains at that time, that the cold upon the mountains was unprecedented and the snow deeper than they had ever known it so early in the year." Williams thought perhaps the party "could manage to get through, though not without considerable suffering."[23] Most of his life had been a succession of difficulties and hard places, which he had overcome; so once more he trusted himself to overcome what obstacles might present themselves on this trip. He still had faith in Old Bill Williams. No doubt he had expected to spend the winter at the Pueblo and entirely recover from his wound, but the call for new adventure was too strong for him—the "old hoss" once again felt the call of the mountains. Little did he expect that in a few short weeks he was to become a principal in one of the greatest disasters in exploration that ever befell any guide engaged during the history of the Rockies—a disaster which was to be the contributing cause of his death, where his ability as a scout and guide would be brought into controversy, and, in the final chapter, result in the perpetuation of his name in Arizona by the naming of a river and a mountain for him.

[23] Narrative of Micajah McGehee, in Private Papers of J. S. McGehee, II, 61.

CHAPTER FIFTEEN

Failure, Retreat, and Starvation

LYING WEST of the Pueblo are the Wet Mountains and the Sangre de Cristo, or Sierra Blanca, Mountains, all part of the Rockies, with an elevation of from seven to fourteen thousand feet. They rise rather abruptly from the plains and had been in sight of Frémont's party since it left Fort Bent. These mountains lie rather in a southeasterly and northwesterly direction, and extend from central Colorado into northern New Mexico. Lying to the west of them are the San Luis Valley and the valley of the Río Grande, the former merging into the latter. In traveling westward from the valley of the Arkansas over the mountains into these valleys, there were three routes used by the trappers. The most northerly crossed the divide at the Williams Pass, named after Old Bill, but since changed to the Music Pass; it has an elevation of 11,800 feet, and on account of its steep ascent and descent never became a used wagon road. The middle route was the Roubidoux Road, crossing at the Roubidoux or Mosca Pass, 9,713 feet in elevation, and the most direct route between the Pueblo and the old Spanish Trail to California; this pass has an easy approach from the east, but is very steep on the descent into San Luis Valley. The most southerly route was by the Sangre de Cristo, now known as the La Veta, Pass; this is 9,382 feet in elevation and constitutes the principal highway through these mountains at the present day.

In traveling west from the passes through the Sangre de Cristo Mountains, there were then two routes known to the mountain men. One was to bear to the north, across the San Luis Valley, enter the Sawatch Mountains by the Sawatch Creek,[1] then turn north into Cochetopa Pass, crossing the Continental Divide. The other was to pass down the San Luis Valley in a southerly direction, then west by the Chama River, and along the foothills north up the San Juan River. Apparently, before leaving Pueblo, the route west by the Cochetopa had been decided upon by Colonel Frémont and Williams.[2]

Accounts of this trip over the mountains come from the diaries and personal letters of Colonel Frémont, Breckenridge, Micajah McGehee, and the three Kern brothers. Frémont never wrote much about this expedition, and what he did record was rather by way of excusing and explaining his failure than a narrative of what took place. Breckenridge covered only a detail of the trip, and his story was related some years afterward. The most reliable sources are the diaries of the Kerns and McGehee. McGehee was a son of Judge Edward McGehee, of Woodville, Mississippi; he was then about twenty years of age and had had the advantages of a good education. Young McGehee, finding himself, in the fall of 1848, in St. Louis, "and having long entertained an insatiable desire to explore the trackless wilds of the far west, the grand prairies, the Rocky Mountains, and California," joined the "party of Colonel J. C. Frémont who was just about to set out on his fourth expedition."[3]

McGehee has left a complete narrative of the entire trip, written after he arrived in California, but from notes made on the way from St. Louis to California.[4] The diaries of Edward M. Kern,

[1] The name has undergone several changes which are due to Mexican and Indian usage. It is spelled Chow-atch, Sho-ouach, Sah-watch, and Saguache.

[2] Letter of R. S. Wootton in *Missouri Democrat* (October 22, 1853). Fort Sutter Papers, Vol. XXXI, No. 130, Letters of Antoine Leroux to E. M. Kern (August 22, 1850). This is the route followed by the Gunnison party in 1853 in their survey.—33 Cong., 1 sess., *House Exec. Doc. 18.*

[3] Narrative of Micajah McGehee, in Private Papers of J. S. McGehee, II, 1.

[4] After arriving in California, Micajah McGehee lived at Big Oak Flat in Tuolumne County, California; he was engaged in California in mining, store

Richard H. Kern, and Benjamin J. Kern,[5] record the trip from day to day, and in most particulars agree with McGehee and Breckenridge. Captain Cathcart and Captain Taplin kept diaries, which have not as yet been found.

With Old Bill in the lead, the party moved out of the Pueblo and started up the Arkansas River. After a day's travel, he led them south to a settlement on Hard Scrabble Creek and about at the foot of the Wet Mountains. Here was a small irrigated area, with some ten or fifteen adobe houses. The previous year the few settlers had raised a crop of corn, which was then stored at the place. This had been purchased by Frémont from the owners, who were stopping below at the Pueblo. In order to carry the corn more readily, all hands turned to and shelled it, working a day and night at the task. It was then sacked and packed, 130 pounds to the animal. Every riding horse was utilized as a pack animal; the mules were all loaded with the baggage, instruments, and supplies, the entire party traveling on foot. At this place Longe, the old French trapper, decided there was too much snow on the mountains and the weather was too cold. His experience having told him the mountains could not be crossed, he turned back, predicting "evil to those who continued."

On the afternoon of November 25, everything being ready, Frémont moved about four miles to the base of the mountains and camped. The plains and the mountains lay deep with snow, and Hibbard, perhaps sensing trouble ahead, said, "Friends, I don't want my bones to bleach upon those mountains this winter amidst that snow." Little did he realize that within sixty days that very thing would happen.

Starting into the mountains the next morning, some of the men took, from an elevation, one last look at the plains they were leav-

keeping, and as justice of the peace for eighteen years, and was a member of the Sixth California Legislature in 1856. He returned to Woodville, Mississippi, in 1872 and died in 1880. He was a noble character and perfect gentleman. It is said he never entirely recovered from the effects of his trip.—From McGehee Family Records.

5 The diaries of Edward M. Kern, Richard H. Kern, and Benjamin J. Kern, in manuscript form, are now in the Huntington Library, San Marino, California.

ing. There the snow spread out level and dead white as far as the eye could reach, and at their backs the mountains they were to cross rose almost perpendicular like a great snow pile. Almost from the time they left Hard Scrabble, it snowed and stormed nearly every day, with the temperature below zero. It was through rough mountain country they were traveling, with no paths or cleared places to help them in climbing; they were even forced to break their way through deep snow, and with the rapid increase in the altitude, they found the going more and more difficult. The snow balled up under the animals' feet and made progress very slow. The drifts were so deep on the bottoms of the canyons that it was necessary to stay up on the sides of the mountains, and with such uncertain footing for the mules, a few slipped down the steep inclines and were lost. From the start there was no feed for the horses, aside from the corn they were packing, and the results of such fare soon began to show in the traveling strength of the animals. At the point of crossing over the summit, the cold became so intense that the mercury sank out of sight in the thermometers and ceased to register the degree of temperature. Old Bill Williams pointed out to the party the place where two men were frozen to death the winter before.

Their route from the Arkansas had been south along Hard Scrabble, then White Oak Creek, striking the Huerfano, and passing over the Roubidoux Pass.[6] Over the pass, the San Luis Valley spread out before them, all covered with snow, and the high Sawatch Mountains loomed up to the northwest, which Old Bill pointed out to Colonel Frémont as their objective. To the southwest could be seen the valley of the Río Grande, an apparent opening between the Sawatch and the San Juan Mountains, lying farther south.

Breckenridge, an old mountain man who bunked with Williams, tells us that there was "a disagreement between Frémont and Williams in regard to the route" the party was to go. Wil-

[6] Mr. Harry H. French, forest supervisor of the San Isabel Forest, Colorado, who is well acquainted with this country, gives it as his opinion that the Frémont party took the route up North Hard Scrabble to the Wet Mountain Valley.

liams told Frémont that "the snow was deeper and the weather more severe than he had even known it to be before . . . he advised a route out of our difficulties to go south around the San Juan Mountains, and then west along what is now the line between Colorado and New Mexico."[7] He was referring to the well-known trail up the Chama, past Abiquiu,[8] and along the San Juan River.[9] The extreme weather conditions caused Old Bill to doubt even the possibility of getting through the Cochetopa Pass, and he advised the safer route to the south. Among Micajah McGehee's private papers is a memorandum which states that George Reed, who was connected with the Quartermaster Department of the army and stationed at Taos in 1849, had seen Bill Williams' notebook. In referring to this notebook, he says, "After his death at the hands of the Utes, his notebook was taken out of his pocket, and in it he [referring to Old Bill] made a note at a camp in the mountains, where he says, 'I wanted to go one way and Frémont will go another, and right here our troubles will commence.' "

Frémont apparently not only declined to follow Williams' advice and counsel, but in effect discharged him, for he placed Alexis Godey in the position of guide for the party. Godey went to the head of the column and led them through the Sand Hills.[10]

The temperature showed no moderation, the snow and storms continued, and added to all this, they now were subjected to driving gales. The party, cold and miserable, continued westerly and a little to the south across the valley toward the Río Grande. A new difficulty here presented itself. There was no fuel except sagebrush, which was almost like burning grass.

On the seventh of December, they got about halfway across this plain, and then camped in the open, with the wind blowing almost a hurricane. Here the hunters succeeded in bringing down five head of deer. An attempt was made to cook some of the meat over the sagebrush fire, but, with indifferent success; it had to be eaten almost raw. The best they could do was to roll up in their

[7] Breckenridge, *op. cit.,* 401.
[8] Also spelled "Abiquiv," and "Albiquiu."
[9] *Letters and Correspondence of J. S. Calhoun,* Map No. 3.
[10] Diaries of R. H. Kern and B. J. Kern, Huntington Library.

blankets, which afforded a little protection from the elements. That night the mules and horses broke loose and started on the back trail. Breckenridge says that he traveled four hours before he finally overtook them. Here Ducatel "came very near freezing to death," with the thermometer registering seventeen degrees below zero. The next day, the eighth, the party made the Río Grande, at a point near where the present town of Del Norte, Colorado, now stands. On the river bottom there was timber, and some game was to be had. The hunters succeeded in killing a few elk and deer. No mention is made in any of the accounts of the trip that there was any shortage of food up to this point. Here McGehee had his feet frozen, because he said, he was wearing boots. These he discarded for moccasins, with his legs wrapped in strips of blankets, in regular mountain fashion, which made traveling easier.

The river here curves to the west; on the north side was the La Garita Range, a part of the Sawatch Range, and on the south the San Juan Range. The valley of the Río Grande, which appeared so alluring from the top of the Sangre de Cristo Mountains, continues open for a distance and gradually narrows, the river heading in the high mountains where the two ranges come together.

Besides those mentioned, a number of the party had had their hands and feet frozen, and the going had been rough and hard. Their breath had frozen upon their eyelashes and whiskers and their faces were stiff from the cold; they could hardly see any distance on account of the driving snow. The stock had given them much trouble, and all of the party had to serve as muleteers. Now, added to all their troubles, they were headed into a cul-de-sac, for so far as any trappers knew, there was no way through the mountains by that route which could be traveled in winter.

The party continued up the Río Grande two or three days, the canyon beginning to offer difficulties of travel, and the mountains becoming higher and apparently more difficult to cross as they went on. It began to be doubtful that they were going to get through. "Colonel Frémont knew it too, for he talked with Williams again, and Williams advised return to the Saguache or south to New Mexico." They still could have taken either route out of their difficulties, but Frémont stubbornly continued in a westerly direction up the river, sticking to the thirty-eighth degree of latitude, along which he had started, "declaring that he wanted to go west by the head of the Río Grande"[11] Return to the "Saguache" (Sawatch) would have meant the retracing of their route up the San Luis Valley with a swing north and then west and through the Cochetopa Pass. Frémont thought he could accomplish the same result by a short cut, for he turned north into the La Garita Mountains.[12] One cannot well guess what was in Frémont's mind, because they were headed into a range of the Rocky Mountains which is about forty miles across, and through which there was no pass known to any man in his company. Nevertheless, he attempted to cross these mountains, and from this point their real troubles began, continuing until the last man straggled into Taos on February 9.

At places the party encountered deep ravines filled with rushing water beneath the snow. These they frequently broke into, getting wet and then freeezing. Storms continued, snows got deeper, mountains higher, and it became more and more difficult to make progress. At one place, with a blizzard raging, they made only a short distance in a day, and here Old Bill Williams nearly froze to death. "He dropped down upon his mule in a stupor and was nearly senseless when they got into camp."[13] Men had their noses, ears, faces, fingers, and feet frozen. The supply of corn being exhausted and no forage available, the poor animals attempted to satisfy their hunger by eating one another's tails and manes and anything loose about the camp. Their resistance about gone, they began to freeze to death in increasing numbers. The strength of the men began to lessen. From the daily fighting with the elements and the high altitude, with their food giving out, on December 17 they found they could not make further progress. Even by beating a path with the mauls, they could make only

---

[11] Breckenridge, *op. cit.*, 401.
[12] *Ibid.*, 402.
[13] Narrative of Micajah McGehee, in Private Papers of J. S. McGehee, II, 69.

half a mile in a day. It snowed night and day and they were at an elevation of twelve thousand feet. The temperature continued much below zero. At this point a few of the men went ahead and thought they could see some level ground covered with grass, but it turned out to be small trees sticking out from the deep snow. They attempted once more to go over the summit of the mountains, which they were near, but human endurance could not withstand the forces of nature, and they were obliged to drop back into their camp of the seventeenth.

In this camp they laid up for five days for the storm to subside. Frémont divided the party into messes and each dug a hole in the snow, with a campfire in the center. The snow was so deep that one group could not see the other. Frémont still had supplies sufficient to last the party about twenty days. It must have been apparent to him that he could not get through the mountains, and the main topic of conversation was how to get relief. On the twenty-second, he began to move camp back towards the Río Grande, packing all the baggage, instruments, and remaining supplies on foot. The remaining mules were left in the mountains. Doctor Kern felt that in leaving the mules, they had sacrificed much "good provisions."[14] They did not directly retrace the route they had taken up the mountains, going rather over the top of a mountain to the east and south. It took about a week to move the baggage and supplies a distance of about two miles.

A few years ago, Professor Frank C. Spencer, with a few companions, traced a part of the trail of the Frémont party into the La Garita Mountains. They located a camp up in the mountains to the north of the Río Grande, near the head of a creek now called Wannamaker Cañon and at an elevation of twelve thousand feet. Professor Spencer found many mule bones and other evidence of the Frémont party's camp, including some stumps of trees cut off as high as eighteen feet from the ground. One other camp was located on the headwaters of Embargo Creek, which flows into

[14] Letter of Benjamin J. Kern to Joe, February 20, 1849, MS in Huntington Library.

the Río Grande. This agrees in the main with the route described by Frémont, Breckenridge, McGehee, and the Kerns.[15]

On Christmas Day, the Colonel decided to dispatch a party down the Río Grande for supplies. Just why Frémont figured that he should have supplies brought into the mountains, rather than take his party to the supplies can only be explained by the fact that he still hoped to get provisions in and continue west along the thirty-eighth parallel. Frémont picked King, Breckenridge, Creutzfeldt, and Bill Williams for this trip, and although they were 160 miles from the settlements, they started on foot with "one blanket apiece, a few pounds of frozen mule meat, about one pound of sugar, a little macaroni, and a few candles." They had with them "three Hawkins rifles for defense against the Indians, about fifty bullets, and a pound of powder." They "also had one shot gun."[16]

Bill Williams has been criticized for not getting through to the settlements for help and supplies. With the conditions under which Williams and his companions traveled, the chances of their getting through were slight indeed. Frémont allowed them sixteen days to go and return, approximately 320 miles, thus placing upon them the responsibility of making the round trip with an average travel of over twenty miles a day. It seems as if good judgment would have demanded of Frémont that he do as many a band of mountaineers had done before—cached their goods, taken all the food they had and such meat as they could manage, and the entire party stay together and travel toward Taos, the stronger helping the weaker. Then, too, it must have been evident to the leader that

15 Spencer, *op. cit.*, 141–46; Breckenridge, op. cit., 400–408. Diaries of R. H. Kern and E. M. Kern, MSS in Huntington Library.

16 Doctor Kern, in a letter to Joe, dated February 20, 1849, stated that they "started for a settlement called Albiquiu, distant some 160 miles."—MS in Huntington Library. This refers to the Village of Abiquiu situated on the Rio Chama, on the west side of the Río Grande, about opposite Taos.—See Map of the Territory of New Mexico, by Lt. Jno. G. Parke, U. S. T. E., 1851. Map No. 3 accompanying *The Official Correspondence of J. S. Calhoun.* This was not Albuquerque, as stated by Micajah McGehee, page 73 of his narrative.—*Cosmopolitan Magazine* (August, 1896), 408.

the route they had traveled was impossible for a railroad. He was not ready to admit mistaken judgment.

With the Bill Williams party off on their relief expedition, the main party continued toward the Río Grande, packing their baggage, saddles, and other implements on their backs through the snow. They could hardly make a mile a day at times, the snow was so deep. The men could get no solid footing, breaking through and occasionally plunging into a deep place which appeared level by reason of the drifted snow. The high altitude told on the men, some of them bleeding at the nose, because of the rarity of the atmosphere. At last their rations were practically gone, and only a little macaroni and sugar were left. They had recourse to eating the "parfleches" and rawhide, which they cut into strips and boiled until it was soft enough to masticate. There was no sign of living animals, and the snow and storm continued. Before they reached the river, Raphael Proue gave out and lay down beside the trail and froze to death. They could not even stop to bury him. The men could carry only a small amount at a time, and for a short distance. At one place the storm was so bad that Andrews and McGehee stayed two days in a cave of rocks, and in getting wood to burn, McGehee was almost swept off a high point by the gale. In the cave they found a small roll of rawhide snowshoe strings left by others of the party. These they boiled up with some dry bones that they found in an old wolf's den near by. At last, on January 2, a portion of the party reached the Río Grande, where they expected to find game, as they had found about three weeks before, when they crossed it. In this they were disappointed. The snow was so deep that the game had left for the south. The outlook was indeed discouraging.

The sixteen days, the allotted time for the King party to return, had passed; then they waited two days more, and on the eleventh of January Frémont decided that he would go himself for relief. He took with him Charles Preuss, Alexis Godey, Theodore McNabb, Godey's nephew, and his man-servant, Sanders Jackson. His plan was twofold: to find out what had become of the Williams party and to push on to the nearest settlement for relief.

Precious time had been wasted in trying to save their baggage and equipment, which they had been packing and which finally had to be cached; so these extra efforts went for naught. Through their exertions and the lack of food, the men were reduced to such a weakened condition that the privations they had to endure in the next seventeen days were too much for ten of the party. Before leaving, Frémont appointed Vincent Haler to take charge of the men, with directions to "finish packing the baggage to the river, and then hasten on down as speedily as possible to the mouth of Rabbit River," where relief would be sent in to them. Frémont here apparently abandoned his idea of getting through the mountains, and decided he would "proceed to California by a southerly route," for he left word with the men remaining to "be in a hurry about it as he was going on to California."[17]

The party was thus split into three groups. Williams, King, Breckenridge, and Creutzfeldt had been gone eighteen days, nothing having been heard from them. Colonel Frémont with the four men proceeded south, and the main party, now comprised of twenty-four men under Vincent Haler, followed them. All three groups were on the Río Grande, going south toward the settlements farther down the river.

The first of these groups, the Williams relief party, after leaving Frémont on Christmas Day, proceeded directly to the river, taking three days in reaching it, and at this point all the food they had was consumed. They followed the river, but they encountered difficulty in traveling because of the snow and cold, and their progress was slow. There was no game, and for three days they were without any food. Then a small hawk was killed and that was divided among the four. Then a dead otter was found. They suffered with frozen feet, the traveling was slow, and they were reduced to eating the leather they had with them. Old Bill's experience in many a trying place could not help him; moreover, he was well along in years, and lack of food and exposure soon

[17] Narrative of Micajah McGehee, in Private Papers of J. S. McGehee, II, 77; also copy of letter from Frémont to Vincent Haler in *Missouri Republican* (May 25, 1849); part of R. H. Kern diary.

reduced this relief expedition to a point where they themselves became very much in need of relief. Their situation was desperate.

On the twelfth of January, they were still about fifty miles short of the settlements. King played out and could go no farther. He urged the others to go on and he would follow. They proceeded for a short way, and then Creutzfeldt went back to help him, but King was dead. The three remaining men struggled on for another day and camped. Creutzfeldt gave out, and Old Bill sat down by his side to await his end. In the meantime Breckenridge started alone, Williams promising to follow as soon as his companion had died. A short distance away Breckenridge saw five deer and succeeded in getting one. They were saved. His first act was to cut out the liver and eat it raw, and then cutting off some meat, he struggled back to camp where Old Bill "took the meat in his long bony hands and began tearing off great mouthfuls of raw flesh like a savage animal." Creutzfeldt was brought back to life by the smell of the meat and resuscitated. The remainder of the carcass of the deer was brought in, and for the time they feasted.[18]

Frémont and his companions, after leaving the main party on January 11, proceeded rapidly down the river. They came across a Ute, a relative of the Ute chief, Walker, known to Frémont, and he conducted them to the village, where horses and food were procured. Frémont then pushed on toward the settlements, and on the thirteenth came across Williams, Creutzfeldt, and Breckenridge while they were feasting on their deer. Frémont describes them as "the most miserable objects he had ever seen," and says that "by aid of the horses" he "carried these three men" with him to the "Red River settlement."[19] Breckenridge's account does not accord with Frémont's letter to Mrs. Frémont, however, for he says Colonel Frémont remained just "long enough to cook some venison, then pushed on, ordering us to follow as fast as we could." According to Breckenridge's account it took the three of them

[18] *Cosmopolitan Magazine* (August, 1896), 408.
[19] Frémont's letter to his wife (January 27, 1849), in John Bigelow, *Life of Frémont*, 371.

ten days to go the remaining forty miles on account of the frozen condition of their feet, and "for nearly the entire distance," he says, "we crawled on ice or through snow."[20]

When Frémont and his companions arrived at Taos on January 20, they went to the home of Kit Carson and stayed there until they left for California in February. Godey immediately got together thirty animals, supplies and four Mexicans, and started back to aid his comrades. In the meantime, since January 11, the suffering of the party under the leadership of Vincent Haler almost beggars description. Their supplies were entirely gone and there was no game. They did succeed in getting one small buck, but it apparently was not evenly divided. A couple of prairie chickens were killed. The remains of a dead wolf were found. This seems to have constituted all of the meat the party was able to get. The leadership of Vincent Haler resulted only in dissension and discouragement. They struggled along down the river, with no organization or direction, until the twenty-first, when Vincent Haler "resigned all command of the party and declared it broken up, and said each man must take care of himself."[21] That night the two French mountain men, Moran and Sorel, did not make camp. Later they were found together, having frozen to death.

On January 22, Vincent Haler, Hibbard, Ducatel, Rohrer, Martin, Scott, Bacon, Ferguson, Beadle, and the two Indians, Gregorio and Joaquín, the stronger members of the party, "started on ahead, determined to leave" the others and proceed on down the river. Vincent Haler gave as a reason for breaking up the party into smaller groups that they could better take care of themselves and were more likely to get game, and in any event, the stronger men could go through without waiting for the weaker; otherwise all would perish. "This piece of rascality was almost without parallel," to the mind of R. H. Kern. He also stated that Vincent Haler, the man left in charge, "was totally unfit on account of want of tact and experience in correct principles to be left in charge of

---

20 *Cosmopolitan Magazine* (August, 1896), 408.
21 Diary of R. H. Kern, MS in Huntington Library.

the men; besides, his conversation did as much to discourage the men as did the situation itself."[22]

This left the three Kerns, Captain Cathcart, Captain Taplin, Micajah McGehee, Steppenfeldt, and Andrews, the weakest of the entire party; yet with spirit and determination they agreed not to leave each other while life lasted. Soon Rohrer, who had started with Vincent Haler, had to drop out and rejoin the Kerns. This latter group all arrived in Taos, except Andrews and Rohrer, who died on the way, their companions faithfully staying with them to the end. Micajah McGehee has left a vivid account of the trials of the next few days.

It is likely other parties on the plains and mountains suffered as they did, but it is doubtful that any group of men went through more than they did and lived to tell of their hardships. The party was reduced to utter starvation and in their extremity ate any stray piece of leather they had about them. They became snow blind and frozen and could not walk more than thirty steps at a time. They searched for bugs and roots, and what was the most fatal, hope began to diminish. Finally, one of the party suggested that they resort to eating their dead companions, but this plan was not approved by the others and it was not mentioned again.[23] Later Frémont made the charge that they had resorted to cannibalism, a charge which was utterly out of keeping with Frémont's usual custom of reporting events, because there was no foundation for it. On the twenty-eighth, Godey reached the McGehee and Kern party, first having passed them. The arrival of the relief party was dramatic. Their strength gone, the men who had remained in the mountains could no longer chop wood, but were obliged to build fires of what they could find. McGehee tells us hope had about gone. "We remained around the fire, stirring as little as possible, and firing guns at frequent intervals during the day. Rohrer died. Two days passed, and no relief came. Several times we imagined we heard an answer to our signals, and would rise up to listen, but being as often disappointed, we had ceased

[22] *Ibid.*
[23] Narrative of Micajah McGehee, in Private Papers of J. S. McGehee, II, 83, 84.

to notice. The morning of the third day, January 25, arrived and was far advanced toward midday, and we sat in the deepest gloom. Suddenly we thought we heard a call. 'Hush,' said one, and we all listened intently. Another call. 'Relief—by God,' exclaimed one of the men, and we all started to our feet, and relief it was, sure enough, for directly we spied Godey riding toward us followed by a Mexican. We were all so snow blind that we took him to be the Colonel until he came up, and some saluted him as the Colonel. We shook him by hand, heartily."[24]

Godey, showing good judgment, gave them each a little bread, then prepared some boiled corn meal and began to feed the men a little at a time. The party was then 70 miles from the nearest settlement, or 120 miles from Taos. They could not walk; so they were put on mules, and in this manner they arrived at the Little Pueblo of the Colorado on February 9, and then went on to Taos. All of the saddles, instruments, and baggage, including the natural history specimens which the Kerns had been collecting, and their books and papers, and the $1,200 in coin belonging to Breckenridge, had been cached in the mountains.

Of the thirty-two men, including Colonel Frémont and Old Bill Williams, who started over the mountains at Pueblo, only twenty-one came out alive. Raphael Proue had frozen to death on January 9. The others who had lost their lives had died from starvation: Henry King on January 12; Henry Wise on January 17; Manuel, the California Indian, probably on January 21; the mountain man Vincent Sorel on January 22, and his partner Joseph Moran between the twenty-second and the twenty-eighth of January; Carver probably on the twenty-seventh of January; Midshipman E. T. Andrews and Henry Rohrer on January 22; Benjamin Beadle on January 26; and George A. Hibbard on January 27.[25] The remainder, exhausted and extremely reduced in physical condition, had arrived at Taos without any means.

Naturally, since this was Frémont's expedition, he was the one who was responsible. At this point, nevertheless, he showed that

[24] *Ibid.*
[25] Diary of Richard H. Kern, MS in Huntington Library.

he was not the Frémont of the previous expeditions or of the California campaign, for instead of assuming the full responsibility of the disaster, he wrote an explanation of his failure to his wife on January 27, even before all of the party had gotten in. "The error of our journey was committed in engaging this man," referring to Bill Williams. "He proved never to have in the least known or entirely to have forgotten the whole region of country through which we were to pass. We occupied more than half a month in making the journey of a few days, blundering a tortuous way through deep snow which already began to choke up the passes, for which we were obliged to waste time in searching."[26]

This attempt to shift the blame to Old Bill was bad enough, but in 1854, when on his final expedition and his party was reduced to scant fare, he made reference to this trip and told his companions that on a previous expedition, his men had been reduced to eating each other.[27] He must have referred to Williams, for Senator Benton, his father-in-law, mentions in after years that King had died of exposure or famine and his comrades had fed upon him.[28] It is not much wonder that with statements like this, a talented writer and one of our able biographers of Frémont should conclude: "Kit Carson and Frémont both strongly suspected that Williams deliberately led the party astray, hoping that they would lose their baggage in the deep snow before emerging on the other side, and that he could come back the next spring to claim it," giving Frémont's manuscript memoirs as reference.[29] Old Bill Williams was charged with incompetence as a guide, cannibalism, and deliberate and premeditated treachery.

[26] Bigelow, *Memoir of John Charles Frémont*, 367.
[27] *Ibid.*, quoting S. N. Carvalho, 439.
[28] *Ibid.*, quoting from Benton, 363.
[29] Nevins, *op. cit.*, II, 404.

CHAPTER SIXTEEN

The End and Vindication

OLD BILL WILLIAMS did not live to deny personally the charges made against him by Colonel Frémont, for in less than two months from the time he arrived in Taos with the survivors of the party, he met a violent death at the hands of the Utes, at a place in the mountains he had traveled over only a short time before.

The evidence is that Colonel Frémont made the trip into the mountains in the dead of winter, against the advice and counsel of all those who were best informed. At Bent's Fort, Old Bill Hatcher told the Colonel the mountains could not be crossed. Another veteran mountain man, Tom Biggs, then at the fort, was of the same opinion, as well as all "who were acquainted with the country."[1] Dick Wootton refused to undertake piloting the party through the mountains, because he was of the opinion it could not be done.[2] Colonel Frémont ignored these opinions and went on to the Pueblo. There he may have himself entertained some doubt about crossing the mountains, for at that point he added Williams to the expedition as guide. Even old Bill was doubtful whether the crossing could be made. Most of the old trappers who were wintering there at the time felt that the attempt should

1 Fort Sutter Papers, Vol. XXXI, No. 126, in Huntington Library.
2 Breckenridge, *op. cit.*, 400.

not be made.[3] The determination to proceed in the dead of winter rested squarely on the decision of Colonel Frémont, and Bill Williams had nothing to do with it.

Once through the Sangre de Cristo Mountains and down the San Luis Valley, with the snow and weather conditions continuing as they did, Williams was in a position to know definitely that the trip north, through the Cochetopa Pass,[4] should not be attempted, and so advised.

John Scott, a mountain man of many years and one of the party, tells how, when they got to the point where Colonel Frémont could see in the distance the mountain chain through which he was to pass, he inquired of Williams where the pass was through which he was to go, and that "Williams pointed him a passage bearing to the north." Frémont then told him that pass was "too far to the north, the he wanted to go a more direct course, and that that passage, pointing to the one further south, must therefore be the one." Williams at the time made it clear to the Colonel they "could not by any possibility go through by that pass" indicated by Frémont, and that even regarding the Cochetopa Pass, "it was a matter of doubt" if they could get through.[5]

Dr. H. R. Wirtz, an army surgeon stationed at Taos at the time, deriving his information "from disinterested persons" says that "Bill Williams lost the confidence of Frémont, and a discussion having arisen as to which was the proper course to take to get through the Cochetope Pass, Frémont took the advice of a man named Godin [Godey] a hunter and mountain man, but young and inexperienced compared with the veteran Williams. This Godin was consequently put in the advance, and Bill Williams sent to the rear."[6] This accords with the R. H. Kern diary, for he tells us that Godey took the lead through the Sand Hills.

"Uncle Dick" Wootton, who was himself well acquainted with

[3] Narrative of Micajah McGehee, in Private Papers of J. S. McGehee, II, 61.
[4] Also spelled Coo-che-to-pa, Cochetope, and Cochatopy.
[5] Memoranda of E. M. Kern, July 23, 1849, Fort Sutter Papers, Vol. XXXI, No. 126, MS in Huntington Library.
[6] "How Bill Williams Was Killed," *Arizona Miner* (Prescott, Arizona, Aug. 20, 1870).

these mountains, through the experience of crossing by this same pass, was at Taos at the time the Frémont survivors came in, and took an active part in the rescue. He talked with Frémont, for he took him to Kit Carson's house and discussed the property left in the mountains with Williams and others. He had sat around camp fires a hundred times with Williams, and his statement must carry conviction. "Williams knew every pass into the mountains, and almost every foot of the Rocky Mountain country, and if General Frémont had taken his advice, he would never have run into the death trap." Wootton says, "General Frémont had picked out the route which he wanted to travel in crossing the mountains. Williams told him it was impractical to cross the range in the winter season by the route which he had selected, but the great 'Pathfinder' listened to an inexperienced member of the party, who volunteered to pilot him over."[7]

Antoine Leroux, a mountaineer, to whom Colonel Philip St. George Cooke referred as a "most sensible and experienced" guide[8] and who conducted Captain J. W. Gunnison over this pass in 1853,[9] after digesting stories he heard from the survivors and from such other information as he could gather, wrote a letter to E. M. Kern. The letter, in his own handwriting, states: "Bill Williams has himself traveled it [referring to the Cochetopa Pass] several times in company with me. His knowledge of that part of the country was perfect. The course which was taken by Colonel Frémont was an impracticable one in winter, and no sensible mountaineer would ever for a moment have entertained the idea of taking it, as no road ever existed there known either to the trapper or to the Indian."[10]

From all of these accounts, we can conclude that as Colonel Frémont came over the Sangre de Cristo Mountains, after having endured several days of extreme hardship, cold, and snow, and Bill Williams pointed out to him the bleak range of the La Garita

---

[7] Conard, *op. cit.*, 198.
[8] 30 Cong., 1 sess., *House Exec. Doc. 41*, 416.
[9] 33 Cong., 1 sess., *House Exec. Doc. 18*, 5, 6.
[10] Letter of Antoine Leroux to E. M. Kern (Aug. 22, 1850), Fort Sutter Papers, Vol. XXXI, No. 130, in Huntington Library.

Mountains lying to the southwest, with the valley of the Río Grande presenting an apparent opening between these two ranges, he decided the latter was the way to go. Lieutenant Beckwith, who afterwards wrote up the report of Captain Gunnison's trip of 1853, tells us that when his party came to the point opposite the Roubidoux Pass, R. H. Kern, F. Creutzfeldt, and Captain Charles Taplin, who had been with the Frémont expedition, pointed out to him "the promising opening of the Sierra San Juan to the southward which allured Colonel Frémont to the disaster of 1848–1849."[11] It is clear that he did not even consider Bill Williams' suggestion to go "south around the San Juan Mountains, and then west along what is now the line between Colorado and New Mexico."

It would seem Frémont took charge of the guiding of his party and determined the route which they were to follow, against the advice of the old mountain man. After Frémont assumed this responsibility, Williams could not be blamed for what thereafter happened. There have been some attempts to relieve Frémont from the blame, which he should have shouldered like a man. Frémont's friends came to his aid in 1856 when he was running for the presidency by publishing a letter over the signature of Godey, but the attempt was futile. The letter was published in the New York *Evening Post*. In it Godey stated he "had the honor of being in command under Colonel Frémont." The letter stated there were many discussions between Colonel Frémont, Williams, and himself with respect to the route they were to travel after they reached the Del Norte. The Colonel, the letter says, "preferred to turn off and go through the Coehatopy, a pass some thirty miles to the left," but that Godey and Williams persuaded the Colonel to go on west and that if there was any fault to be attached in the selection of routes, it lay squarely on the shoulders of Old Bill Williams and himself.[12] This letter was written during the campaign of 1856, when Frémont was a candidate for the

[11] Reports of Exploration and Surveys for a Railroad. Report of E. G. Beckwith, 33 Cong., 2 sess., *House Exec. Doc. 19*, II, 44.

[12] Letter signed by Alexander Godey, published in the New York *Evening Post*, (October 30, 1856).

presidency, and refuted many other campaign charges made against Colonel Frémont besides the one mentioned. It would seem, from language, style, and content, that some ardent supporter of Frémont prepared it and attached Godey's name. Godey was not accustomed to writing, could scarcely sign his name, and when he did sign, it was "Alexis" and not "Alex";[13] surely, he never was the author of that political document. This conclusion is borne home when the letter refers to the "Coehatopy Pass" as being on the "left of the party," for at no time after leaving the Pueblo until Frémont turned around and started out of the mountains on the twenty-second of December was that pass on their left.

The expedition was a failure; the route was not practicable for a railroad; but when the Colonel sought to shift the blame for the failure from himself to the old mountain man, then the old scout had defenders. It must be admitted Old Bill did fail when he attempted to go for relief, but that was due to the fact that the human frame could no longer withstand cold, starvation, and fatigue. He was directed to perform a task, the success of which was dependent on many factors over which he had no control. It was a task for a young man with strength, and not for one who was over sixty years of age. His failure to get through in no wise reflected on either his ability as a guide or his knowledge of the mountains.

The other charge that Old Bill had resorted to eating his companions is not supported by any creditable evidence. Cannibalism had been resorted to on several occasions in the history of the development of the West, when starvation had forced it, but there is nothing to show that Old Bill had resorted to it on this trip. It could be only in connection with the death of Henry King that the charge was made. King played out, Breckenridge tells us, and "sadly we left him lying in the trail 'to rest' " as he said, "but 'at rest' would more probably convey the idea of our feelings." After they had traveled on, Creutzfeldt started back to help King into camp, but Williams told him it was no use, he was dead, as a buz-

[13] See Probate File in Estate of Alexis Godey, Clerk of Court, Kern County, California.

zard was circling about and that was a sure sign that life was about gone. Creutzfeldt nevertheless went back, but returned in a few hours and reported King was dead, and that from the position of his body, he had not moved after Williams and his companions had left him. The three continued on down the river to a camp, distant several miles from where King had died, and it was at this latter place that Frémont came across them.[14] The next day Breckenridge killed a deer, and that saved the life of the three. This agrees with what Frémont afterwards wrote to his wife, when he stated "King had starved to death a few days before. His remains were some six or eight miles above, near the river."[15] It is entirely likely that Frémont did find the body of King partly devoured. It could well have been animals, but more likely was the work of the buzzards Williams had noticed flying about. Bill Williams was never near King after he died. Whatever the shortcomings of Old Bill were—and he had many to answer for—the charge of eating human cadaver during that terrible trip cannot be listed.

There was a suggestion made by a member of the McGehee party during the terrible days of their starvation that they save themselves by eating the body of one of their dead comrades. The suggestion, however, was not entertained by other members of the party. It should be pointed out further that Williams was not a member of this group.[16]

This charge savored of pettiness and evidently was made by Frémont's friends to becloud the issue and divert attention from the disastrous failure of the expedition.

We can pass over the suggestion of certain writers that Williams had deliberately misled the expedition, thereby hoping the party would be compelled to leave the baggage in the mountains so that he might be able to return in the spring and profit by such as he might salvage. All the facts in the case render it so absurd and so out of keeping with the truth that the mere statement contains

[14] Breckenridge, *op. cit.*, 406, 408.
[15] John Bigelow, *op. cit.*, 370, quoting from Frémont's letter to Mrs. Frémont, dated January 27, 1849.
[16] Narrative of Micajah McGehee, Private Papers of J. S. McGehee, II, 83.

its own refutation. For many years Old Bill Williams had roamed the mountains, hunted, trapped, fought Indians; had been on every sort of an expedition; had drunk and gambled; and was known personally to every trapper or mountain man of any consequence over a long period of years. When Williams joined a party there was at once a feeling of security which lasted so long as he remained with them. There is yet to be recorded an act of treachery on the part of Old Bill against his own race. Frémont himself could never have believed that suggestion, for the Colonel offered to mount and equip all of the party who would accompany him to California, including Williams. Bill Williams, the three Kerns, Captain Cathcart, and Steppenfeldt, of their own accord, declined to go. This accusation of treachery, it should be pointed out, was not made until half a century had elapsed; yet it was a natural result of the charges of incompetence made against Old Bill Williams.

Edward M. Kern had been a trusted assistant of Colonel Frémont on the California campaign, and had served with distinction as the commander of Fort Sutter during that war. It was he for whom Kern River, Kern County, and Kern Lake in California were named. Kern had gone back from California after Frémont's trouble with Kearny, taking the private papers of Colonel Frémont to Washington, where he assisted and aided him in the court-martial. In 1848, Edward M. Kern was returning to California with many of these papers in his possession. On this expedition he had arranged for Richard H. Kern, his brother, to go as artist and topographer, and another brother, Dr. Benjamin J. Kern, as the doctor for the party. The three Kern brothers were serving without pay; they started out ardent, enthusiastic admirers and supporters of Colonel Frémont, but they came into Taos embittered and of a mind to have nothing further to do with him. Edward M. Kern said, " 'Twas best to part before coming to a rupture with him, which certainly would have been the case had we continued together."[17] The Kerns were of the opinion that Frémont

---

[17] Letter of Edward M. Kern to Mary (February, 1849). MS in Huntington Library.

was alone responsible for the failure. When, therefore, he attempted to shift the blame onto the old scout's shoulders, the Kerns joined his defenders.[18]

Shortly after the Colonel arrived in Taos, he made an effort to regain the lost instruments and baggage which had been cached in the mountains. A party was sent into the mountains, but the deep snow prevented their getting through, and their efforts came to naught, with a loss of some ten head of mules.[19] Just before Frémont left for California, he arranged, without any consultation with his men, for Dick Wootton to bring out the goods cached on the Del Norte. When the latter learned that the Kerns were owners of a portion of the property, he decided to let them get it themselves and not to become involved in any controversy.[20] The Kern brothers had been making a collection of "birds and other specimens of natural history"[21] on the trip, on which they had their instruments and valuable papers. They were anxious to recover their property and as soon as they had convalesced from the effects of their trip, began to lay plans for going back to the cache in the mountains. It was arranged. Bill Williams and Dr. B. J. Kern and a few Mexicans, with a pack outfit, started out the last of February,[22] and retraced their route back up the Río Grande. The snow was still deep and the progress slow. For various reasons it had been deemed wise not to let the party's departure be generally known and the military station at Taos was not informed of their purpose. This oversight was attended with fatal results to Williams and Kern, and the complete failure of the plans for recovery of the goods.

[18] Fort Sutter Papers, Vol. XXXI. MSS in Huntington Library.

[19] Letter from Frémont to Senator Benton (February 24, 1849), Bigelow, *op. cit.*, 377.

[20] Conard, *op. cit.*, 199.

[21] Letter from R. H. Kern to J. R. Bartlett (March 8, 1851), Fort Sutter Papers, No. 138. MS in Huntington Library.

[22] On February 20, 1849, Doctor B. J. Kern wrote to Joe he was slowly recovering from the effects "of our starvation," and a letter written in February, 1849, from E. M. Kern to Mary stated they were anxiously awaiting the return of Doc who had gone back into the mountains to recover their lost property.— MSS in Huntington Library.

For some time prior to the departure of the Williams and Kern pack outfit from Taos, the Utes had been on the warpath against both the whites and their enemies, the Arapahoes. The summer before, they had attacked their Indian foes, but had been worsted; this had not improved their feelings. Besides, they had been carrying on depredations for some time against the whites. A portion of the tribe had been with the Apaches when Major Reynolds had come in conflict with those Indians in the Raton Mountains. Things had come to such a point that Major B. L. Beall, the commanding officer of the First Dragoons, stationed at Taos, decided it was time to bring the Utes to order. He ordered Lieutenant J. H. Whittlesey to take the field and make the Utes understand that the army required peace. From the manner in which the orders were carried out, it was apparent the military men were of a mind that the Utes required a real licking. Lieutenant Whittlesey, with a command of thirty-seven men of Company G, First Dragoons, and with Antoine Leroux, the brothers Tom and Charles Orterbis, and Lucien Maxwell[23] as scouts, started up the valley of the Del Norte on the eleventh of March.

On the second day out, when about fifteen miles north of the Río Colorado, they discovered the smoke of a Ute village on the west side of the river, in a grove of piñons. They headed for it. The ground was still covered with deep snow, making travel and maneuvering difficult. As the soldiers approached the village, a few of the chief men came out to meet the advancing column and wanted to know what was wanted; the Lieutenant said, "I came to fight," to which the Indians replied, "It is well." Without further parleying a sharp engagement took place in which the Utes were worsted and "fled precipitously from their camp, abandoning nearly everything they possessed, excepting their animals." The Lieutenant took possession of the village, but had not had time to unsaddle when at a distance he could make out a band of Indians coming towards the village, evidently unaware of the

[23] Lucien Maxwell, mountain man, worked for Bent as a trader; was a son-in-law of Judge Beaubien; and succeeded to the large range in New Mexico known as the Maxwell Grant; served with Frémont in 1815; among the Cheyennes was known as "Big Nostrils"; lost his land and possessions and died poor in 1875.

fight that had taken place. Lieutenant Whittlesey now turned his attention to the second band. He was able to approach them without exciting suspicion, and then attacked and scattered them. The soldiers were savage in their attack, pursuing them for several miles, but the depth of the snow and the condition of the men and horses compelled an abandonment of the chase.

The young officer and his men and guides had carried out their orders to the letter. After the second engagement was over, he summed up the results of the day in his report as follows: "I killed 10 of the enemy and from the blood on the snows I feel confident that many must have been wounded who were carried off. The greatest part of their provisions and camp equipage in a village of more than fifty lodges fell into my hands and were destroyed. I captured, killed and wounded about 20 horses. I also captured 2 women and a son of one of their chiefs, all this I accomplished with a loss of only two men and 3 horses, and at no time had more than 23 men in action." He concludes with thanks to Assistant Surgeon H. R. Wirtz, and to his guides and others of the command, "for their valuable services."[24] The Indians were driven, pell-mell through the snow, away from their village, traveling in all directions.

Dr. Wirtz kept a notebook, and from this record we get the happenings immediately following the Utes' defeat, as related to him by the Mexicans who were with Old Bill. He tells us that about a dozen of the band fled in the direction of the upper Del Norte, and during that night or early the next morning came upon the party encamped at Frémont's cache.[25] "Old Bill and Dr. Kern were sitting by their campfire, after having opened the cache and packed everything preparatory to starting on their return to Taos. Williams and the Doctor were unsuspicious of any evil design and treated the Indians well. But the savages had prepared a dire revenge for the death of their friends, and while the two white men were conversing, seated on the ground, two of the

[24] Report of Lieutenant J. H. Whittlesey to Major B. L. Beall (Taos, New Mexico, March 15, 1849). MS in files of War Department, Washington, D. C.

[25] Doctor Wirtz says it was "at night" the Utes came upon the party. Dick Wootton says: It was early the next morning.—Conard, *op. cit.*, 200.

Utes suddenly raised their rifles and fired. One bullet struck Bill Williams in the forehead, and another passed into the heart of the Doctor. The Mexicans prepared to fly, but the Indians called to them and said they were at war only with the whites, and did not intend to harm them. The murderers, however, took possession of the mules and packs, and ordered the Mexicans to remain where they were until morning."

Dr. Wirtz had come to know Old Bill Williams and had often conversed with him. He says that Williams had a firm conviction, based on a dream he had had, that if ever a bear laid its paw on him, he would be killed by an Indian. The old scout had since that time been careful not to let a bear get near him. A short time before he had started up the Del Norte he told Dr. Wirtz and some friends he had had another dream in which a bear had laid his paw on his shoulder. The Doctor said that Old Bill didn't consider the second dream of importance in the light of the first dream; yet, "in a week he had an Indian bullet in his brain." At the time of his death, the Doctor tells us, Bill Williams' hair was gray, his figure somewhat bent; he had a fine profile, with quick restless eyes and with strong marks of humor about his mouth.[26]

On March 14, 1849, Old Bill Williams paid the supreme penalty, and his score with the Utes was even. The Utes felt they were justified in killing Old Bill and Dr. Kern, for the Indian agent, after investigating the circumstances, reported that they claimed "that the murders, with which they are charged, were subsequent to the murders which they charge upon Lt. Whittlesey, and thus they balance that account current."[27] It is likely the members of the band of Utes who killed Old Bill did not recognize him at the time they came upon him. Afterwards, when it was discovered who it was they had killed, he was given a chief's burial by the Indians, and this notwithstanding his having led the soldiers against them the summer before.[28]

One of the newspapermen of his day says of the old mountain

---

26 "How Bill Williams Was Killed," *Arizona Miner* (Aug. 20, 1870).
27 *Correspondence of James S. Calhoun*, 77.
28 Hamilton, *op. cit.*, 196.

man's passing: "Thus died Bill Williams—a fair specimen of the old mountaineer—a set of men now nearly extinct; a set of men who possessed warm hearts, as noble purposes, and as courageous spirits as could be found in any state of society. Rude and unpolished, but tender and true; firm in fight, but gentle as a woman to misfortune and distress—true Paladins of the mountains and the plains."[29]

Following the death of Williams and Dr. Kern, the two remaining brothers carried on a diligent search to recover their property, taken by the Indians at the time of the death of Williams and their brother. The officers stationed at Taos did all they could. J. S. Calhoun, the Indian agent at Santa Fe, took an active part in the search. On January 27, 1852, they were still searching.[30] Just how or where the papers were at last turned up is not known, but, many years after, they were brought to light and are now in the manuscript department of the Huntington Library at San Marino, California, and have been edited and published in thirty-nine volumes under the title of *Fort Sutter Papers*. They bear silent testimony to the details of the disastrous expedition and of the death of Old Bill Williams.

Edward M. Kern and Richard H. Kern found employment in the next few years with the several expeditions being sent out from Santa Fe under the direction of the Topographical Corps of the Army. Richard H. Kern accompanied Colonel J. H. Simpson in the fall of 1849 in his reconnaissance into the Navajo country. Returning from the expedition, he was in 1851 employed by Captain Lorenzo Sitgreaves to go with him as a topographer on an expedition to survey a wagon road from Zuñi westward to the Colorado. In this party Antoine Leroux went along as guide and

[29] John H. Marion, who wrote this eulogic passage, was born in Louisiana in 1835; as a young man he went to Oroville, California; engaged in mining and newspaper work; moved to Arizona in 1865; prospected, fought Indians, edited the *Arizona Miner*, and the Prescott *Courier* from 1866 to the time of his death, July 27, 1891. He was an editor of ability, and his newspaper exerted a powerful influence on affairs in Arizona during his years.—T. E. Farish, *History of Arizona*, V, 347.

[30] Letter from H. L. Dickison to E. M. Kern, Fort Sutter Papers, Vol. XXXI, No. 129, MSS in Huntington Library.

Frederic Remington, "Utes Watching for the Relief Column,"
from *The Century Magazine* (October, 1891)

"It is likely the members of the band of Utes who killed Old Bill did not recognize him. Afterwards, when it was discovered who it was they had killed, he was given a chief's burial."

"As a result of . . . Williams' death, Richard H. Kern, acting on information received from Antoine Leroux, a mountaineer, named a . . . mountain in Arizona after the old trapper." (Bill Williams Mountain, Coconino County, elevation 9,265 feet.)

hunter. On the Sitgreaves expedition, as was his custom, R. H. Kern kept a diary wherein he minutely set down day by day all the details of the country passed over and the party's doings.[31] The report of the expedition was practically copied from Kern's diary, to such an extent, in fact, that in places the report and the diary are identical. On this expedition, the party passed down the Zuñi River, now known as the Río Puerco, to its junction with the Little Colorado, near the present town of Holbrook, Arizona, and thence down the Little Colorado to a point where it begins to fall off into the Grand Canyon of the Colorado. Here the party turned south to the San Francisco Mountains, and passed north and west of these peaks, thence in a westerly direction to the solitary mountains lying about forty miles from the peaks.

In the diary and report this mountain is not designated by its present name, "Bill Williams Mountain"; they merely recite they were "keeping along the side of the mountain in the hope of meeting with water," until they descended into the bed of a small stream which Leroux said was called Bill Williams Fork. Leroux told Kern he had met Williams on this stream in the year 1837.[32] On the map attached to the report, the mountain is marked "Bill Williams Mt.," and the river, "Bill Williams Fork," is also shown on the map as heading on the mountain.

The map attached to this report with these designations of the mountain and the river is the first instance in which they were designated by their present names. Up to that date the official map of this country was the Disturnell Map, published in 1847, and referred to in Article V of the Treaty of Guadalupe Hidalgo of February 2, 1848. The river R. H. Kern drew on the Sitgreaves map as the Bill Williams Fork is shown on the Disturnell Map as the Santa María. Anyone well acquainted with the topography of the country knows that Bill Williams Fork does not head on Bill Williams Mountain, and that there is a watershed between the mountain and the Bill Williams Fork. The headwaters of the Bill

31 Diary No. 2 of R. H. Kern, on the Sitgreaves Expedition, MS in Huntington Library.
32 *Ibid.* See also *Report of An Expedition down the Zuñi and Little Colorado Rivers by Captain L. Sitgreaves. 32 Cong., 2 sess., Senate Exec. Doc. 59.*

Williams Fork are some fifty miles from the mountain of the same name. The Verde River, then called the San Francisco, does head on Bill Williams Mountain and pursues a westerly course for a way. It was this that misled Mr. Kern in drawing this stream on his map. Antoine Leroux had been familiar with all the streams and mountains in Arizona for many years, and it is doubtful that Richard Kern showed Leroux the map after it was finished, or this error would have been corrected. It was due, nevertheless, to Richard H. Kern[33] and Antoine Leroux that Old Bill Williams' name is perpetuated as it is in Arizona. It seems probable that in this act they signified their regard for the old mountain man.

Dr. Robert H. Wilson, of Saline County, Missouri, who knew Old Bill Williams during his lifetime, told Judge John J. Hawkins, himself a native of Missouri, and later of Prescott, Arizona, in the early eighties when Judge Hawkins was on a visit to his old home town, "I knew Bill Williams. He was a great trapper and scout. The mountain and river in your state are named in memory of his greatness. It was a fitting tribute."[34]

Old Bill Williams did not live to deny the charges made against him, that he was the cause of the failure of the Fourth Frémont Expedition. His hunting and trapping companion, and a member of that ill-fated expedition of 1848, did that for him. So stands today the beautiful, green, wooded mountain, a towering solitary peak above the foothills at its base, characteristic of Bill Wil-

[33] In the summer of 1853, Captain J. W. Gunnison of the Topographical Engineers, conducted an expedition through the Sangre de Cristo Mountains through the Cochetopa Pass, seeking a railroad route to the west. He employed Richard H. Kern as topographer, F. Creutzfeldt as botanist, Charles Taplin as wagon master, and for a time Antoine Leroux as guide. When in western Utah and after striking the Spanish Trail, a smaller party made a side trip to Sevier Lake. At this place, on October 26, they were surprised at daybreak by the Pah-Utes, and Captain Gunnison, R. H. Kern, Creutzfeldt, William Porter, a Mormon guide, Privates Caulfield, Liptook, Mehrteens, and an employee, John Bellows, were slain and mutilated. Captain Gunnison had received fifteen arrow wounds.—33 Cong., 1 sess., *House Exec. Doc. 18*, 3, 5, 6.

[34] Dr. Robert H. Wilson was born on March 4, 1829, in Timbridge, Rockbridge County, Virginia, in the same house in which Sam Houston was born, on the day Jackson was inaugurated the second time. He lived in Saline County, Missouri, all of his life, with the exception of eight years spent in California. He practiced his profession in that county and died October 8, 1907.

liams—Old Solitaire—and not far distant is the mountain stream, now quiet and peaceful, now a rushing torrent, emblematic of the human career of Old Bill, whose life as a mountain man helped to save the plains and the mountains of the Louisiana Purchase to this country.

BIBLIOGRAPHY

I. Manuscript Materials

Baptismal Records of St. Francis Church, St. Paul, Kansas. These are the records made by Fr. De la Croix and others during their trips into the Osage country before the establishment of the Osage Missions on the Neosho River in 1847.

Brown, Joseph C., Report of, dated October 27, 1827, containing a "Map of the Road Surveyed and Marked out, from Fort Osage to San Fernando in the Valley of Taos, near Santa Fe, New Mexico," —Old Map Files of the Chief of Engineers, U. S. Army, War Department, Washington, D. C.

Clark, William, Superintendent of Indian Affairs, St. Louis, License issued by, to Antoine Robidoux to pass through the Indian country to Council Bluffs, Dec. 29, 1823. Huntington Library, San Marino, California.

Deeds, Book I of, City Hall of Records, St. Louis, Missouri.

Fort Sutter Papers, Vol. XXXI. Huntington Library, San Marino, California. The Fort Sutter Papers are correspondence and other papers of Edward M. and Richard H. Kern, relating to the California campaign, Colonel Frémont, and the fourth expedition. They were acquired by the Huntington Library from dealers in manuscripts, and later bound into a number of volumes, although the papers are numbered consecutively. A small number of copies were printed.

French and Spanish Archives, Vol. IV, No. 1. City Hall of Records, St. Louis, Mo. The Archives in the City Hall of Records at St. Louis contain all the recorded legal papers of the pre-American and earlier American periods in St. Louis County. The papers were many of them recorded years after their original dates, and due to the many disputes arising from unrecorded deeds, mortgages, leases, etc., Congress finally passed a law in 1845 creating a statute of limitations on such recording.

Godey, Alexis, Records in the Probate of the Will of. Office of the Clerk of Court, Kern County, Court House, Bakersfield, California.

Houck Papers, Spanish MSS "A," 1784–1805. Wisconsin Historical Society, Madison, Wisconsin. Copies of Documents in *El Archivo de las Indias,* Seville, Spain. These were made by Louis Houck in his study of the early history of Upper Louisiana.

Indian Agents, Accounts of, 1822–25. Kansas Historical Society. This is one of a series of old record books from the office of the Superintendent of Indian Affairs, St. Louis, which were purchased a number of years ago by the society. Duplicates are no doubt in Washington, as these seem to be the records of the office at St. Louis for its own use.

Kern, Benjamin J., Diaries of, on the Frémont expedition, 1848–49. Huntington Library, San Marino, California.

Kern, Benjamin J., Letter of, to Joe, Taos, N. M., February 20, 1849. Huntington Library, San Marino, California.

Kern, E. M., Diary of, on the Frémont expedition of 1848–49. Huntington Library, San Marino, California.

Kern, E. M., Letter of, to Mary, Taos, N. M., February, 1849. Huntington Library, San Marino, California.

Kern, R. H., Letter of, to J. R. Bartlett, March 14, 1851. Fort Sutter Papers, No. 138. Huntington Library, San Marino, California.

Kern, Richard H., Diaries of. His diary while on the Frémont expedition of 1848–49 and that of the Sitgreaves expedition of 1851 were used in this work. Huntington Library, San Marino, California.

Leavenworth, Col. Henry, Commanding Officer in Charge of the Post at Council Bluffs, Permission of, to Antoine Robidoux to pass through the Indian country lying between "this place and the boundary line between the Territory of the United States and New Mexico, in the direction of Santa Fe." Huntington Library, San Marino, California.

McGehee, J. S., Private Papers of, Vol. II, Narrative of Micajah Mc-Gehee. The McGehee papers are in the possession of Mrs. James Landis, of Cambridge, Mass., and Washington, D. C. Mr. Stewart McGehee, of Laurel Hill, Louisiana, has a copy of the narrative. A copy of the narrative and some of the papers are also in the library of the writer. Portions of the narrative were published in *The Century Magazine* (March, 1891), and in *Outdoor Life* (May, 1910).

McNair, Alexander, Letter of, to President James Monroe, dated January 30, 1825. In Miscellaneous Letter Files for January, February, March, 1825. Office of Secretary of State, Washington, D. C.

Martin, Thomas S., Narrative of (taken down by E. F. Murry in 1876). Bancroft Library, Berkeley, California.

Pardons, Vol. IV, in Office of Chief Clerk of Office of Secretary of State, Washington, D. C.

Private Claims, Vol. B. Records of the Land Department of Secretary of State, Jefferson City, Missouri.

Purchase of Louisiana, Collection of Correspondence relating to, in the Library of Mr. Joseph W. Walton, St. Davids, Pennsylvania.

Records of the General Accounting Office, Records Division, Washington, D. C.

Records of the General Land Office, Volume XIII, Allottees under Treaties with the Indians. Department of the Interior, Washington, D. C.

Reeves, B. H., and Mather, Thomas, Report of, concerning the Survey of the Road to Santa Fe in New Mexico, dated Nov. 5, 1825, Franklin, Missouri, and sent to Hon. James Barbour, Secretary of War. Library of Congress, Washington, D. C.

Retired Files of Indian Fur Trade, Library, Office of Indian Affairs, Department of the Interior, Washington, D. C. The records of the Trade under the Factory System are kept in bundles according to the year and the tribe of Indians to which the papers pertained. No effort has been made to designate or classify these papers.

Reynolds, Maj. W. W., Report of, to Lt. W. E. Prince, August 11, 1848. Files of the Adjutant General's Office. U. S. Army, War Department, Washington, D. C.

Sibley, George C., Letters of, to Pedro Martínez, Alcalde of Taos, New Mexico, August 19 and 23, 1826. Huntington Library, San Marino, California.

Sibley, George C., Papers of, Vol. III. Missouri Historical Society. St. Louis, Missouri.

Treaty dated Fort Smith, Arkansas, August 7, 1822, between the Cherokee Nation and the Big and Little Osage Nations. Records of the Indian Office, Department of the Interior, Washington, D. C.

Union Mission Journal, 1820–26. Typewritten copy of the MSS in the Oklahoma Historical Society, Oklahoma City, Oklahoma. The original is also there.

Vaughan, C. E., Records in Family Bible in the possession of. Mr. Vaughan lives at Owensville, Missouri, and is a grandson of Arabella Williams, the younger sister of William S. Williams.

Whittlesey, Lt. J. H., Report of, to Major B. L. Beall, dated Taos, N. M., March 15, 1849. War Department, Washington, D. C.

Williams, Joseph, Will of, Records in the Probate of the Will of. City Civil Court of St. Louis, Mo., Probate Division, Case No. 350.

2. Printed Diaries, Reminiscences, Travels, etc.

Beall, Thomas J. "Recollections of Wm. Craig," *Lewiston* (Idaho) *Tribune* (March 3, 1919).

Breckenridge, Thos. E. "The Story of a Famous Expedition," as related to J. W. Freeman and Charles W. Watson, *Cosmopolitan Magazine* (August, 1896).

Clyman, James. "James Clyman, His Diaries and Reminiscences," *California Historical Society Quarterly*, Vol. IV, No. 2.

Disturnell, J. *Map of the Republic of Mexico* (Mapa de los Estados Unidos de Republica de Mejico, según lo organizado y definido por las varias actas del Congreso de dicha República y construído por las mejores autoridades). New York, J. Disturnell, 1848.

Dupré, E. *Atlas of the City and County of St. Louis by Congressional Townships*. St. Louis, E. Dupré, 1838.

Fort Sutter Papers. See above, *sub* Manuscripts.

Grant, Blanch C., ed. *Kit Carson's Own Story of His Life*. As dictated to Col. and Mrs. DeWitt Clinton Peters about 1856–57. Taos, New Mexico, 1926.

Gregg, Josiah. *Commerce of the Prairies*. Reprint of the first edition (1844). Dallas, Texas, Southwest Press, 1933.

Hamilton, William T. *My Sixty Years on the Plains*. Edited by E. T. Sieber. New York, Forest and Stream Publishing Company, 1905.

"How Bill Williams Was Killed," *The Arizona Miner* (Aug. 20, 1870). This article was taken from the notebook of Dr. H. R. Wirtz, then stationed at Whipple, Arizona. The last two paragraphs are apparently the comment of John Marion, the editor of the paper, and additional notes from the information furnished by Dr. Wirtz. In file of Prescott Historical Society, Prescott, Arizona.

Kennerly, James. *See* Wesley, Edgar B.

McGehee, Micajah. "Rough Times in Rough Places," from the Narrative of Micajah McGehee, *The Century Magazine*, Vol. XLI (March, 1891).

McKenney, Thomas L. *M'Kenney's Memoirs and Travels among the Indians*. New York, Daniel Burgess & Co., 1854.

Pike, Zebulon M. *The Southwestern Expedition of Zebulon M. Pike*. Edited and annotated by Milo Milton Quaife from the first edition published at Philadelphia in 1810. Chicago, The Lakeside Press, 1925.

Russell, Osborne. *Journal of a Trapper*. Boise, Idaho, Syms-York Company, 1921.

Ruxton, George Frederick. *Life in the Far West*. New York, Harper & Brothers, 1849. Reprinted as *In the Old West* (edited by Horace Kephart), New York, Outing Publishing Company, 1916.

——. *Adventures in Mexico and the Rocky Mountains*. London. John Murray, 1847; New York, Harper & Brothers, 1848.

Stewart, Sir William Drummond. *Altowan, or Life and Adventure in the Rocky Mountains*. Edited by J. Watson Webb. New York, Harper & Brothers, 1846.

Thwaites, Reuben Gold, ed. *Early Western Travels*, Vol. V. Cleveland, The Arthur H. Clark Company, 1906.

Wagner, W. F., ed. *Adventures of Zenas Leonard*. (Original edition edited by John F. Short, *Clearfield Republican*, Clearfield, Pennsylvania, 1839.) Cleveland, Ohio, The Burrows Brothers Company, 1904.

Wesley, Edgar B., ed. *The Diary of James Kennerly*. Missouri Historical Society Collections, Vol. VI, No. 1.

3. PUBLIC DOCUMENTS

American State Papers: Public Lands, Vols. II, VIII; *Foreign Affairs; Indian Affairs; Miscellaneous*. Washington, by order of the Congress, 1834.

Annals of Congress, 1 Cong., 1 sess. Washington, Gales and Seaton, 1834.

Annual Report of the Commissioner of Indian Affairs for 1873. Washington, Government Printing Office, 1874.

Calhoun, James S. *The Official Correspondence of James S. Calhoun While Indian Agent at Santa Fe and Superintendent of Indian Affairs in New Mexico.* Compiled by Annie Heloise Abel. Washington, Office of Indian Affairs, Department of the Interior, 1915.

The Congressional Globe, (March 5, 1845), 28 Cong., 2 sess. Washington, Blair and Rives, 1845.

Emory, Lt. Col. W. H. "Notes on a Military Reconnaissance from Fort Leavenworth in Missouri to San Diego in California," 30 Cong., 1 sess., *House Exec. Doc. 41.*

Graham, George, late agent for settling the concerns of the United States trading establishments with the Indians, reporting "Progress Made in the Execution of the Act to Abolish the Indian Trading Establishments," October 1, 1824. 18 Cong., 1 sess., *House Exec. Doc. 61.*

Gunnison, J. W. *Report of the Expedition of Captain J. W. Gunnison through Colorado,* 33 Cong., 1 sess., *House Exec. Doc. 18.*

Heads of Families, First Census of the United States, 1790, North Carolina. Washington, Department of Commerce and Labor, Bureau of the Census, 1908.

Heitman, Francis B. *Historical Register and Dictionary of the United States Army, from its Organization, September 29, 1789, to March 2, 1903.* Washington, published under Act of Congress, approved March 2, 1903.

Hempstead's Court Reports of Arkansas Cases. Boston, Little, Brown & Company, 1856.

Hodge, Frederick Webb, ed. *Handbook of American Indians North of Mexico,* Bureau of American Ethnology, Bulletin No. 30, Part 2. Washington, Government Printing Office, 1907–10.

Kappler, Charles J., ed. *Indian Affairs, Laws and Treaties.* 57 Cong., 1 sess., *Sen. Doc. 452,* 2 vols. Revised edition, 70 Cong., *Sen. Doc. 53.*

McNair, Governor Alexander, of Missouri, to the Secretary of State, "In Relation to the Trade and Intercourse now Carried on Between the United States and the Mexican Provinces," April 27, 1824. 18 Cong., 1 sess., *House Exec. Doc. 155.*

Marcy, Randolph B. *Exploration of the Red River of Louisiana.* 32 Cong., 2 sess., *Sen. Doc. 54;* also 33 Cong., 1 sess., *House Exec. Doc.*

Report of the Secretary of War Conveying a List of Licenses to Trade with the Indians as issued during the quarter ending September 30, 1826. 19 Cong., 2 sess., *House Exec. Doc. 86.*

Reports of Explorations and Surveys, etc., for a Railroad, Vol. II. 33 Cong., 2 sess., *House Exec. Doc. 91.* Washington, A. O. P. Nicholson, Printer, 1855.

Reports of Explorations and Surveys, etc., for a Railroad, Vol. XI. *Sen. Exec. Doc.* Washington, George W. Bowman, Printer, 1861.

Rives, John C., ed. *An Abridgment of the Debates of Congress from 1789 to 1856.* New York, D. Appleton and Company, 1856.

Secret Journals of the Acts and Proceedings of Congress, Vol. IV. This series contains the records of the Continental Congress, 1775–89. It was published by order of the United States Congress. Boston, Thomas B. Wait, 1820–21.

Sitgreaves, Captain L. *Report of an Expedition down the Zuñi and Little Colorado Rivers.* 32 Cong., 2 sess., *Sen. Exec. Doc. 59.* Washington, February 12, 1853.

State Papers and Correspondence bearing upon the Purchase of the Territory of Louisiana. Printed Pursuant to House Concurrent Resolution of May 13, 1902. Washington, Government Printing Office, 1903. This material is also to be found in *American State Papers on Foreign Affairs,* Vol. II.

United States Statutes at Large, Vols. III, IV, VII, VIII, XIX. The Statutes at Large are printed at various times by the order of the Congress and contain such acts of Congress, Treaties, etc., as make up the Federal Statutes of the United States. Appropriation bills are included.

United States Supreme Court Reports. *Strother* vs. *Lucas,* 12 Peters 410; 9 L. Ed. 1137.

Wold, Ansel, comp. *Biographical Directory of the American Congress, 1774–1927.* 69 Cong., 2 sess., *House Doc. 783.*

4. NEWSPAPERS AND PERIODICALS

American Missionary Register, The, Vols, I–VI. New York, J. J. Harper, 1820–25. This magazine was a monthly publication of the United Foreign Missionary Society and some other like societies. It was published for six years. At the end of that time the Society was merged with the American Board of Commissioners for Foreign Missions (ABCFM), and its work is from then on recorded in the *Missionary Herald,* but in far less detail. The historical value of the *Register* is great; it is the best source for frontier history in the Missouri and Arkansas borderland, 1820–25.

Arkansas Gazette, The, October 19, 1824, and October 26, 1824. Files in the Congressional Library, Washington, D. C.

Colorado Magazine, The, Vols. VI and VII, 1929–30. The Colorado Historical Society, Denver, Colorado.

Globe-Democrat, St. Louis, Missouri, December 24, 1911.

Kansas State Historical Collections, Vol. XVI, 1923–25. Material on the Santa Fe Trail and the Council Grove Treaty. Kansas Historical Society, Topeka, State Printer, 1925.

Missouri Democrat, The, October 22, 1853.

Missouri Gazette, The, St. Louis, Missouri, 1808–25. Files in the Missouri Historical Society, St. Louis, Missouri.

Missouri Intelligencer, The, 1820–24. Files in the Missouri State Historical Society, Columbia, Missouri.

New York *Evening Post,* October 30, 1856.

St. Louis *Inquirer,* 1820–21. Files in the St. Louis Mercantile Library, St. Louis, Missouri.

Santa Fe (N. M.) *Republican.* Files for 1848 in New Mexico State Museum and Historical Society, Santa Fe, N. M.

5. SECONDARY SOURCES

Adams, James Truslow. *Epic of America.* Boston, Little, Brown and Company, 1932.

Allsopp, Fred W. *Albert Pike.* Little Rock, Parke-Harper Company, 1928.

Alter, J. Cecil. *James Bridger.* Salt Lake City, Shepard Book Company, 1925.

Ashe, Samuel A'Court. *History of North Carolina.* Greensboro, North Carolina, Charles L. Van Noppen, 1908.

Atkeson, W. E. *History of Bates County, Missouri.* Topeka and Cleveland, Historical Publishing Company, 1919.

Bancroft, Hubert Howe. *Collected Works,* Vols. I, III, XVII, XX, XXV; *Native Races,* Vols. I, III; *History of Arizona and New Mex-*

ico; *History of California*, Vol. III; *History of Nevada, Colorado and Wyoming*. San Francisco, The History Company, 1889.

Barker, Eugene C. *Life of Stephen F. Austin*. Nashville and Dallas, Cokesbury Press, 1925.

Bigelow, John. *Memoir of the Life and Public Services of John Charles Frémont*. New York, Derby and Jackson, 1856.

Blair, Walter, and Franklin J. Meine. *Mike Fink, King of the Mississippi River Keelboatmen*. New York, Henry Holt and Company, 1933.

Bolton, Herbert Eugene. *New Spain and the Anglo-American West*, Vol. II. Los Angeles, Privately Printed, 1932.

———. *The Spanish Borderlands*. ("Chronicles of America," Vol. XXIII.) New Haven, Yale University Press, 1921.

Bonner, T. D. *The Life and Adventures of James P. Beckwourth*. New York, Harper and Brothers, 1856.

Branch, E. Douglass. *Westward*. New York, D. Appleton and Company, 1930.

Bryan, William Smith, and Robert Rose. *History of the Pioneer Families of Missouri*. St. Louis, Bryan, Brand and Company, 1876.

Burrard, Major Gerald. *The Modern Shotgun*, Vol. II. New York, Charles Scribner's Sons, 1931.

Channing, Edward. *A History of the United States*, Vol. II. New York, The Macmillan Company, 1905–25.

Chittenden, H. M. *A History of the American Fur Trade of the Far West*. New York, Francis P. Harper, 1902.

Conard, Howard Louis. *Uncle Dick Wootton*. Chicago, W. E. Dibble and Company, 1890.

Contributions to the Historical Society of Montana, Vol. III. Helena, State Publishing Company, 1900.

Coutant, C. G. *History of Wyoming*. Laramie, Chaplin, Spafford and Mathison, 1899.

Dellenbaugh, F. S. *Breaking the Wilderness*. New York, G. P. Putnam's Sons, 1905.

———. *Frémont and '49*. New York, G. P. Putnam's Sons, 1914.

Denton, Doris. "Harmony Mission, 1821–1837." Unpublished Master's thesis, University of Kansas. Copy belonging to W. W. Graves, St. Paul, Kansas. *Dictionary of American Biography*, Vol. IV. New York, Charles Scribner's Sons, 1930.

Duffus, R. L. *The Santa Fe Trail*. New York, Longmans, Green and Company, 1930.

Duncan, R. S. *A History of the Baptists in Missouri*. St. Louis, Scammell and Company, 1882.

Farish, Thomas Edwin. *History of Arizona*, Vols. II, V, and VI. Phoenix. Printed and Published under the Direction of the Second Legislature of the State of Arizona, 1915.

Foreman, Grant. *Pioneer Days in the Early Southwest*. Cleveland, The Arthur H. Clark Company, 1926.

———. *Indians and Pioneers*. New Haven, Yale University Press, 1930.

Garraghan, Gilbert J., S. J. *St. Ferdinand de Florissant*. Chicago, Loyola University Press, 1923.

Garrard, Lewis H. *Wah-To-Yah and the Taos Trail*. Edited and annotated by W. S. Campbell, and reprinted from the 1850 edition. Oklahoma City, Harlow Publishing Company, 1932.

Graves, W. W. *Life and Letters of the Early Jesuits at Osage Mission*. St. Paul, Kansas, W. W. Graves, 1916.

———. *Rev. Father John Schoenmaker, S. J.* Parsons, Kansas, The Commercial Publishers, 1928.

Hafen, LeRoy R. and W. J. Ghent. *Broken Hand*. Denver, The Old West Publishing Company, 1931.

Hall, Sharlot M. *Pauline Weaver, Trapper and Mountain Man*. Prescott, Arizona, Prescott Courier Print, 1929.

Hallum, John. *History of Arkansas*, Vol. I. Albany, Weed, Parsons and Company, 1887.

Hibbard, Benjamin Horace. *History of Public Land Policies*. New York, The Macmillan Company, 1924.

Hill, J. J. "Ewing Young and the Fur Trade in the Far Southwest," *Oregon Historical Quarterly*, Vol. XXIV (March, 1923), 7.

History of Cole, Moniteau, Morgan, Benton, Miller, Maries, and Osage Counties, Missouri. Chicago, Goodspeed Publishing Company, 1879.

Hobbs, Captain James. *Wild Life in the Far West*. Hartford, Wiley, Waterman and Eaton, 1875.

Hockett, Homer C. *Political and Social History of the United States, 1492 to 1828*. New York, The Macmillan Company, 1925.

Houck, Louis. *History of Missouri*, Vol. I. Chicago, R. R. Donnelly and Sons, 1908.

Howland, Charles P., ed. *Survey of American Foreign Relations.* New Haven, Yale University Press, 1928.

Inman, Henry. *Old Santa Fe Trail.* New York, The Macmillan Company, 1898.

Irving, Washington. *Adventures of Captain Bonneville.* (*Works of Washington Irving,* Vol. X, New Edition, Revised.) New York, G. P. Putnam, 1861.

———. *Astoria, or Anecdotes of an Enterprise beyond the Rocky Mountains.* Caxton Edition. New York, Belford, Clarke and Company, n.d. (First published in two volumes, Philadelphia, 1841.)

James, Marquis. *Andrew Jackson, the Border Captain.* New York, The Literary Guild, 1933.

Lewis, William Terrell. *A Genealogy of the Lewis Family in America from the Middle of the Seventeenth Century down to the Present Time.* Louisville, Courier Journal Job Printing Company, 1893.

McAnally, D. R. *Methodism in Missouri.* St. Louis, The Advocate Publishing House, 1881.

Maples, J. C., and R. P. Rider. *Missouri Baptist Biography.* Liberty, Missouri, Missouri Baptist Society, 1916.

Marsh, J. B. *Four Years in the Rockies, or The Adventures of Isaac P. Rose.* New Castle, Pennsylvania, W. B. Thomas, 1884.

Morehouse, George P. "An Historic Trail through the Southwest," *Journal of American History,* Vol. III, No. 3 (1909).

Musick, John R. *Stories of Missouri.* New York, American Book Company, 1897.

Nevins, Allan. *Frémont.* New York, Harper and Brothers, 1928.

Ogg, Frederick A. *The Opening of the Mississippi.* New York, The Macmillan Company, 1904.

Parkman, Francis. *The Oregon Trail.* New York, Grosset and Dunlap, 1927.

Peck, Rev. J. M. (An Old Pioneer). *Father Clark, or The Pioneer Preacher.* New York, Sheldon, Lamport and Blakeman, 1855.

Peters, DeWitt Clinton. *Pioneer Life and Frontier Adventures.* An authentic record of the romantic life and daring exploits of Kit Carson and his Companions, from his own narrative. Boston, Estes and Lauriat, 1884.

Pike, Albert. *Prose Sketches and Poems.* Boston, Light and Horton, 1834.

Prince, L. Bradford. *A Concise History, of New Mexico.* Cedar Rapids, Iowa, The Torch Press, 1912.

Riemaecker, Alfred de. *Joseph et Charles De la Croix.* Ghent, Belgium, Typographie A. Siffer, 1894.

Roosevelt, Theodore, *The Winning of the West.* New York, The Current Literature Publishing Company, 1906. There are several other well-known editions of this work.

Rose, John Holland. *Life of Napoleon I.* New York, The Macmillan Company, 1902.

Ross, Alexander. *The Fur Hunters of the Far West.* Edited and annotated by Milo Milton Quaife, from the first edition published in London, 1855. Chicago, The Lakeside Press, 1924.

Sage, Rufus B. *Rocky Mountain Life.* Boston, Estes and Lauriat, 1880.

Sanders, James U., ed. *Register of the Society of Montana Pioneers.* Helena, State Publishing Company, 1809.

Scharf, John Thomas. *History of St. Louis City and County.* Philadelphia, L. H. Everts and Company, 1883.

Semple, Ellen Churchill. *American History and Its Geographical Condition.* New York and Boston, Houghton Mifflin Company, 1903.

Stillson, H. L., ed. *A History of Free Masonry and Concordant Orders.* Boston and New York, The Fraternity Pub. Co., 1904.

Sweet, W. W. *Religion of the American Frontier.* Vol. I, "The Baptists." New York, Henry Holt and Company, 1931.

Templin, Lucinda de Leftwich. *The Sibleys, Two Illustrious Pioneers in the Education of Women in Missouri.* St. Charles, Missouri, Lindenwood College, 1926.

Treat, Payson Jackson. *The National Land System, 1783-1820.* New York, E. B. Treat and Company, 1910.

Triplett, Frank. *Conquering the Wilderness.* New York, N. D. Thompson & Company, 1883; Minneapolis, The Northwestern Publishing Company, 1888.

Upham, Charles W. *Life, Explorations and Public Services of John Charles Frémont.* Boston, Tichnor and Fields, 1856.

Van Tramp, John C. *Prairie and Rocky Mountain Adventures.* Columbus, Segner and Condit, 1867.

Victor, Mrs. Frances Fuller. *The River of the West.* Hartford, Columbian Book Company, 1870.

Wells, Frank Evarts. *Story of Old Bill Williams.* A collection of stories about Old Bill printed and sold at Williams, Arizona, in pamphlet form.

Wilson, Woodrow. *History of the American People*, Vol. III. New York, Harper and Brothers, 1902.

Wissler, Clark. *North American Indians of the Plains.* New York, American Museum of Natural History, 1920.

Young, F. G. "Ewing Young and His Estate," *Oregon Historical Quarterly*, Vol. XXI, No. 3, 196, 200, 203.